The New Creation

ٱلخَلْقُ ٱلجَدِيدُ

The New Creation

Akram al-Majid

الأستاذ أكرم الماجد

ترجمه وقدّمه

الدكتور مختار علي

Translation and Introduction by

Mukhtar H. Ali

ISBN: 978-0-9837517-8-6

الكتاب: الخلق الجديد
تأليف: الأستاذ أكرم الماجد
مراجعة: الدكتور مختار علي

1440 / 2018

Title: *al-Khalq al-Jadīd*
Author: Akram al-Majid
Translator: Mukhtar H. Ali
Cover Design: Huda Ali

Contents

الفهرس

الفهرس

Jesus said, "None can ascend to the heavens unless he has been born twice." "How can someone be born when they are old?" Nicodemus asked. "Surely they cannot enter a second time into their mother's womb to be born!" Jesus said, "Flesh gives birth to flesh, but the Spirit gives birth to spirit" You should not be surprised at my saying, you must be born again."

(John 3:3-8)

Introduction

This visionary treatise of the venerable sage, scholar and gnostic, Professor Akram al-Majid, contains a great many secrets of the spiritual way (*al-ṭarīq*) and highlights its salient features. Each of the author's written works intimates a certain aspect of his particular spiritual methodology. For example, the focus of his work *Taj al-mulūk fī ādāb sayr wa al-sulūk* (The Crown of Kings in the Disciplines of Spiritual Wayfaring) is literary and moral, even if it is replete with spiritual mysteries. His work *Manāzil al-sā'irīn: bāb al-firāsa*, a part of which is translated in English as *The Principles of Correspondences*, is an academic work on natural philosophy, defining the human being vis-à-vis his relation to the various planes of existence in God's creation. He has given hundreds of lectures on topics such as theology, philosophy, mysticism, spiritual psychology, dream interpretation, physiognomy, and jurisprudence, each expressing the literary, legal, moral, philosophical or mystical dimensions of his teachings. Each lecture in this treasury evokes the spirit of the path which can be articulated in its simplest form: the pursuit of Truth and the realization of reality.

Should one come across a spiritual master, the first question one might ask is, "What is the way?" The answer to that question will differ, of course, according to the teacher, the methodology, the level of his or her attainment, the power of expression and finally, the capacity and needs of the student. If the questioner is searching for an answer that will satisfy his mind, then there are many definitions for the 'Way' in the books of Sufism, Taoism, and other spiritual traditions. However, since true spirituality has both a theoretical and practical dimension, it may be better to say that the way is 'finding,' or something the seeker must realize within himself. In other words, the way is finding Truth and reality, on the tablet of the heart inwardly, and on the plane of creation, outwardly. The Qur'ān alludes to both aspects in following verse, "We shall show them Our signs in the horizons and in themselves, until it is clear to them that He is the Truth" (41:53). 'Horizons' refer to the planes of outward existence in the macrocosm, the material, the imaginal, and the intellectual, and 'in themselves' are the same material, imaginal and intellectual in the microcosm, which is the human being.

How does one find Truth (*al-ḥaqq*)?[1] Is Truth self-evident or does it require verification? These are essential questions upon which to reflect and one must be certain that the seeker of Truth will ultimately find it, as God has confirmed in the verse above—He will show them His signs so that they come to realize Truth. In other words, he who seeks God finds Him. God shows Himself to the one who seeks Him,

1 "The term '*al-ḥaqq*' has many meanings such as truth, reality, fact, rightness, the established and necessary. It is also one of the epithets of God, referring to the fact that He is the sole reality, the truth, the established, the necessary, the opposite of falsehood, and one whose existence and reality are proved to be true. It also refers to absolute Being,the divine Essence, or that through which all things are known, so that the gnostic who obtains awareness of God, distinguishes that which is real and that which is false and illusory in existence." See Ali, *Foundations of Islamic Mysticism*, p. 212.

because He created the world *only* so that the creatures would find Him. The famous *hadith qudṣī* states "I was a hidden treasure and I wanted to become known, so I created the creatures so that I would become known," and as the Bible says, "The God who made the world and everything in it is the Lord of heaven and earth and does not live in temples built by human hands. And He is not served by human hands, as if He needed anything. Rather, He Himself gives everyone life and breath and everything else. From one man, He made all the nations, that they should inhabit the whole earth; and He marked out their appointed times in history and the boundaries of their lands. God did this so that they would seek Him and perhaps reach out for Him and find Him, though he is not far from any one of us." (Acts 17:24)

The Present Work

The following introduction is an instructional commentary, derivative of Professor Al-Majid's lectures as he taught the present text to his students. Because the work already contains the author's footnotes, I decided to place this material in the beginning, rather than the end of each chapter. I have attempted to record his words as faithfully as possible and with minimal intrusion on my part. However, the lessons do not cover the entirety of the work, but aptly end with the chapter "Finding and Losing." It seems providential that the lessons ended at this juncture, but perhaps one day the Shaykh will finish teaching the entire book. Fortunately, the last few chapters are relatively straightforward and contain ample footnotes to guide the reader.

The book is designed in such a way as to give the reader access to the original Arabic alongside the author's annotations. It will be helpful to use the introduction as a running commentary on the original text/translation and follow along where possible.

Summary of the Work

The essence (*sirr*) of the book is contained in its title, 'The New Creation' and concerns the Intellect, light and darkness. The Intellect is the original creation of God, as the hadith states, "The first thing that God created was the Intellect."[2] It is pure light, awareness, life and power. Its light radiates from itself and transforms all that it touches, endowing everything with light, awareness, life and power. When the Intellect illuminates the soul, it transforms into a new creation, rising from the darkness of its material origin to the sublimity of the light of perfection, suspended by the Intellect's majesty. When the soul becomes luminous, the body in which it inheres also becomes luminous and the spiritual properties of light dominate its materiality. Thus, there are successive creations formed anew from the light of the Intellect.

The hallmark of a spiritual work is that it is an elixir of the soul, the heart[3] and the Intellect. It should produce real effects in those who engage with it, ponder its meanings and apply it. One gradually

---

2 Bursī, *Mashāriq anwār al-yaqīn*, p. 13; Āmulī, *Jāmiʿ al-asrār*, p. 347.

3 The root meaning of the term heart (*qalb*) is to overturn, to return, to go back and forth, to fluctuate and to undergo transformation. As its name suggests, the heart has two aspects, one that faces the spirit and one that faces the corporeal body. The aspect that faces the body is called 'soul' and the aspect that faces the spirit is called 'Intellect'.

Najm al-Dīn Rāzī describes the heart's significance in the spiritual landscape of man, "Know that the relationship of the heart to the body is like that of God's Throne to the world. In the same way that the Throne is the plane of manifestation for the repose of the attribute of compassion in the macrocosm, so too the heart is the place of manifestation for the repose of the attribute of spirituality in the microcosm... The heart, however, has a property and nobility that the Throne does not possess, for the heart is aware of receiving the effusion of the grace of the spirit, while the Throne has no such awareness". Rāzī, *Mirṣād al-ʿibād*, p. 201.

becomes enlightened by its meanings as its words provide solace to the seekers of Truth. This is because truly spiritual words are light, having arrived through gnosis and divine reception. This book speaks to the individual intellect, strengthening and refining it, affords it power, agency and awareness and connects it to the universal Intellect. Just as the source of all worldly power is the Sun, the source of spiritual power is the divine Intellect. Fire is the highest elemental nature and it is the Sun that heats the coldness of earth and water, ripening and transforming dense matter through its subtle rays and giving it life. Similarly, the Intellect's rays and life-giving power animate the entire human reality, bringing new life.

However, the Intellect's light is not a physical light but a spiritual and divine light that is the source of material light. Just as material light is one of the pillars of existence, spiritual light is from the divine attribute, the Light (*al-nūr*), and the Intellect emanates from a hidden, treasured light in the ancient knowledge of God. The Qur'ān says, "God is the Light of the heavens and the earth. The example of His light is like a niche within which is a lamp, the lamp is within a glass, the glass is as if it were a glittering star lit from a blessed olive tree, neither of the east nor of the west, whose oil would almost glow even if untouched by fire. Light upon light. God guides to His light whom He wills. God speaks to mankind in parables and He is the Omniscient" (24:35).[4]

---

4 Commenting on the Verse of Light, 'Abd al-Razzāq Kāshānī writes, "The heart is a luminous, disengaged substance halfway between the spirit and the soul. It is that through which true humanity is realized. The philosophers refer to it as the rational soul. The spirit is the inward dimension, and the animal soul is its mount and its outward dimension, halfway between it and the body. Thus, the Qur'ān [24:35] compares the heart to a glass and a shining star, while it compares the spirit to a lamp. The tree is the soul, the niche is the body. The heart is the intermediate reality in existence and in levels of descents, like the Guarded Tablet in the cosmos. The glass is an allusion to

The Intellect is the first principle of existence, a divine reality that manifests in all of creation and ultimately in the human being. The prophets have the greatest share of Intellect, as stated in the hadith, "God has not sent a prophet except with Intellect, one that is superior to his entire nation."[5] Some prophets are the perfect manifestation of the Intellect, such as Abraham, and exemplify the attribute of life and the new creation, such as Jesus. Among the spiritual mysteries of this work is that it exemplifies the principle of Jesus. This is because Jesus had a mother but no father and cannot rightly be included in the children of Adam. He is, therefore, a new creation like Adam, whom God created without precedent similar to Eve, who was created from Adam. Related to this thesis are the miracles of Jesus such as reviving the dead[6] and walking on water, water being the very origin and source of life.[7] Those who were dead and given life by Jesus were

---

the heart that is illumined by the spirit and illuminates everything around it by shining light upon them." Kāshānī, *Iṣtilāḥāt al-ṣufiyya*, pp. 167-168, cited in Murata, *The Tao of Islam*, pp. 299-300.

5 Kulaynī, *Uṣūl al-kāfi*, v. 1, p. 13

6 "Then God will say, 'Jesus, son of Mary! Remember My favour to you and to your mother: how I strengthened you with the Holy Spirit, so that you spoke to people in your infancy and as a grown man; how I taught you the Scripture and wisdom, the Torah and the Gospel; how, by My leave, you fashioned the shape of a bird out of clay, breathed into it, and it became, by My leave, a bird; how, by My leave, you healed the blind person and the leper; how, by My leave, you brought the dead back to life; how I restrained the Children of Israel from [harming] you when you brought them clear signs, and those who disbelieved said, "This is clearly nothing but sorcery" (5:110).

7 I heard Imam al-Ṣādiq say, "Fear God and do not envy each other. Jesus the son of Mary used to wander the land with his sacred law. So, he went out and among his companions was a short man who was very much attached to Jesus.

When Jesus arrived at the sea he said with certainty, "In the Name of God" and walked on the surface of the water. Seeing Jesus, the man also said

the manifestations of the new creation. Both Abraham and Jesus share the principle of life: Jesus epitomizes the Spirit and Abraham epitomizes the Intellect since the Intellect is light of the world of Spirits. The Intellect, therefore, not only endows with power but also life, as we clearly see in the miracles of both Jesus and Abraham.

Any foundational work that pioneers new knowledge must be ready to answer to the critiques of philosophy, theology, law, hadith and intellectual reasoning and should not be simply a compilation or exposition of a pre-existing ideas.The tripartite division of knowledge contained in the *The New Creation*, is one of the most sophisticated expositions in mysticism. If this spiritual path had only this work to its credit, it would have been sufficient.

The first seven chapters set the foundation for the eighth chapter, which is the aim of the work, *The Form of the Intellect and its Contents.* This book has a theoretical, practical and spiritual dimension, and is divided into two sections. The first seven chapters set the foundation for the second half of the book, starting from chapter eight, which is the key chapter in the whole work. Those who wish to develop the intellect can study the rational sciences and philosophy even though philosophy is only the shadow of the true Intellect which is pure light.

The aim of this book is to develop the true Intellect and beautify the inward dimension of the human being. Because this path is the path of the Intellect one must strive to revive the Intellect and perfect it through engaging with this work as wind ignites the ember!

---

with certainty, "In the Name of God" and walked on the water and followed Jesus. But he was filled with pride..."' Majlisī, *Biḥār al-anwār*, v. 14, p. 254.

Once someone asked Jesus , "How are you able to walk on water?"Jesus replied, "With certainty."Then someone said, "But we also have certainty!"Jesus then asked them, "Are stone, clay and gold equal in your eyes?" They replied, "Certainly not!" Jesus responded, "They are in mine." Ibn Ḥanbal, *Musnad.*

Commentary

Emulating the Qur'ān, the work begins with the doxology "In the name of God, the Merciful, the Compassionate" or *basmalla*, which is very first verse of its opening chapter, *al-Fātiḥā*. Then the author quotes a supplication relating to the subject of the book which is to be found among the narrations (hadith) of the Prophet's family (*ahl al-bayt*), "O Turner of the hearts and eyes, confirm my heart in Your religion. Do not make my heart swerve after you have guided me and bestow on me a mercy directly from You, for You are most generous."[8] This is a befitting prayer since the heart (*qalb*) and the eyesight (*baṣar*) fluctuate more than anything else, the former fluctuating spiritually and the latter physically. "The hearts of the children of Adam are between the two fingers of the Merciful. He directs them wherever he wills."[9] The eyes fluctuate the most from the physical faculties. From one perspective, the hearts and eyes refer to the spiritual and physical worlds, respectively. Alternatively, *abṣār* may also refer to

8 Tirmīdhī, no. 2140; Qummī, *Mafātiḥ al-jinān*, p. 49.

9 Muslim, Qadar, 17

insight which is the vision of the heart and not the physical eyes, as it says in the verse, "God alternates the night and day; There is a lesson in that for those who have insight (*al-abṣār*)" (24:44).

Thus, the supplication says, "confirm my heart on Your religion," since the heart is the *imām* (leader) of the body. If the *imām* is sound then the body will be sound. Asking for the heart's confirmation on the path, then mercy relates to the divine names of majesty and beauty, respectively. The first type is the mercy of guidance and second type is the mercy of protection since "God's mercy encompasses all things" (7:156). The prayer states, "God, increase my lifespan so that I may further enrich my life." One prays for long life so he can avail himself of divine munificence. "Expand my sustenance lest I become preoccupied in other than You. If you provide for me then You are sufficient!"

When it is said, "If I have been written among the wretched in the Mother of the Book, then make me among the felicitous" we can glean that the Mother of the Book (*umm al-kitāb*) is subject to renewal (*ja'l*), like the Tablet of Effacement and Establishment (*al-lawḥ al-maḥw wa al-ithbāt*), even if it is the origin of every book.

The prayer also relates to the fluctuation of the hearts and eyes, since the heart fluctuates between the two fingers of God and the night and the day are in alternation. This also informs the reader that the subject of this book concerns darkness and light, the definitive features of the night and day, which of themselves provide many lessons.

Imam 'Alī said, "Through reflection (*istibṣār*) one learns lessons (*i'tibār*)," and "Constant reflection leads to enlightenment." He said, "May God have mercy on a person who reflects, takes lesson, then perceives. If one does not realize the mystery, secret and wisdom of a thing he cannot learn a lesson from it since '*ibra* literally means 'crossing over'. Imam 'Alī said, "He who finds wisdom (*ḥikma*), learns a lesson." The lesson (*i'tibār*) arises from the wisdom that reveals its quintessence (*zubda*) and summary (*khulāṣa*). The way one learns lessons from the alternation of the night and day and the fluctuation of the heart is by receiving divine light and not turning away from it, as the Qur'ān says, "How many a sign in the heavens and the earth that they pass by and yet turn away" (12:105). Some signs are not contained in the written Book, but are existential verses written in the heavens and the earth, "We will show him our signs on the horizons and in the souls" (41:53). If one ponders the signs and understands their significance, it is knowledge that helps one arrive. A person who is guided benefits himself and a person who is blinded harms only himself. Blindness and sight here relate to insight (*baṣīra*) of the heart, not the eyes of the body. The verse states, "It is not the eyes that are blinded but the hearts that are in the chests" (22:46).

Some people are blinded of eyesight and some blinded of insight. Mu'āwiya said to one of the Banī Hāshim, your eyesight will be afflicted. He replied, but you, O Banī Umayyah, your insight will be afflicted, that is, your hearts and intellects. Spiritual wayfaring (*sayr wa sulūk*) and mysticism (*'irfān*) are based on the heart's vision not the eyesight, which is why the Qur'ān exhorts people to open the eyes of the heart. One cannot ignore the Qur'ān's counsel and rely on rational arguments of the scholars. Wayfaring only occurs through insight (*baṣīra*), which is guidance through the heart's vision. Imam 'Alī says that wisdom leads to understanding lessons and is acquired after one becomes sincere. "Whoever becomes sincere for the sake of God for forty days, springs of wisdom emerge from his heart and onto his tongue."[10]

Again, the criterion for obtaining wisdom is the heart. He who heeds lessons is among the foremost, traveling on the arc of ascent and returning to the hereafter through light and insight. Rational proofs, that are no more than conjecture will not lead a person to reality. But the path of the wayfarer, the existentially awake person

10 Ṣadūq, *'Uyūn akhbār al-Riḍā*, p. 258; Ḥillī, *'Uddat al-dā'ī*, p. 170; Kulaynī, *Usūl al-kāfī*, v. 2, p. 16

in the arc of ascent and descent, depends on insight, the heart and light, all of which are key themes in this book.

The Path of God

The introduction begins with the prayer, "In the name of Light..." which revolves around the theme of light. In Arabic, it is called *barāʿāt al-istihlāl*, which is a skillful opening that contains allusions to the main themes of a work or summarizes the entire book. Some prayers and hadith have weak chains of transmission but their meaning and content accord with scripture and agree with the Intellect so we cannot reject them on this basis alone. Relying solely on chains of transmission to authenticate hadith ignores the critical role of content and meaning. This prayer is found in both Sunnī and Shīʿī hadith collections and is called the supplication of light which has been narrated by Salmān, from Fāṭima al-Zahrā.

God is the light of light, or that the first Intellect is light, or that it has been created by light. All of the terms mentioned in this prayer allude to various theophanies (*majālī*) and manifestations, conforming with the approach of mysticism, which is unveiling (*kashf*) and witnessing (*shuhūd*), and the methodology of philosophy, law (*sharīʿa)* and rationality. Since the content of the hadith is not in conflict with any of the various types of knowledge mentioned above, there is no need to exclusively rely on its chain of transmission.

The prayer is not just the opening statement but also intimates the theme of the book, which is light. If a saint utters such words, it is not rhetorical, but for the purpose of imparting knowledge. He is able to describe reality with a natural eloquence. These words are taken directly from the Qurʾān, "By the Mount (Tūr), and the Inscribed Book (*kitab mastūr*), and the Unfurled Parchment (*raqq manshūr*)," (52:1-3). God swears by the Tūr, the sacred mountain where He spoke to Moses. *Mastūr* means written, *raqq*, that which is written on, *habr* means happiness (*surūr*) as in the verse, "Enter the garden, you and your spouses, rejoicing (*tuḥbarūn*)" (43:70). It also means blessing (*ni'ma*) and to be honored greatly.

The next section identifies and defines the true nature of the path of God, which is the first step in traveling the path. The author identifies the methodology by which one traverses the path. For example, if one wishes to go to the Ka'ba, he cannot arrive through speculation. In the past, it required many months of travel before one reached Mecca. Even now, one cannot simply board a plane and guess the direction in which he should travel. If you rely on speculation you will not arrive and will certainly waste resources, time and lifespan. In other words, life is not long enough to tread the path through guesswork and conjecture. Similarly, the path of God cannot be fathomed through conjecture but perceived only by certainty. God has, in fact, forbidden conjecture, saying that conjecture is not knowledge and cannot benefit one in the pursuit of Truth, as the verse states, "They have no knowledge of it, but follow conjecture. Conjecture cannot avail against Truth in the least" (53:28). Thus, the text reads that the path of God cannot be perceived by conjecture. There is, however, a type of conjecture that is acceptable, one that is endorsed by light, not one acquired by the rational mind, as in, "Those who suppose (*yaẓunnūn*) that they will meet their Lord" (2:46). Here, the Qur'ān praises this type of 'supposition' which is endorsed by light and identifies reality, albeit from afar.

One cannot traverse the path to God through blind conformity (*taqlīd*), since traveling the path is equivalent to attaining perfection. Lexically, *taqlīd* means following in the footsteps of one's forebears without the slightest deviation. In legal terms, it means accepting the statement of another without proof. It is self-evident that blind conformity is a sign of ignorance, since one imitates another *because* of ignorance. Therefore, the path of God cannot be attained through blind conformity because knowledge is essential to the path. One must have knowledge of its stations, the maladies of the soul and visionary experience in order to arrive at individual perfection. There is no place for ignorance on the path of perfection. *Taqlīd* is the suspension of the Intellect and limited by the level of learning of the one who is being imitated. Both conjecture and blind conformity are types of darkness and one cannot arrive through darkness, nor a mixture of darkness and light, nor shadow (*ẓill*) and shade (*fay*).

Ẓill is shadow before noon, and *fay* is the afternoon shadow. *Ẓill* contains light but it still has darkness and the path of God is only light. Because God is Light, the path of God is a ray emanating from the source of that light. This ray is not a mixture of light and darkness, shadow, conjecture, or blind conformity. "God is the light of the heavens and the earth" (24:35). The path is identical to its goal, a theophany from its source and the sun of reality, which is light. If the source of this path is light, then its path is also light, and its people are also clothed in a garment of light when they walk this path. They call upon God with insight from His command.

A mystical path supported by evidence is the correct way to proceed. Those who do not have light are alive outwardly but dead inwardly, as the verse states, "Is he who was dead and We revived, having given him a light by which he walks amongst people, like one who is in inexorable darkness? Thus, the deeds of the unbelievers are made to seem alluring to them" (6:122). Since, the goal is God, who is absolute perfection and Light, the true path to God is the path of light—all else is a form of darkness. God is the one who places a light before them so they walk with it among people, and life is equated with light. "Do not consider those who have been killed on the path of God as dead, but they are alive receiving sustenance from their Lord" (3:169). In this case, people consider them to be dead but God says that they are living. They are truly alive, even though their bodies are dead and those who are in darkness are considered dead even though their bodies are alive. The verse states that they walk amongst people with light, that is, they walk the path to God while still amongst them. This has been made very clear by the Qur'ān and the verse does not require a large apparatus of commentary and interpretation. In fact, all religions would confirm the idea that a person cannot travel the path of God without light.

From the following passages in the Bible, we see the corresponding Christian view. Jesus addresses his companions, "You are the salt of the earth. But if the salt loses its saltiness, how can it be made salty again?" When we come across such words from the Bible, we should look at it with a view of its spiritual content not its chain of transmission. As long as these verses agree with the message of the Qur'ān, the spirit of the hadith and the dictates of reason, then they should be deemed valid. These verses and others should be accepted on the basis of their content not on the false premise that the entirety of the Bible has been altered.

Jesus says, "It is no longer good for anything, except to be thrown out and trampled underfoot. You are the light of the world. A town built on a hill cannot be hidden. Neither do people light a lamp and put it under a bowl. Instead they put it on its stand, and it gives light to everyone in the house." In the same way, let your light shine before others, that they may see your good deeds and glorify your fathers in heaven" (Matthew 5:13, 14). Therefore, if you have received some of the divine teachings then put yourself in the appropriate place that God has chosen for you. Again, these verses are self-evident and correspond to original nature (*fiṭra*). Those who dispute these teachings on the basis that the Bible has been altered have failed to see truth and have, in effect, falsified the signs God. The Bible says, "Let your light shine before others," because you are a light amongst people, in your speech or your person, since God has made you a light. You will have chosen silence when God has chosen speech for you. If you do not act with light, you have opposed what God has done for you. Why do you choose darkness when God has chosen light for you?

When the Bible says, "Glorify your fathers in heaven," the word father and son do not denote physical paternity. Even the Qur'ān uses the word '*ibn*' metaphorically, as in *ibn al-sabīl* to mean traveller. Moreover, Jesus is not the only son of God, but every luminous thing is the son of God, and all those who have been born from light. The Bible states, "To all who did receive him, to those who believed in his name, he gave the right to become children of God, children born not of blood, nor the will of the flesh nor the will of man, but born of God" (John 1:12-13).

"Jesus said, 'None can ascend to the heavens unless he has been born twice.' 'How can someone be born when they are old?' Nicodemus asked. 'Surely they cannot enter a second time into their mother's womb to be born!' Jesus said, 'Flesh gives birth to flesh, but the Spirit gives birth to spirit' You should not be surprised at my saying, you must be born again'" (John 3:3-8). The second birth is not physical, but luminous. Jesus outright denies being born physically from God, so how can it be claimed that he is the son of God? The belief that Jesus is the physical son of God is based on a material approach to theology and blind conformity to the scholars of religion, described in the Bible verses condemning the Pharisees, who were the exoterically minded professional scholars of religion and ardent legalists. They denied Jesus because he opposed their blind conformity to their customs and traditions. They also opposed Jesus' practice of keeping company with the downtrodden and the sinners. They were oblivious to the fact that the Messiah would need to impart his teachings to these groups, particularly the sinners in need of reform. These objections originate from ignorance, hypocrisy and misguided erudition, so we seek refuge from ignorance and its people.

The ignorant are defined as those who rely on conjecture and blind conformity. Their movement occurs in complete darkness, or a mixture of light and darkness or through shadows. The ignorant are members of the same family tree, born of their fathers and mothers, just as the spiritual have their fathers and mothers. Some of them are the *imāms* of unbelief.

Just as spiritual birth is from light and a pure, luminous womb, there is a birth from ignorance, and a dark, impure womb. While some are born of light, others are born of darkness from the fathers and mothers of ignorance. Just as the people of light are the eyes, hands or hearts of their spiritual parents, the people of ignorance are the eyes, hands and hearts of the progenitors of ignorance. The Qur'ān states, "Or, like the depths of darkness in a vast, abysmal sea covered by wave upon wave with clouds above. Layer upon layer of darkness, when he holds out his hand he can barely see it. He whom God gives no light has no light at all" (24:40). The ignorant person is in a state of darkness, as if he is in a deep ocean and when he sticks out his hand, metaphorically speaking, he can barely see it. The ship of his soul is sailing on the vast ocean of Being and it is enveloped in layers of ignorance in a deep ocean of darkness. Since light is given by God, he who does not have a light from God has no light. One must strive to acquire divine light. Thus, it is said that the path is from God, with God, and in God.

The Spiritually Veiled

Those who are veiled fall under three types: the ignorant, the hypocrite and the misguided scholar. The ignorant is one who has had little or no contact with religion and spirituality, the simple minded like the elderly, or the imitator and conjecturer, as the verse states "They have no knowledge of it, but follow conjecture. Conjecture does not avail against Truth in the least" (53:28). The author has sought refuge in God from being included among the ignorant, the hypocrites and the conjecturers. The ignorant person is in complete darkness, as the Qur'ān says, "Or like the depths of darkness in a vast, abysmal sea covered by wave upon wave with clouds above. Layer upon layer of darkness, when he holds out his hand he can barely see it; He whom God gives no light has no light at all" (24:40). There are many categories of the ignorant, the simple, the imitator, and so on, although it could be said the conjecturer possesses a certain amount of light.

The second type among the veiled is the hypocrite, whom the Qur'ān describes, "Some say, 'We believe in God and the Last Day,' but they do not really believe. They try to deceive God and the believers but they only deceive themselves without realizing it. There is a disease in their hearts, to which God adds more. Agonizing torment awaits them for their persistent lying. When it is said to them, 'Do not cause corruption on earth,' they say, 'We are but reformers!' They are indeed the agents of corruption, but they do not feel it. When it is said to them, 'Believe, as others have believed,' they say, 'Should we believe like fools?' *They* are the fools, but they do not realize it. When they meet the believers, they say, 'We believe,' but when they are alone with their devils, they say, 'We are really with you; we were only mocking.' God is mocking them, and giving them respite to wander blindly in their insolence. They have bought error in exchange for guidance, so their trade reaps no profit nor are they rightly guided. They are like people who kindle a fire, and when it lights up everything around them, God takes away all their light, leaving them in utter darkness, unable to see — deaf, dumb, and blind, they will never return." (2:8-18). These verses state that the hypocrites kindle a fire that gives off light. They reap the benefit of the first light of faith. However, because of their hypocrisy that light is put out. They become deaf, dumb and blind, or remain in darkness with respect to their hearing, speaking and seeing so they cannot find their way back.

The verses describe yet another state of the hypocrites, using the metaphor of thunder and lightning in a storm. They are walking in a dark storm, when they hear the thunderclaps, they put their fingers in their ears out of fear. But when lightning illuminates their path, that is, when they meet the believers, their vision returns briefly, but are blinded as soon as they leave their company. This type of veiled individual is the misguided scholar. These categories are derived from the Qur'ān and hadith. "Have you seen the person who has taken as a god his desire, whom God allows to stray in the face of knowledge, sealing his hearing and heart and covering his sight? Then who can guide him after God? Will you not take heed?" (45:23). The three types of veiled individuals, the ignorant, the hypocrite and the misguided scholar also have a parallel in the Bible.

The Bible condemns these people saying, "Woe to you, teachers of the Law and Pharisees, you hypocrites." In Arabic, the term '*wayl*' is used to mean perdition, humiliation, or signifies a valley in hell. The Qur'ān states, "No! We hurl truth against falsehood, striking it on the head (*yaḍmaghuhū*) and suddenly vanishing! Woe to you for the way you describe God!" (21:18). '*Ḍamagha*' means a fatal strike to the head. The word used in the Arabic rendition of the Bible is '*murāʿūn*', which means to display what one is not. The word occurs in the Qur'ān, in the verse, "They show off in front of people and remember God only a little" (4:142). We can glean from these verses of the Bible that the message of Christianity is to call people to the kingdom of heaven, or the spiritual and unseen realms, which requires a wakeful heart and a path of gnosis and illumination. Christianity calls people to gnosis since the kingdom of heaven refers to spiritual mysteries and unseen realities. A person cannot grasp the reality of a thing without spiritual light. The Qur'ān also invites people to the kingdom of heaven, spiritual life and wayfaring, "Thus, We showed Abraham the kingdom of the heavens and the earth, so that he might be among those who have certainty" (6:75). "Do they not contemplate upon the kingdom of the heavens and the earth and all that God has created?" (7:185). While contemplating on the kingdom of the heaven and the earth requires certain discipline, it requires, most of all, a spiritual way.

Jesus says that they close the doors to the kingdom of heaven and want people to follow them blindly, forbidding them from seeking the kingdom of heaven. The legal doctors and scholars of the Israelites were following the outward form of their law, but Jesus rebuked them saying that they neither enter the spiritual way nor allow others to enter. The Bible is filled with statements of Jesus warning the people, especially the so-called scholars of law and those who lead people blindly. The Bible says, "Woe to you, teachers of the Law and Pharisees, you hypocrites! You shut the door of the kingdom of heaven in people's faces. You yourselves do not enter, nor will you let those enter who are trying to" (Matthew 23:13). Jesus severely criticized their fanatical adherence to the letter of the law while entirely disregarding its spirit. The Pharisees of yesterday are rampant today in every religion, those who outwardly appear as tidy and chaste but inwardly reek of impurity and death.

Jesus also called them snakes and vipers. Even among snakes some are dreadful and others are beneficial, such as the snake of Moses which helped him vanquish the Pharaoh's magicians. "'Moses, what is that in your right hand?' 'It is my staff,' he said, 'I lean on it; restrain my sheep with it; I also have other uses for it.' God said, 'Throw it down, Moses.' So he threw it down, and all of a sudden it was a snake moving swiftly'" (20:17-20). In this verse, it was called *ḥayya*, a small snake, but when he confronted the Pharaoh, it was called *thuʿbān*, or a serpent, to display a miracle and also invoke fear. "Moses said, 'Pharaoh, I am a messenger from the Lord of all the Worlds, duty-bound to say nothing about God but the truth, and I have brought you a clear sign from your Lord. Let the Children of Israel go with me.' He said, 'Produce this sign you have brought, if you are telling the truth.' So Moses threw his staff and, lo and behold, it was a snake, clear to all" (7:104-108).

The blood of every prophet from Abel to Zakariya—who was the last martyr during Jesus' life—is on the hands of those he condemned. He cursed them, and that curse continues from one generation to the next because each perpetuates the wickedness of his forefathers. Similarly, those living today who acquiesce to the killing of the prophets and saints of the past are also cursed because there is an inward correspondence with those deeds. Therefore, the bridge that links the sins of the fathers to their children must be severed. The branch of evil must be cut so there is new growth on fresh earth.

The Path of Pure Light

The path can only be attained through pure light, not a mixture of light and darkness, shade, shadow, rational deduction and discursive thought, even if they prove to be correct. The philosophers, theologians, and rationalists use deductive reasoning, words and concepts but these can never reach the true nature of reality. One reaches the true nature of reality through light. Imam 'Alī says, "He who does not know me through light does not know me."[11] This is confirmed by the

---

11 Ibn al-Ḥadīd, *Sharh Nahj al-Balāgha*, v. 2, p. 450. Salmān and Abū Dharr relate that Amīr al-Mu'minīn said, "O Salmān and Jundub, he whose allegiance to me (*wilāya*) is greater outwardly than it is inwardly is weak in deeds. The believer's faith is not complete until he recognizes me through light, and if he knows me through light, then he is a believer whose heart God has tested for faith, expanded his breast for Islam. He has acquired gnosis of religion and so he perceives. He who falls short of that remains in doubt and misgivings. O Salmān and Jundub, knowing me through light is knowing God through light, and knowing God is knowing me—and that is true religion, as God says, 'They were commanded only to worship God, becoming sincere for Him in religion'"(98:5).

verses of the Qur'ān which state, "He walks among humanity with a light" and "Guidance has come to you from your Lord" (10:57). Rational thought is limited by the concepts but real perception through light is the way of the saints.

One might ask, how does one see through light? This sort of perception is self-evident for the people of God. It requires knowledge, training, spiritual discipline and a divine connection. The people of God witness it first-hand and the hadith clearly states the primacy of light, "Knowledge is not extensive learning, it is but a light that God casts in the heart of whomever He wishes to guide."[12] Therefore, whatever knowledge one possesses, philosophical, theological, legal, or otherwise, it is not considered knowledge until it reaches the level of luminosity. This is because the reality of knowledge is divine light, one that God casts in the hearts. In another hadith, "Knowledge is a light and brightness that God casts in the hearts of the saints," and, "Every servant has two eyes of the heart which are unseen and perceive the Unseen." When the Qur'ān and hadith insist that the spiritual path is tread with divine light and the opening of the heart's eyes, the exoteric scholars of every religion continue to focus on its legal and rational aspects, shutting the door to true spirituality. If the religious scholars are truly the divine emissaries then where are the prescriptions for treating the soul? Where are the attainments to spiritual stations, the attachment (*ta'alluq*), assuming of divine attributes (*takhalluq*) and realization (*taḥaqquq*) of the divine names? Quoting these hadith from the Imams are not for the sake of beautifying speech but are remedies for spiritual illnesses. The Imams were spiritual physicians, writing prescriptions for people, yet the religious scholars blindly take from their pharmacy without understanding.

When a saint claims to have received knowledge directly from God, most people dismiss it and accuse him of heresy even though

12 Majlisī, *Biḥār al-anwār*, v. 1, p. 225.

the Qur'ān clearly states, "Have God consciousness and God will teach you" (2:282). Dismissing a saint is equivalent to dismissing the Qur'ān, because when one who receives knowledge from God receives the signs (*ayāt*) of God. Just as the Qur'ān is composed of verses (*ayāt*), the saint becomes the manifestation of those divine signs. In fact, the saint is the very manifestation of the Qur'ān, since its verses require an external paradigm, one who applies its meaning in the world. Thus, if one rejects the saint, one rejects the Qur'ān itself.

The saints take God as the first and only teacher, based on the verse, "Be God-conscious (*taqwa*) and God will teach you" (2:282) and the hadith, "Knowledge is a light that God casts in the heart of whomever He wishes to guide." This *taqwa,* which includes its degrees and stations on the plane of the five outward senses and the inward faculties, refers to its true reality, not a superficial degree that allows anyone to learn directly from God. Those who learn directly from God are few in number. Nonetheless, everyone should strive to earn this privilege. Elsewhere, the Qur'ān says, "Whoever is God-conscious, God will find a way out for him, and provide from an unexpected source. Those who put their trust in God, He is sufficient. God achieves His purpose; He has set a due measure for everything" (65:2-3).

Divinely inspired knowledge is light. It is self-evident and does not need an external proof. This is because light is, by definition, luminous and illuminates others. The Qur'ān says, "There are those who dispute about God without knowledge and follow every rebellious devil" (22:3) and, "There are those who dispute concerning God without knowledge, guidance or a luminous Book" (22:8). Here, knowledge refers to true knowledge, not one founded on faulty reasoning or weak hadith transmission or a general type of guidance that one obtains after reaching certain conclusions. Real guidance is one that produces certitude that it is indeed God-given. Thus, knowledge is light, its people are light, the path is light and the goal is light.

After providing evidence from the Qur'ān and hadith to establish the thesis of the book, namely, that the only path that leads to perfection is the path of light, a discussion of its manifestation follows. Light is a single reality which at times, manifests outwardly as expression (*'ibāra*), at times allusion (*ishāra*) and at times as reality (*ḥaqīqa*) itself. Those who attain it are but a few as Imam 'Alī says, "Do not feel lonely on the path of guidance due the paucity of its followers. People have gathered around a feast whose satiation is brief and whose hunger is prolonged."[13] Loneliness (*waḥsha*) is a type of constriction and its opposite is intimacy (*uns*), which is expansiveness. The Bible says, "Enter through the narrow gate. For wide is the gate and broad is the road that leads to destruction, and many enter through it. But small is the gate and narrow the road that leads to life, and only a few find it" (Matthew 7:13-14).

The gate that leads to perdition is wide open because of the multitude of people who will enter it, as Qur'ān says, "Most of them are averse to the Truth" (43:78). Those who follow light are few but the misguided are many. The wayfarer on the path to God faces trials and hardships in confronting his own soul—this is the narrow gate. The Bible says, Someone asked him, "Lord, are only a few people going to be saved?" He said to them, "Make every effort to enter through the narrow door, because many, I tell you, will try to enter and will not be able to. Once the owner of the house gets up and closes the door, you will stand outside knocking and pleading," (Luke 13:22-30). Jesus will disown them and cast them out.

---

13 *Nahj al-Balāgha*, sermon 201.

The Knowledge of Reality

As mentioned earlier, light is a singular reality but manifests as expression (*ishāra*), allusion (*'ibāra*) and reality (*ḥaqīqa*). Since the subject of our discussion is reality, which is the station of the Intellect, the knowledge of reality was mentioned first, followed by the manifestation of reality and then the station of reality.

'Ḥaqīqa' is the essence (*kunh*) of a thing. Here, it refers to the Intellect,[14] which is the first thing that God created and the most beloved and noble of His creation. It is also called the world of Intellect, in contrast to the Imaginal and material worlds. All things have a reality and the Intellect is the source of all realities. As for the knowledge of reality, the hadith states, "Knowledge is the lantern of the Intellect."[15] This chapter describes the knowledge of reality which is the lantern of the Intellect. The language of the world of Intellect originates in divine knowledge, as the hadith describes in chapter eight. The Prophet said, "God created the Intellect from a hidden, treasured light in His ancient knowledge, of which neither a sent messenger nor a proximate angel had any awareness." This chapter is an exposition of the knowledge of reality, expressing certain concepts, signs, or specific qualities of the language of the world of Intellect.

The people of the Intellect do not engage in interpretation. This is because the world of Intellect is the essence and source of light. It reveals itself without form, materiality, image, or representation. Since God created the Intellect first and foremost, it is pure light. There are some individuals who are associated with the world of Intellect

---

14 The word in Arabic for intellect is *'aql*. The lexical meaning of *'aql* is to tie, fetter or bind, which also indicates its function, that is to tether ideas in the mind through limiting and defining them, or as the Prophet states, "The intellect is a fetter against ignorance." Majlisī, *Bihār al-anwār*, v. 1, p. 117.

15 *Ghurar al-ḥikam*, p. 536.

directly and do not engage in interpretation. Those who speak from the plane of the Intellect speak without interpretation. Their vision accords with their being and their affiliation with the pure light of Intellect. Abraham was of this station and would state things exactly as he saw them in the world of Intellect. The Prophet said, "God show me things as they truly are." Similarly, Abraham glanced at the stars in the material plane and immediately understood that he was ill. "He took one look at the stars and said, 'I am ill'" (37:88-89). Similarly, a person looks at the face of another and sees light. Those who have this sort of luminous insight (*firāsa*) immediately look at a face then see light emanating from it, or they see light manifesting on the face of a believer.

There is some discrepancy in the interpretation of Abraham's statement. Some scholars hold that in order to extricate himself from the company of certain people, Abraham said that he was ill. Others claim that Abraham lied on three occasions and that, according to certain hadith, this was the first. The second time was when he was questioned about breaking the idols, to which he replied, "the largest of them," and a third time was when he said that Sarah was his sister, whereas, in fact, she was his wife.

These commentators try to rationalize Abraham's statements through hadith that permit lying for the sake of a greater good. If a person averts a greater harm through lying, then it is not considered a lie in the *sharīʿa*. However, even if Abraham lied on this occasion, his speech was still based on some reality existing in the world of Intellect, which then manifested on the material plane.

In the Imaginal world, he saw himself sacrificing his son in a dream, but he did not resort to interpreting the dream. Since the Intellectual world is the world of meaning and the Imaginal world is the world of forms, Abraham's speech predominantly expressed meaning rather than form. "We gave Abraham sound judgement from before, and We were aware when he said to his father and his people, 'What are these images to which you are devoted? (21:51-52). His words also emphasize the return to original nature (*fiṭra*)[16] because *fiṭra* originates from the world of Intellect, "He said, 'Your true Lord is the Lord of the heavens and the earth, who engendered (*faṭara*) them, and to Whom I am a witness'" (21:56). Abraham also saw a reality in the Imaginal world, but one which originated in the Intellectual world. Abraham spoke through the language of the Intellect, which consists of divine proofs originating in the lights of reality. Having smashed the idols, Abraham's argument against the idolaters originated from the luminous Intellect, even if those same arguments can be made from the rational mind.

The divine Intellect is light but the rational mind is a veil, even if it reaches a correct conclusion. As such, theology, jurisprudence and philosophy use the rational mind to discover truths. In Imam 'Alī's conversation with the Jewish man we find that even though Imam 'Alī never learned philosophy he spoke 'philosophically' through the heart's light. The mystic, therefore, speaks philosophically through light but the philosopher imitates the words of the mystic yet remains veiled. In this example, the Jewish man was amazed by the Imam's philosophical discourse inasmuch as he considered him to be a philosopher, but the Imam spoke from the heart's light that simply resonated with the listener.

---

16 *Fiṭra* means creation, initiation and origination. It is that God engendered the creatures with innate knowledge of Himself or it is the nature with which He created them in their mother's wombs. God says, "So turn your face sincerely towards religion, the original nature in which God has fashioned mankind—there is no altering of God's creation! This is the true religion, though most people do not realize it." [30:30]. "I worship Him who originated me and He will certainly guide me" [43:27]. "Why should I not worship the One who originated me" [36:22]. It is said that every person originates with the innate knowledge that God is Lord and Creator. Al-Majid, *The Principles of Correspondences*, p. 188.

Since Abraham's station is that of the Intellect and the Intellect is described as being clear, the Qur'ān juxtaposes the Intellect's clarity to his nation's clear (*mubīn*) misguidance. "He said, 'You and your fathers have clearly gone astray' (21:54). His trial was also clear, "This was indeed the clear trial" (37:106), as it was for his progeny, the righteous and one who has wronged himself, We gave Abraham the good news of Isaac—a prophet and a righteous man—and blessed him and Isaac too: some of their offspring were good, but some clearly wronged themselves" (37:112-113).

The World of Intellect

Some of qualities of the world of Intellect were mentioned in the previous section, namely, that it is the world of proof, evidence and meaning. Abraham epitomizes this world and is among the people of proofs, evidence and meanings. Furthermore, the world of Intellect is the world of lights and Abraham's place of witnessing, as stated in the Qur'ānic verse, "When the night grew dark over him he saw a star and said, 'This is my Lord,' (6:76) but when it set, he said, 'I do not like things that set'" Abraham is from the world of lights because the Intellect is pure light.

It is said that Abraham's nation were the Sabeans, an ancient Semitic civilization who used to worship the stars. Abraham argued from the light of original nature (*fiṭra*)—not the rational mind, that God is not a setting star (*āfilīn*) because that which sets is created. God is eternal and cannot be described as rising or setting, which are signs of the engendered. After maintaining that God is neither star nor sun, giving examples of luminous bodies, he said, "I have turned my face as a true believer towards Him who created the heavens and the earth—I am not one of the polytheists" (6:79). He returned to original nature (*fiṭra*) stating that God originated and created the world without precedence.

Abraham used the divine name, *al-Fāṭir*, one of the names of original being that corresponds with the Intellect. In religious discourse, the world of Intellect is called the world of spirits, since the Spirit is the origin of creation, followed by the Imaginal and material worlds. Thus, the world of Intellect is the world of Spirits.[17]

Abraham said, "My Lord, show me how you revive the dead." He desired to advance from the knowledge of certainty to the vision of certainty, so he resorted to the name, the Living (*al-Ḥayy*), which governs the world of spirits and the Intellect. The world of Intellect is the world of lights, the world of lights is the world of spirits and the world of spirits is the world of life.

Several examples of the power of life vested in Abraham are given in the Qur'ān, such as reviving the birds, sparing his son's life, and engaging in the debate with Nimrod ibn Canaan, the first human to claim Godhead. The Qur'ān says, "Have you not seen the one who disputed with Abraham about his Lord because God had given him kingship? When Abraham said, 'My Lord is the one who gives life and death" (2:258). This verse represents all of the names that governed Abraham's being and epitomized his existence, such as life, light, the sound argument and potent speech. Nimrod's arguments claiming to have the power to kill or spare a life were weak in comparison to Abraham's. Yet Abraham was the one to revive the birds, with God's permission, and did not claim Godhead. He argued that if you claim that you can take life, you cannot do so without injury. That is, you take life through killing through some intermediary such as a sword

---

17 When the spirit is engaged in thought, discernment, knowledge and truth it is called intellect. The Prophet states, "The very basis of man is his intellect, and the man devoid of intellect has no religion."(*Rawḍat al-wā'iẓīn*, p. 9).

It is the most luminous dimension of the human being for which the Prophet said, "The Intellect is a light that God has created for mankind and has made it illuminate the heart, so he may know the difference between manifest things and unseen things." Aḥsā'ī, *'Awālī al-la'ālī*, v. 1, p. 248, no. 4.

or strangulation, but God can take life without intermediary and without injury to the body. Secondly, you cannot revive those you have killed or give life to those who are already dead.

The Manifestations of Reality

The word *majālī* (manifestations) comes from *jalīy* which means manifest, as opposed to *khafī*, which means hidden. *Ḥaqīqa* means essence, epitome (*khulāṣa*), mystery (*sirr*), origin (*aṣl*), inscription (*naqsh*), or source (*nab*ʿ). After describing the names and signs of the world of Intellect and Abraham being its complete manifestation, we investigate the manifestations of the Intellect. The text reads, "Know that Reality is the unveiling of a phenomenon in its true form. It is a luminous unveiling in any world and in any language." The people of Intellect perceive things through light, as they truly are. Theirs is a luminous unveiling in any world, spiritual, imaginal or material, whether in wakefulness, sleep or a half-sleep state. They perceive the real, essential or luminous aspect of a thing.

Similarly, their dreams inform them of reality, like the break of dawn. These dreams do not need interpretation, presenting themselves without distortion and being clothed in any other form. They are considered firm signs (*ayāt muḥkamāt*) not ambiguous ones (*mutashābihāt*), being that they are luminous realities. Even though the Imaginal is a luminous world, it necessitates interpretation. However, an entity in the Imaginal world has a luminous reality which is its mystery or essence, because as the Prophet stated, "For every truth there is a reality."[18] The Imaginal world is a truth but it also possesses a reality, which is its essence and luminous aspect. The same is true for the material world, which is a truth but possesses a reality, source and light.

---

18 Isfahānī, *Mufradāt alfāẓ al-Qurʾān*, p. 247

The three, Intellectual, Imaginal and material, worlds originate in a single reality, light, which is present in each world. When light descends into a particular world, it becomes colored by that world, and although the source is one, its colors differ according to each world. Thus far, we have been discussing the universal manifestation of reality, namely its outward referent.

As mentioned, the complete manifestation of the world of reality (*ḥaqīqa*) is the world of Intellect, personified in Abraham. In each of these worlds, there is a vision of reality *in* that very world. Because each world is a reality in itself, the vision of reality is not interpreted in another world. However, if it crosses from the Intellect to the Imaginal or from the Intellect to the sensory, there is no interpretation because it is a single reality manifesting in different worlds. In other words, not everything that is seen in the Imaginal world requires interpretation. The people of reality see it as it truly is, in the Imaginal or sensory worlds even if it is colored by those worlds. The vision of reality occurs in descending or ascending degrees, from the Intellectual to the Imaginal or the Intellectual to the sensory or from the Imaginal to the sensory. It can occur in ascending degrees like one who sees the sensory as a reality in the Intellect, or in the Imaginal.

Thus, there are six divisions, three descending and three ascending. In whichever world the reality appears, it takes on the color of that world, but retains its reality and original luminosity. It is neither interpretation, shadow, suspension (*ta'ṭīl*) or a confused dream (*aḍghāth aḥlām*) and is seen with the luminosity of the beholder's insight. This type of seeing is physical, referred to by the word, *ru'ya*, with the feminine ending '*tā*'. There is another type of seeing in the dream world, referred to by the word, *ru'ya*, ending with the long *alef*. One may see a dream, as is, without needing interpretation, like one who sees a dream within a dream. There is no interpretation because the second dream remains in the Imaginal world and does not cross over to another world. One may also have a sensory Imaginal vision which is realized in the sensory world and is interpreted there as well, like one who sees milk in a dream and interprets it as milk. Then, there is one who has a sensory vision and it is as if he is seeing a dream within a dream. Because wakefulness is also a type of dream, as Imam ʿAlī says, "People are asleep and when they die, they wake up."[19] Just as one may see a dream within a dream in the Imaginal world, one can see a 'dream' within a 'dream' in the sensory world. From this perspective, the sensory world is like the Imaginal even if it is perceived by the senses. However, the people of reality are awake vis-à-vis reality even though they are asleep from another perspective, as it is said, their eyes sleep but their hearts are awake. Therefore, the sensory world is considered sleep and the Imaginal world is wakefulness, whereas normally, one would consider the sensory world as wakefulness and the Imaginal world as sleep. The same relationship exists between the Imaginal and Intellectual worlds. The Imaginal corresponds to sleep and the Intellectual to wakefulness, whereas it was said that the Intellectual corresponds to sleep and the Imaginal to wakefulness.

There are many permutations of sleep and wakefulness between each of these three worlds. The same can be applied to the half-sleep state (*sina*). The gnostic might see a dream within a dream, witness the sensory within the sensory, or reality within a reality in the Intellect or *sina* within *sina*; each reality is seen in its own world without crossing over to another world. Witnessing the sensory within the sensory is also called 'reading of the signs' (*qirāʾat al-āyāt*). For example, these permutations can be understood by contemplating on the number five, which is always preserved in any of its multiples. When it is squared the result is twenty-five, and each square thereafter preserves the number

---

19 Majlisī, *Biḥār al-anwār*, v. 4, p. 43; Mazandarānī, *Sharḥ Uṣūl al-kāfī*, v. 2, p. 192; ʿIrāqī, *Takhrīj aḥadīth iḥyā ʿulūm al-dīn*, v. 4, p. 28; Suyūtī, *al-Durr al-manthūr*, p. 133.

twenty-five. In other words, five and its 'child' which is twenty-five, are both preserved in their squares. Similarly, reality preserves itself in every world, while acceding to the color of that world. Five is considered one of the numbers of circularity that indicate perfection and give rise to 'offspring'. Similarly, reality is always present in every world, as a 'firm sign', even if it is colored by the particularities of a realm. The reality of six-hundred and twenty-five is five. The people of reality recognize it as five since it is the origin but a person of another world may perceive it as six-hundred and twenty-five. Both are correct but the latter is considered interpretation. Ibn al-ʿArabī maintains that interpretation is a necessary feature of the Imaginal world. However, the author has expanded on this and stated that there are many more permutations and interrelationships between the worlds which engender multiple levels of interpretation.

The Station of Reality

As mentioned earlier, the worlds are three, the material, Imaginal, and Intellectual. The people of reality have a firm station belonging to the station of the Intellect. As they are primarily engaged in this station, it is their point of departure; they are not limited by it and explore other stations as well. The station of reality is the world of the Intellect, which is pure light, one which originates from the hidden, treasured, light in the divine knowledge. It is not obscured by the darkness of materiality nor shadowed by the Imagination, since the Imagination is the shadow of the Intellect and materiality is a shadow of the Imagination. There is no shadow in the world of Intellect, nor is there is suspension (*taʿṭīl*), such as confused dreams, which leads to falsehoods. The gnosis of the people of this station is not obfuscated by the darkness of nature and the shadow of the Imagination, even if the Imagination has some light.

Shadow (*tadhlīl*) can be used in a general sense to mean any type of darkness, or in a specific sense to mean the shadow of the Imaginal world (*barzakh*), because the material world is darkness (*ẓalām*). In any case, the world of Intellect is pure light and there is nothing more luminous than the Intellect. It is the greatest theophany of its Creator, which the Qur'ān describes as light, as in the verse, "God is the light of the heavens and the earth. The parable of His light is the lamp-niche (*mishkāt*)..." *Mishkāt* is a niche in a wall where one places a lamp, or it means the candlestick that houses the wick. This verse provides evidence that the original source of the Intellect's light is God.

The Qur'ān refers to people as 'dead' since they are far from the life-giving light of Truth. The people of reality are the people of light. They are surrounded by light so their witnessing is also light, whether it is with their physical eyes or in the world of dreams. What they see at their station requires no interpretation whereas those at the station of the *barzakh* require interpretation and are governed by shadows, and an admixture of light and darkness and confused dreams, which occurs for those who are veiled.

Perception in the world of Intellect is clear to its perceiver like the break of dawn, without the slightest veiling or confusion. It is said that whenever the Prophet saw a dream it was like the break of dawn. The people of the station of Intellect are themselves luminous so they see with light and what they see is light. Since the Intellect originates from the divine names of original being, a person on the plane of the Intellect has a share in these divine names, such *al-Nūr* (the Light), *al-Muḥyī* (the Life-Giver), *al-Fāṭir* (the Originator), *al-Khāliq* (the Creator), according to their degree of attachment (*ta'alluq*), assumption of traits (*takhalluq*) and realization (*taḥaqquq*). Whoever exemplifies this station externally has a share in some or all of these names.

The qualities of the people of Intellect consist of the conclusive argument, an exaltedly truthful tongue, clear speech, an upright mind and a sound heart, which are all qualities of the Intellect. It will be mentioned in a later chapter that the Intellect is a creature obedient to God, in the foremost position, the Imām, and the divine argument. These attributes are present in those who are at the station of the Intellect like Abraham, but even they differ in degrees, "We favored some messengers over others" (2:253). If there were a thousand people at the station of the Intellect, they would all differ in degrees, even though they would originate in a single source, in the same way that children originate in their father. They only see and witness God because the Intellect was the first creation whom God addressed.

Since Abraham was of this station, these names also manifested in him. God says, "Peace be upon Abraham" because he was free from all defects, so he was in peace and safety. Just as the entire creation returns back to the Intellect, all religions return back to Abraham. The people of God incline, because *ḥanīf* means to 'incline', from their particular religion and creed to the religion of Truth, which is the religion of Abraham. Thus, Abraham is the highest source, just as the Intellect is the highest source and the purest light.

Following an authority must be on account of light, because light unveils darkness. If someone claims to be an Imam then he must have light. Likewise, if someone claims to be a legal authority in religion (*marjʿa*), he must also have light. Of course, there are certain types of authority that do not necessitate light, but with respect to spiritual perfections, wayfaring, ascent, and reaching the ultimate station with God, this all requires light. True spiritual light is one which reveals hidden mysteries of existence.

God created the Intellect from the divine treasure, which is hidden and undisclosed to anyone in the divine knowledge. The nobility of the Intellect is evidenced by the fact that none knows its reality. Neither prophet, messenger nor proximate angel knows the reality of the Intellect because it originated in God's hidden treasure. It is not the case that the Prophet knew everything, because this is the endpoint of the knowledge of every prophet.

Light is the language of the Intellect and its speech is reality, not interpretation, or even the speech describing the mysteries of nature. All Abrahamic realities was expressed with this tongue, that is, the speech of reality, whether it was his dream or his argument against the idolaters. His arguments were not from the rational mind like those posited by the philosophers and theologians. Even if his conclusions were the same, they came from the station of light, like one looking with divine insight (*al-firāsa al-ilāhīya*) because his vision is through the light of God, as the hadith states, "Beware of the believer's insight (*firāsa*) because he sees with the light of God,"[20] and as the Qur'ān says, "Had we wished, we could have shown them to you and you would have known them by their marks, but you will certainly recognize them by the tone of their speech. God knows your deeds" (47:30).

Those who have spiritual insight ascertain a hidden reality at first glance. They are certain of the reality as it is seen and do not engage in interpretation. The reality of their knowledge is light as the hadith states, "Knowledge is not extensive learning but a light that God casts in whomever He wishes to guide."[21] Since, the essence of the path is light, their path is light and their knowledge is light. They are light and they see only light.

When realities become established in the hearts of the people of God by way of certitude and tranquillity, they speak of those realities accompanied by evidence, as the Qur'ān says, "Can they be compared to those who have clear proof from their Lord, bringing evidence from Him?" (11:17). These proofs are the signs in outward existence and inwardly in the self. When realities manifest in their hearts, whether through divine bestowal, casting or inspiration, perceived with or without words, the hearts become illuminated. Divine signs and evidences in the external world confirm what they witness inwardly.

---

20 *Kanz al-'ummāl*, hadith no. 30731; Majlisī, *Biḥār al-anwār*, v. 24, 128.

21 Majlisī, *Biḥār al-anwār*, v. 1, p. 225.

Abraham's place of witnessing was light so he saw divine proofs in the stars, moon and sun, since these are the most striking signs of light in creation. He was at the highest station of light and the exemplar of the divine name, the Light. He turned towards the greatest of luminous bodies in stages as evidence of divine light and had comprehensiveness in identifying the signs of light, from the weakest to the strongest. His method of reasoning can be summarized in the following: This is light, My Lord is light therefore this is my Lord. However, he negates this argument saying that all that sets cannot be the Lord.

When Abraham says, "I am not among the polytheists," it means that there can never be polytheism at his station of the Intellect. This is because polytheism is darkness and the Intellect is pure light, being the first, highest and greatest of God's creation. It was alone with its Creator from its very inception and there was no other creation that might suggest another deity. Therefore, polytheism cannot exist, by definition, on the plane of the Intellect and the station of Abraham. Any person who arrives at this station can never entertain polytheism.

The hadith describes the greatness of the Intellect in the following words, "By My honor and majesty, I have not created a creation greater than you, nor more obedient to Me than you, nor higher, nor nobler, nor majestic. I give and take through you, through you My unity is recognized, through you I am worshipped, supplicated, yearned for, hoped for, feared, cautioned against. By you I reward and punish." This is the reason why one should honour the Intellect, obey its dictates and repudiate those who cause one to depart from it. This is also why, the greatest darkness covering of the Intellect is blind conformity (*taqlīd*), which is completely antithetical to religion, the Qur'ān and spiritual wayfaring. There is no religion that calls for blind conformity, but when one follows a person of Intellect it is adhering to spiritual authority (*wilāya*), which is to follow through light, unlike blind conformity, which is following in darkness.

The world of Intellect in philosophy, is what religious discourse (*lisān al-sharʿ*) refers to as the world of Spirit. This is why the station of Abraham also includes the world of Spirits. If the manifestation of the Spirit reaches its climax and perfection, it realizes the divine name, the Life-giver (*al-Muḥyī*) and one is endowed with life-giving power (*iḥyā*), on account of the Intellect's governance of the entire human kingdom. While death has been ascribed to the human being, "Is he who was dead and We revived..." (6:122), when the Intellect governs the human being, it becomes resurrected and revived through the infusion of the Spirit. The origin of this life is the Intellect which is also identified as the station of Spirit.

Thus, if the Intellect governs a person, he assumes (*mutakhalliq*) and realizes (*mutaḥaqqiq*) the divine name, the Living (*al-Ḥayy*). The author writes, "This occurs when the Intellect governs the entirety of the human kingdom becoming the wellspring of all things manifest and hidden, in particular, the Spirit's governance of the body, the source of physical life and the human faculties." The correspondence between light and darkness, or life and death respectively, is reiterated in this verse above; light corresponds to life and darkness corresponds to death.

There is no station beyond the station of the Intellect, the station of Reality, because it is the first thing that God created. It is the Intellect that communes with God. Beyond the Intellect, there is only God.

Everything in Abraham's discourse reveals his place within the station of the Intellect. He speaks of life, death, lights, the sun, the moon, the east, the west, etc. Why does Abraham speak of these things and their qualities? Because Abraham's station is the Intellect, the world of Spirits and the world of light and life. Thus, he says, "My Lord is the one who gives life and death" (2:258). He argues that God is life-giver, since this is one of the names of original creation which is substantiated by his own state of being, stating that God makes the sun rise, which is an example of light. In the Qur'ānic account, Abraham argues that God gives and takes life without intermediary whereas the king takes life through killing or gives life through sparing. God gives life from nothing and takes life without killing and in reality, the king neither has the power to give life or take life. Abraham's argument focuses on the divine name, the Life-giver (*al-Muḥyī*), and in the Qur'ān's account, he actualizes this name when he produces life. The second of his arguments involves light, saying, "God brings light from the East so now bring it from the West. So the unbelievers were dumbfounded" (2:258). Those at the station of Reality give evidence that originate from their own qualities, namely, light, life, origination, etc. Their actions accord with their existential realities and their corresponding station.

Abraham's objection to the idols is due to his relation to the names of original being, the Creator (*al-Khāliq*). Thus, he says, how can you worship something that is created and disregard the Creator? Just as God chose the Intellect, he also chose those who have arrived at the station of the Reality. Just as God says in the hadith, "God created the Intellect from a hidden, treasured light in His ancient knowledge, He says in the Qur'ān, "We gave Abraham sound judgement and were aware of it from before." Just as God chose the Intellect, he chose Abraham and the Intellect's origin in the hidden, treasured light in His ancient knowledge, as if He were saying "We were aware of it from before."

These are the attributes of Abraham, the Intellect and in general, the station of the Intellect. Whoever forsakes the Intellect, whether it be through exclusive attention to the rational sciences, scientific, academic, religious thought, or via blind conformity (*taqlīd*), forsakes Abraham and his creed (*milla*). The Qur'ān says, "Who but a fool forsakes the creed of Abraham?" (2:130). The word '*safiha*' in Arabic refers to ignorance and stupidity. "We chose him [Abraham] in this world and he is among the righteous in the Hereafter" (2:130). Just as God chose the Intellect, he chose Abraham and made him among the righteous in the Hereafter. Just as God created Abraham upon light, he will be so in the Hereafter. This is the station of universal Intellect whose complete manifestation is Abraham. This is the reason why we must sanctify the Intellect, the luminous Intellect confirmed by God, not the rational mind. The Intellect can only submit to the people of light with respect to their spiritual authority (*wilāya*). One must differentiate between blind conformity and the statement, "The believers are guardians of one another"(9:71) inasmuch as light follows light and corresponds with light.

Just as God made the Intellect the leader of all things so he made its perfect manifestation, Abraham, an Imam in existence. Just as the Intellect is the collectivity of all things, Abraham is the collectivity of all people so God called him a nation (*umma*). All of the attributes of the Intellect are present in Abraham because he is its perfect manifestation. Even Prophet Muḥammad follows him in this regard. God has guaranteed this station for Abraham but not for his descendants.

He said, 'I will make you a leader of people.' Abraham asked, 'Will You make leaders from my descendants too?' God answered, 'My pledge does not hold for the evildoers" (2:124). "Abraham was a nation (*umma*), devoted to God, sincere in faith, and he was not of the idolaters" (16:120). Abraham reiterates that he was not among the polytheists because it is impossible for the Intellect to commit polytheism.

If the Intellect appears, then obedience to it becomes necessary. If its light appears in another, then *wilāya* of that person also becomes necessary, whether or not they share the same religion. This is because it is divine light and the true meaning of *sharīʿa*. Thus, one must follow the Intellect according to the strength of its luminosity, never departing from its dictates either with respect to *sharīʿa* or the principles of spiritual development (*sulūk*). They are, in fact, one and the same.

Another aspect of the Intellect is to furnish proofs. Abraham came to his people with proofs and a decisive argument such that his word would not be overcome, especially in matters of divinity. This is because God is the one who prepared Abraham with proofs whose origin is light. "Such was the argument We gave to Abraham against his people – We raise in rank whomever We will. Your Lord is All-wise, Omniscient" (6:83). "We granted Our grace to all of them and gave them a noble reputation" (19:50). "We gave Abraham sound judgement from before and of which We had foreknowledge" (21:51). That is, he was all light and not misguided in the least.

Why did Abraham negate the idols of his father? He wanted them to worship God directly, not through something else. He opposed idolatry not from the perspective of being a prophet but existentially, since his station is pure light and idolatry is pure darkness. The first form of darkness is the blind following of one's forefathers, that is, blind conformity (*taqlīd*) mentioned in the Qur'ān, "'We found our fathers worshipping them.' He said, 'You and your fathers have clearly gone astray'" (21:54). True religion is at war with blind conformity because it diametrically opposes the Intellect. While adherence to a spiritual authority (*wilāya*) is necessary it must occur through knowledge, light, guidance and evidence. Essentially, *wilāya* is returning to God and it exists for a prophet, Imam and even believers towards each other. There can be no *wilāya* for the corrupt or ignorant person because *wilāya* is light. It should be the *wilāya* of light not the *wilāya* of darkness. In other words, if someone walks in the dark behind another who is carrying a lantern, he may not have light but he is holding the hand or cloak of a person who has light. This does not apply to blind conformity because there is no guarantee that the leader has light.

The following verses concerning Abraham smashing the idols and facing his people demonstrates Abraham's method of argumentation. He concludes saying, "You know very well that these gods cannot speak.

'How can you worship what can neither benefit nor harm you, instead of God? Shame on you and on the things that you worship instead of God. Do you not think?'" (21:51-67). All of this stems from the inspired Abrahamic Intellect—May God make us among those who follow the religion of Abraham, in truth (*ḥaqq*) and reality (*ḥaqīqa*)!

It was mentioned earlier that the station of Reality is the essence of truth and its engraving (*naqsh*). Thus, one must arrive at both truth and reality not simply truth. "The path has been made easy for that which you have been created."[22] In other words, if one strives for a station for which he has not been created, it will only result in weariness, angst and disappointment. However, since ones does not know the full scope of his own existence, the only way forward is to strive and illuminate the heart until one's true station is revealed. You will then know your state.

God gave everything a unique nature and mode of being then guided it along the path of the completion of its reality. We strive to follow Abraham's religion because Abraham is the epitome of this station. Thereafter, the rest of humanity have a share. Those who are most worthy of it have the greatest share of light. Similarly, those who are worthiest of Prophet Muḥammad are the most complete in light. "Indeed, the worthiest of Abraham among the people are those who followed him, this prophet and those who believe. God is the Guardian (*walī*) of the believers" (3:68). All who follow Abraham's truth and reality are worthier of him.

What does it mean to follow Abraham? It is to be at his station, tread his path, walk his way and embody his spirit. How does one follow Abraham? Through light! The key principle here is to illuminate the Intellect and acquire an Intellect confirmed by divine light. This is the very purpose of our creation. We have not been created to enlist in an army and simply obey commands, to follow blindly and

---

22 Bukhārī, 4949.

keep silent in the face of false authorities. Rather we have been created to revive the Intellect which will illuminate the rest of the human kingdom. Original creation has been founded upon the principle of the Intellect and it is the reason for being. It is self-evident that the Intellect stands in opposition to blind conformity and ignorance. The Intellect can only follow light and its dictates and all else is considered a loss and a waste of life, just as Imam ʿAlī has said, "Be careful of wasting what remains of your lives for what has passed will not return."[23] He also said, "You are but a certain number of days, each day that passes a part of you is gone. So lessen your desires and beautify your attainments."[24] So, lessen your desires. Do not burden your soul with attachments that distance yourself from the real goal because one cannot ascend to the higher planes of being except through a certain correspondence to those realms. Since God, the angels and paradise are light, those in darkness cannot approach them. Darkness is the fuel for hell, which is fire not light. The path described in this work is the Abrahamic path. That is why its methodology is Intellectual, but one that is endorsed (*muʾayyad*) by light. Every path speaks from the vantage point of its methodology.

The Knowledge of Allusion

The knowledge of allusion (*ʿilm al-ishāra*) relates to the Imaginal world, which follows the world of Intellect. The text focuses on the Intellect in three chapters: the knowledge of reality, the manifestation of reality and the station of reality. Thereafter, it describes the knowledge of allusion and the knowledge of expression in separate chapters. The reason for this is that the principle of the book relates to the luminous Intellect, whereas allusion and expression are subordinate to the Intellect.

---

23 *Ghurar al-ḥikam*, p. 92, hadith no. 39.

24 *Ghurar al-ḥikam*, p. 129, hadith no. 3028.

The Imaginal world is an isthmus between Intellectual and material worlds, like the Connected Imagination (*al-khayāl al-muttaṣil*), the human imagination, and the Discrete Imagination (*al-khayāl al-munfaṣil*), which is the macrocosmic imagination. Given that the human being is endowed with an intellect, imagination and senses, one may see something in the external world as a reality in imaginal form, like the Prophet saw the angel Gabriel as Diḥya al-Kalbī, who appeared as a man in Imaginal form. If Gabriel was seen only by the Prophet, then he was in Imaginal form, but if he was also seen by others, then he appeared in sensory form either for the Imaginal eye or for the sensory eye.

Similarly, a person might see an Imaginal reality, through a vision (*mukāshafa*), externally. One sees an external reality with the Imaginal eyes, which is not perceptible to others because it is not sensory. While one is having a vision, others will not be able to see the same thing with their sensory eyes. This is because the human being has two sets of eyes, Imaginal and physical. He sees with the former, Imaginal realities and with the latter, sensory things.

The world of Imagination, or the world of *barzakh* has a specific language that differs from the language of Reality, or the language of the Intellect. The knowledge of allusion is expressed in the language of the Imaginal world. The 'Imaginal' here is referring to the true Imaginal realm and not the 'imagination' which creates figments or confused dreams, like when someone says, "You are imagining things." The false imagination does not have an external reality and is considered fantasy.

The Imaginal in this chapter refers to the existential plane of reality related to the *barzakh* and its mode of expression. Both the Connected and Discrete Imagination are rooted in the Intellect and therefore, the treasured light of God. The language of this Imaginal world also originate in the treasured light, in the ancient knowledge of

God, except that it has form. This world requires interpretation unlike the Intellectual which is pure light and requires no interpretation.

Interpretation exists for the sensory world as well. This interpretation relates to the knowledge of expression (*'ilm al-'ibāra*), which reveals a hidden meaning (*kashf sirr*). Just as Khidr revealed the hidden reasons for his actions, as he says, "That is the interpretation for those things you could not bear patiently" (18:82). So Khidr called it interpretation (*ta'wīl*), even though interpretation is the use of a concept to explain another. For example, if a person sees himself flying in the sky along with the birds it could mean freedom, intellection, or the soul's lightness. In any case, we use one concept to elucidate another. However, in the case of Khidr and Moses, Khidr did not explain his actions through a concept but gave the reason for damaging the boat. He revealed its hidden meaning and this is not considered interpretation. Here, interpretation means to return to the origin (*al-aṣl*). The knowledge of allusion involves interpretation, or producing another form or meaning, whereas the knowledge of reality is seeing things as they are. Thus, *ta'wīl* encompasses both meanings, interpretation or the revelation of a mystery—whether it is witnessed in a dream or in wakefulness. The former concerns the knowledge of allusion and the latter concerns the knowledge of expression.

The epitome of the station of reality is Abraham and Joseph is the epitome of station of allusion, "Thus will your Lord choose you and teach you the interpretation of events (*ta'wīl al-aḥādīth*) and complete His favor upon you and upon the family of Jacob, as He completed it upon your fathers before, Abraham and Isaac" (12:6). *Ta'wīl al-aḥādīth* means dream interpretation according to some, and according to others includes speech as well. Whether or not Prophet Joseph was able to interpret both dreams and events in the external world remains unknown. Obviously, he did not interpret all of life's events even if this was the predominant aspect of his station.

One important point of this verse is that the word 'father' also refers to grandfathers. Both physical and spiritual fathers are referred to as 'father', in the same way Christians call their priests, 'father'. Joseph was the son of Jacob, the son of Isaac, the son of Abraham. The issue of spiritual fatherhood is also present in Islam, since the Prophet said, "O 'Alī, you and I are the fathers of this nation."[25] God taught Joseph the interpretation of events (*ta'wīl al-aḥādīth*) and strengthened him in the land of Egypt. God raised Joseph from a pit deep within the ground and sat him upon a throne. No one could have imagined that he would go from pit to a throne or that he would become a prince. God manages the affairs for each individual and He is the Master of His own affairs, as the Qur'ān states, "God reaches His purpose and yet most people do not realize" (12:21).

Everything happens according to the will of God but most people do not realize it. This is because people have not grasped its reality and have not witnessed God's omnipotence over life and its affairs. When we contemplate on the Qur'ān we find that the whole purpose of religion is to fathom realities which only occurs through light. Only light, not concepts, can unveil reality. The essence of religion is that the human being should arrive at the appropriate station, realize with his light and ascend. The purpose of religion is not to simply obey commands or fill a void. The religion we know is a set of commandments and prohibitions, or what we *believe* to be its commandments and prohibitions.

The essence of creation is to obtain light, to illuminate the lamp of the Intellect. One might say that the Intellect is itself a lamp so why then does it need to be illuminated? The answer to this is found in the following example: The Intellect is a lamp but their luminosity differs just as a night-light differs from a regular lamp. A night-light is designed to let people sleep even though one might still be able

25 Ṣadūq, *'Uyūn akhbār al-Ridha*, v. 2, p. 91

get up and move around. This is why it is said, "People are asleep and when they die they wake up." Spiritual wayfaring is the process of lighting the lamp of wakefulness. Through knowledge and wisdom, the lamp of the Intellect becomes lit and increases in brightness. Each soul differs with respect to brightness and luminosity. Some people's light is so bright that it illuminates the entire human kingdom. Those who have rational knowledge are like those who move around in a room with a night-light. There is just enough light to move around but the room is still considered dark and suitable only for sleep. The gnostic has ignited this lamp and has arisen, as the Qur'ān says, "Say, I only advise you of one thing and that is to stand up for God, singly or in pairs" (34:46).

Joseph says, "My Lord! You have given me authority, You have taught me about the interpretation of events. Creator of the heavens and the earth, You are my protector in this world and in the Hereafter. Let me die in submission (*muslim*) to You and join me with the righteous" (12:101). Notice that Joseph prays to be taken from this life as an adherent of Islam, which is the original religion of every prophet. The Qur'ān states, "It is the religion of your father, Abraham. God has called you Muslims—both in the past and in this [message]—so that the Messenger can bear witness about you and so that you can bear witness about other people" (22:78).

Interpretation applies to physical vision as it applies to dreams, as evidenced in the case of Joseph when he was in the prison. Just as the station of the Intellect is the station of Abraham, it is also the station of Jesus because he was also governed by the names of original being, such as healing, creation, reviving the dead through the name the Living (*al-Muḥyī*), as well as informing without interpretation. Abraham and Jesus are both at the station of the Intellect but each with different coloration. Jesus says, I will inform you of what you eat and what you store in your homes, whereas Joseph says, I will "inform you of the interpretation" of the food. Jesus is not interpreting but informing, just as Abraham did not interpret his dream. "When the boy was old enough to walk with his father, Abraham said, 'My son, I have seen myself sacrificing you in a dream. What do you think?' He said, 'Father, do as you have been commanded, and God willing, you will find me steadfast.' When they had both surrendered to God, and he had laid his son down on his face, We called out to him, 'O Abraham, You have already fulfilled the vision!' This is how we reward the virtuous" (37:102-105). Normally, this would be interpreted as the greater *jihād*, which is warring against the lower self and is supported by the hadith, "Die before you die." But Abraham, being at the station of reality, did not interpret the dream and proceeded to apply it exactly as he saw it. Thus, his place of witnessing (*mashhad*) is the world of reality even though he saw it in a dream.

Likewise, some of the Prophet's dreams came to him like the break of dawn, as the hadith states, "The advent of revelation was a true dream. He never saw a dream except that it came like the break of dawn."[26] Nabulsī, the greatest scholar of dream interpretation, writes that these types of the Prophet's dreams would not need interpretation. This is because the Prophet saw these dreams from the station of Abraham. Some dreams of the Prophet, however, did require interpretation, in the case where he interpreted milk as knowledge, and in the verse, "The dream We showed you was only a test for people..." (17:60). These types of dreams are of the Imaginal world whose place of witnessing is the knowledge of allusion.

The knowledge of reality originates from a hidden, treasured light in the ancient knowledge of God. The same can be said concerning the knowledge of allusion, except that it is seen through the lens of the Imaginal world and described in a language specific to it. For example, if a lamp is covered by green glass, the light will appear

26 Bukharī, *Ta'bīr*, 1

green even though the original light is white. White light is hidden, as it were, behind the green light. The light from this lamp is colored by the green glass even though it is essentially white light. Similarly, the knowledge of allusion originates in the knowledge of reality but its color and language is different.

There may be a person who is created for the Intellectual world to the exclusion of others, while another might comprehend all of the worlds and engage with each world equally. Another person might comprehend every world, but one world will predominate. Take, for example, a person who has lived half of his life in the West and the other half in the Middle East. This person might be equally proficient in English and Arabic, whereas someone else in the same situation might be stronger in one language. Furthermore, it does not mean that a person who has comprehensiveness commands a higher station than one who is of the sensory world. This is because he might have acquired only a small portion of each world while another person may have acquired the entirety of a single world. Even if comprehensiveness is efficacious, the strength of a person is in their receptivity, in the way that God gave nine out of ten parts of physical beauty to Joseph, and one part He divided amongst the rest of humanity—although true beauty is inward beauty.

The Knowledge of Expression

The knowledge of expression (*ʿilm al-ʿibāra*) relates to the outward, material world, the knowledge of allusion refers to the hidden and the knowledge of reality refers to the hidden of the hidden. But despite being related to the material world, it originates from the light of God. It is not considered one of the rational disciplines but a spiritual knowledge insofar as it relates to unveiling the mysteries within material existence, originating from the hidden, treasured light of God's ancient knowledge. The knowledge of allusion speaks of interpretation, or the form of something other than what is apparent. One may confuse interpretation at the level of allusion from unveiling a mystery within material existence or between the latter and the knowledge of reality. Unveiling a mystery within material existence relates to causality, allusion relates to a form other than what is witnessed, and the knowledge of reality is the vision of the essence or true nature of a thing.

The story of Moses and Khidr is a prime example of the knowledge of expression. Even though Moses was the greatest of prophets, the Interlocutor of God and the among possessors of resolve (*ūl al-ʿazm*), he desired to learn a type of knowledge that encompasses many subtleties known as the knowledge of guidance (*ʿilm al-irshād*) from one of the saints of God, Khidr. Khidr looked into Moses through spiritual insight (*firāsa*) and said that he would not be able to tolerate him at this station. Moses did not lack capacity but was unable to bear that which he had no knowledge. It is natural to ask questions when confronted with unknown existential realities. Moses, having approached Khidr for the sake of learning would inherently be inclined to ask him about his actions.

This verse reveals two important principles of the spiritual path, patience and obedience. Without these two qualities, one cannot keep company with a saint. This is the advice given to all disciples concerning their Shaykhs and students concerning their teachers. The first of Khidr's conditions to Moses was that he would not ask him the reasons for his actions. Similarly, there are times when the disciple must not ask the Shaykh for an explanation. This holds true not only for the student towards his teacher but in general, any person towards God. While there are verses and hadith exhorting people to ask God concerning every affair, there are times when it is discourteous to do so, as in the case of Noah, when he was rebuked for asking about his son. In the Qur'ān, God equated Noah's question with ignorance.

"He said, 'O Noah, he is not of your family, he is an unrighteous deed, so ask Me not about that which you have no knowledge. I warn you, not to be among the ignorant'" (11:46).

If a person is in a state of remembrance (*dhikr*) and God discloses (*yatajalla*) a certain affair to them, they should know when to ask. This principle demonstrates the importance of training at the hands of a Shaykh possessing true gnosis of God. Such a person will excel in his development, companionship and discourse with God. But those who rely on their own understanding of the Qur'ān and hadith or on scholars who understand scripture only through rational concepts without any expertise in spirituality, will never excel. This is generally the case concerning the exoteric scholars who are not the masters of discourse with God, but rely on teachers of the outward. Rational knowledge (*'ilm kasbī*) is useless if it is not accompanied by spiritual knowledge. That is why one must have a spiritual teacher whose heart is illuminated by a light from God with respect to knowledge and learning. This is the real way for a person to reach God.

When Khidr damaged the boat, Moses rebuked him saying that what you have done is a grave (*'imr*) offence, to which Khidr replied, "Did I not tell you that you would not be able to bear with me" (18:75)? We can glean from this verse is that it is possible for the Prophets to forget. In this story, Moses forgot his previous oath to Khidr on three occasions, which is evidence that the prophets are capable of forgetting. He says, "Do not take me to task for what I have forgotten" (18:73). This forgetfulness is in contrast to remembrance (*dhikr*). Some commentators say that forgetfulness here means abandoning the oath or pact of obedience he gave to Khidr, not forgetfulness (*nisyān*) or neglect (*ghafla*). But the apparent meaning of the verses suggests otherwise and such an interpretation (*ta'wīl*) would require further evidence. Forgetfulness here is opposed to remembrance (*dhikr*), which fundamentally does not contravene the Qur'ān, Sunna, rationality and unveiling, and can be taken at face value. Even if it opposes the theological doctrine that the prophets are inerrant in all respects, one is not obligated to ascribe to this view, if the case can be made that this doctrinal view is flawed in and of itself. There is no doubt that positing absolute infallibility for the prophets at the level of divine infallibility is fundamentally flawed.

After the incident of the ship, they arrived at the shore and met a boy who was playing with other children. Khidr took the boy and killed him. Khidr's actions clearly contravene the *sharīʿa*, and are objectionable in the view of the exoterically minded who do have the knowledge of right guidance (*ʿilm al-rushd*) and the knowledge of subtlety (*ʿilm al-laṭāʾif*). This is the very knowledge that Moses sought from Khidr.

Scholars such as al-Ṣadūq and Tabrasī, among the early commentators of the Qurʾān, maintain that this forgetfulness is in contrast to remembrance.[27] After having questioned Khidr's actions when he rebuilt the wall without payment, Khidr dismisses Moses saying this is where we part ways. He tells Moses that he will inform him of its interpretation (*taʾwīl*), which is in fact, the knowledge of expression or the revelation of a mystery (*kashf al-sirr*) in the material world. Moses, despite being God's interlocutor, came to learn at the hands of God's saint and even still, did not reach a very high level of *ʿilm al-rushd*. The Prophet said, "If Moses had been patient, he would have seen thousands of wonders." Even though Moses was among the greatest of prophets, he received very little of the *ʿilm al-rushd* from Khidr. The Qurʾān calls Khidr's explanation as *taʾwīl*, which, in this case, is the knowledge of expression.

Another principle gleaned from Khidr's marring of the boat is that sometimes what appears to be a wrongdoing is actually good, insofar as it repels something worse. It is therefore considered a good

27 See Ṭabrīsī, *Majmaʿ al-bayān*, v. 7.

deed. One must distinguish between the doer and the act itself. The act might be bad but the doer may still be good, as Imam ʿAlī says, "The intelligent is one who chooses the lesser of two evils." Khidr calls it interpretation but it is not interpretation in the sense of the representation of a concept with another. It is the disclosure of a hidden cause. Khidr's killing of the child was also explained in the verses of the Qur'ān, as was his rectifying the wall. In all of these explanations the principle at work here is the disclosure of a mystery in the natural world (*kashf al-sirr*) not the representation of a concept which is the nature of interpretation (*taʾwīl*). This knowledge originates in the light of divine knowledge, not rationality, empiricism, reflection, chance or coincidence. This is why Khidr says, "I did not do this out of my own accord" (18:82).

In addition to revealing the material cause, there is an interpretation on the Imaginal plane associated with each of these events. What is the interpretation of Khidr's marring of the boat? It may mean a defect, a shortcoming in life, or some sort of tearing related to one's house. There are many possible interpretations for this story and each interpretation makes use of a concept different from the original. However, the original story indicates that the reason Khidr marred the boat was because a certain despotic king had plans to seize its contents. Just as there is hidden reason for this event, there is a corresponding Imaginal form, which is its interpretation, and there is also reality on the plane of the Intellect.

Some events in the material world give rise to Intellectual knowledge that go beyond the disclosure of a natural mystery, as Abraham knew that he was ill just by glancing at the stars. There is no logical relationship between the stars and his illness, nor is there a natural cause for it. Abraham simply took one glance at the stars and knew that he was ill, as if the stars were a mirror for his own state. Abraham's statement did not reveal any causality or mystery within the material world but intimated a reality. Thus, one must distinguish between the disclosure of a natural mystery and the knowledge of a reality on the plane of the Intellect, both of which, in this case, have been ascertained from the material plane. Both Abraham's glance and Joseph's interpretation of the inmates' food occurred in the natural world but relate to the planes of Intellect and Imagination, respectively. A glance on the Intellectual plane differs from a glance on the Imaginal.

Among the mysteries of the natural world, some require interpretation and others require commentary (*tafsīr*), which is like removing a mask from a face. Likewise, commentary of the Qur'ān is revealing an aspect of a verse or its expression, like a woman revealing herself behind a veil. Disclosure of a mystery within the natural world is considered the knowledge of expression, irrespective of the station of the saint who witnesses it. The saint may possess multiple stations and can engage with other planes, or be principally at the station of the Intellect and engage with the material. But if the event is interpreted through a form or concept other than the original, beyond the disclosure of a natural mystery alone, then it is called the knowledge of allusion, on the Imaginal plane. If a reality is witnessed directly as it truly is, then it is called the knowledge of reality on the Intellectual plane.

From the previous discussion, it appears that there are only three worlds. However, there are actually five or six worlds as chapter seven describes, but they are called the five universal presences.

Moses had the knowledge of disclosing mysteries of the natural world. However, God wanted to teach him the subtleties that were in apparent conflict with the ordinary, such as Khidr's killing of the child. For example, if someone contracts a disease, Moses might instruct the person to take a particular herb for the illness. This is within the realm of the ordinary. This opposes neither the *sharī'a* nor reason, but Khidr would teach him the 'oppositional knowledge of guidance' which is called *'ilm al-rushd al-mukhālif* in contrast with the 'conforming knowledge of guidance'. Is there a type of knowledge which contravenes the outward form of religion? Yes, the knowledge of Khidr, which resulted in him killing the innocent child.

One must also distinguish between etiquette (*adab*) and knowledge (*'ulūm*). Khidr saying "do not ask me," relates to etiquette. One of the conditions Khidr set down for Moses is to not ask him until he himself gives the reason for his actions. Etiquette is also a type of knowledge, but it is different from the subtleties (*laṭā'if*) of the knowledge of guidance (*'ilm al-rushd*), which is the disclosure of a mystery.

The Universal Worlds and the Five Divine Presences

After having described the three worlds, Intellectual, Imaginal and material, and their corresponding forms of knowledge, the knowledge of reality, allusion and expression, we turn our attention to the universal worlds and five divine presences. They are either five or six in number and each has their individual characteristics. As mentioned, the Intellect is a luminous reality whose origin is the ancient knowledge of God. Everything that follows it, originates from this luminous source, but its manifestations and theophanies are multiple. Similarly, the paths to God is a single luminous reality, each originating in the Intellect.

Each world has a people and a leader (*sayyid*) who speak the language of that world. The people of the Intellect speak without interpretation, the people of the Imaginal speak in the language of allusion and interpretation and the people of material speak in a language that discloses the mysteries of that world. It is a single reality yet multiple in manifestation. It is important to note that those who speak the language of expression, who disclose mysteries of the material world, speak with light, unlike those who acquire rational knowledge and are also able to disclose some mysteries of the natural world. Whether one speaks in the language of expression, allusion or reality, the origin and source is light, not rational thought and discursive learning.

As mentioned, the knowledge of reality, allusion and expression correlate to the three worlds, Intellectual, Imaginal and material which are existential matters. In contrast to these are divine matters. The former related to creation and existence, and the latter relate to God directly. The three worlds originate in the five or six divine presences. The example of the five presences is like a tree hidden in the seed. When it is said, the seed manifests to itself, it means that the roots, trunk, branches or leaves are not taken into consideration when contemplating the seed. There is neither a conceptual nor external distinction to be made here. This theophany is called the first individuation which has neither conceptual division nor external multiplicity. The reality of absolute Being is devoid of every condition, even the condition of absoluteness. The divine Being is disclosed in the degrees of infinite manifestation and theophany but these divine presences are the universal manifestations or individuations (*taʿayunāt*)—otherwise the degrees are endless.

Thereafter, the seed manifests as the root, trunk, branches and leaves so that the whole becomes individuated. There is conceptual division at the second stage, or the second individuation, even if there is no multiplicity in the external world. As mentioned, the first individuation does not possess any conceptual division or external multiplicity and is annihilated in the unity of the Essence. These are matters of the Essence (*shu'ūn dhātī*), also called the unseen of the Unseen, or the first Unseen, because everything other than God is negated therein, as stated, "There was God and nothing else besides Him."[28] This is the plane of Singularity that does not permit any multiplicity; it is called the Singularity of the Essence because it is pure unity. At this plane, the Kingdom, (*al-mulk*) cannot be distinguished from the Dominion (*al-malakūt*) or the Unseen, which is the realm of souls and spirits, also known as the Imaginal world, nor can it be

---

28 Bukhārī, 7418.

distinguished from the world of Invincibility (*jabarūt*), the world of greatness or the divine names and attributes, or the world of immaterial entities, which some refer to as the *barzakh*. The divinity (*lahūt*) is the degree of the Singular Essence (*al-aḥadiyat al-dhāt*).

The second degree is called the Permanent Archetypes (*al-aʿyān al-thabita*)[29] by the gnostics, and quiddities (*al-māhiyāt*) by the philosophers. It is the second unseen or the second individuation and the degree of Unity (*al-wāḥidīyya*), in contrast to the degree of Singularity (*al-aḥadiyya*). The Archetypes do not manifest either for themselves or for others. They are not manifest except for their Knower and possess a relative multiplicity, in the same way that concepts in the mind are present to its knower but nowhere else. This is the degree in which there is conceptual distinction.

The third degree is the manifestation of simple, immaterial realities, such as intellects and universal souls. It is called the degree of spirits or the relative Unseen in relation to the absolute Unseen. Realities at this stage are perceived and distinct from their Archetypes.

The fourth degree is the absolute Imaginal world (*al-khayal al-muṭlaq*), vis-à-vis the limited Imaginal world belonging to the human being, or the Discrete (*munfaṣil*) and the Connected (*muṭṭaṣil*) Imaginal worlds, respectively. It is also called relative Unseen (*al-ghayb al-mudhāf*) or the *barzakh*. This degree, which possesses subtle existent realities—as opposed to dense ones, manifests meanings embraced in a tangible vessel. Meanings become manifest taking shape, color and form. For

---

29 Permanent Archetypes are the realities in the divine knowledge. They are the specific individuations and intellectual forms (*ṣuwar maʿqūla*) of the divine names. They are 'Permanent' insofar as God's knowledge is identical with His Essence and remain in the realm of the Unseen and are governed by the divine names, the Hidden and the First. They do not partake in existence but remain in the state of sheer potentiality. The Permanent Archetypes then become manifest in the external world through the divine names, the Last and the Manifest. See *Muqaddima Qayṣarī*, ch. 3.

example, knowledge is represented in the form of milk or religiosity is represented as confinement because religion is a type of limit and boundary. Even though these forms possess some of the properties of material bodies, they are not capable of division and dissection, but possess some properties of materiality and some properties of the higher spiritual realms.

The fifth degree is the sensory, outward, physical world and the world of dense bodies that are capable of division and dissection. These are the five worlds, and the sixth world is the human being which comprehends all of them, which is called the degree of Comprehensiveness (*jamʿ*). If we enumerate the worlds to be five in number it is because the first two degrees of the divine degrees are considered as one, insofar as both are specifically divine degrees. Alternatively, there is the absolute Unseen (*al-ghayb al-muṭlaq*) in contrast to the absolute manifest (*al-mulk*) and the relative Unseen which possesses both the Invincibility (*jabarūt*) and Dominion (*malakūt*), or the spirits and the souls. These are closest to the absolute Unseen. The relative manifest is the Imaginal world because it is the closest to the material world. The fifth is the comprehensive world of the perfect human.

In *Naqd al-nuṣūṣ*, Jāmī discusses the reasons why these degrees are limited to five. He writes, "There is only one thing in existence, which is the existence of God."[30] This is based on the doctrine of the Unity of Being, which unfortunately, many have misunderstood. It does not posit that God is identical to the entities in existence, external or otherwise, but that entities are the manifestations and theophanies of His Being, like the rays of light emanating from its source. Although divine effusion is limitless, the universal degrees of Being are five. Two of these degrees are related to divinity and three are related to creation. Thus, the world of the Intellect, Imaginal and material which have been the subject of this book are matters relating to creation.

30 Jamī, *Naqd al-nuṣūṣ*, p. 142.

Describing the division of the worlds, Qayṣarī writes, "The world of Kingdom (*al-mulk*) is a manifestation of the Dominion (*al-malakūt*), which is the absolute Imaginal world (*al-khayal al-muṭlaq*). The Dominion is a manifestation of the world of the Invincibility (*jabarūt*), or the world of immaterial beings. The Invincibility is a manifestation of the Permanent Archetypes (*al-a'yān al-thābita*), which are the manifestations of the world of divine names (*al-asmā'*) at the degree of Unity (*al-wāḥidiyya*). The degree of Unity is a manifestation of the Singularity (*al-aḥadiyya*)."[31]

Ibn al-'Arabī says in *Futūḥāt al-Makkīyya*, "The Imaginal presence is the vastest of the presences. The cosmos is two worlds and the presence is two presences, though a third presence is born between the two from the totality. The first presence is the Unseen, and it possesses a world called the world of the Unseen. The second presence is the Visible and the witnessed; its world is called the Visible world and it is perceived by eyesight, while the world of the absent is perceived by insight. That which is born from the coming together of the two is a presence and a world. The presence is the presence of Imagination, and the world is the world of Imagination. It is the manifestation of meanings in sensory forms, such as knowledge in the form of milk, perseverance in religion in the form of a fetter, Islam in the form of a pillar, faith in the form of a handle, and Gabriel in the form of Diḥya al-Kalbī and in the form of the Bedouin, and the Imaginal form of a "well-proportioned mortal" (19:17) before Mary. That is why the presence of Imagination is the vastest of presences, because it brings together the two worlds, the world of the Unseen and the world of the Visible."[32]

It is important to note that even if the Imagination possesses realities of both Intellectual and material worlds, it does not encompass either one entirely. Since the Intellectual world contains pure imma-

31 Qayṣarī, *Sharḥ fuṣūṣ al-ḥikam*, ed. Ḥ. Āmulī, p. 111.

32 Ibn al-'Arabī, *Futūḥāt al-Makkiyya*, v. 3, 42.5.

terial realities, the Imagination can never possess realities as they are in the Intellect, which also holds true for the material world. Objects as they exist in the material world can never be encompassed by the Imaginal and remain material. The Imagination is not vaster than the Intellectual world because it cannot contain pure Intellect. It is a new type of creation that receives the descent of the Intellect. But Ibn al-ʿArabī's statement holds true if the word 'vast' (*siʿa*) is described as comprehensive, insofar as the Imagination merges aspects of the Intellectual and the material, even if its own objects are specific to it. The word *siʿa* in Arabic is in contrast to limit whereas the word encompass (*iḥāṭa)* has no limit, "God encompasses them from beyond" (85:20).

The Imagination is real although it can also create fictional images as well. *Ibdāʿ* means creation from pure non-being. But the Imaginal returns to the Permanent Archetypes so there is no true *ibdāʿ* in it. Even these fictional images are rooted in the Permanent Archetypes because everything in existence has an origin. All things in existence have 'descended' from a higher plane and it can be said that true creativity begins at the plane of the Permanent Archetypes.

It is a erroneous to believe that there is another existence besides the one we are in. There is only a single existence and the Imaginal world is the inward aspect of the material, just as the Intellectual world is the inward of the Imaginal. The inward is not more constricted than the outward rather the Imaginal is vaster than the material and the Intellectual is vaster than the Imaginal. Having described the five universal worlds, it is important to correlate them with the three mentioned in this book: the world of Reality, Expression and Allusion.

The first seven chapters can be considered introductory material to the main ideas of the work which are explored in the remaining chapters, namely, the form of the Intellect and its contents, the form of the soul and its contents, and the form of the body and its contents. One of the practical concerns of the book is that an individual should become a person of light, one who is illuminated by the light of the Intellect who then illuminates the soul and body by its light. Since even the physical body transforms into a luminous being, one becomes light, not metaphorically, but in truth and reality.

The Form of the Intellect

The Intellect is the foundation of creation (*takwīn*), the divine law (*tashrīʿ*) and spiritual wayfaring (*sulūk*). Since God has made it the highest principle, a person's arrival at the highest station requires Intellect. Just as the creation of the human being is contingent upon the Intellect, so is his responsibility (*taklīf*) towards God, because only a person of sound mind is entrusted with divine obligations. When the Intellect is released from the fetters of materiality, the Imagination and the self, it witnesses the light of its Lord, as it had done so in the first instance of its creation.

When God created the Intellect He did so from a hidden, treasured light in His ancient knowledge, 'treasure', referring to the famous *hadith qudsī*, "I was a hidden treasure and I loved to be known, so I created the creation so that I may become known."[33] The Intellect originated in God's hidden, treasured knowledge, of which no prophet or proximate angel had any awareness. Since the Intellect was the first creation when there was nothing else in existence, how could anyone, prophet or angel, have any knowledge of it?

God then filled the Intellect and made knowledge its soul. The Intellect is like a creature that has a soul, spirit, head, eyes, etc. God made knowledge its soul, understanding it spirit, abstention its head, modesty its eyes, wisdom its tongue, compassion its concern, mercy its heart. Then He adorned it and strengthened it with ten things: certainty, faith, truthfulness, serenity, sincerity, companionship, generosity,

---

33 Kashānī, *Laṭā'if al-iʿlām fī ishārāt ahl al-ilhām*, p. 486.

contentment, submission and gratitude. If the Intellect becomes perfected then these qualities appear and it becomes a creature whose soul is knowledge and whose spirit is understanding. That is why it is necessary for a person to become free from the material, Imaginal, and rational limitations so that he returns to God as the original creation. He becomes a balanced and complete human being in the form of the Intellect.

What is the form of the Intellect? It is a divine mystery that even prophets and angels cannot fathom, yet there is no form of the human more perfect than this. Every person, scholar or otherwise, must strive to realize the Intellect and attain the perfect human form. This is not a goal specific to mysticism but is the ultimate pursuit of humanity.

When God commanded the Intellect to retreat, it retreated, and when He commanded it to approach, it approached. This indicates that the Intellect has complete obedience to God's commands and prohibitions. Then God said, "Speak!" So, the first words it spoke corresponded with its essential nature that is founded on divine unity. It said, "Praise be to God who has neither an opposite, nor contrary, nor similar, nor equal, nor substitute, nor equivalent, and before whom all things are humble and abased." These words arose from its very existence and lofty station for which every human in this world must strive to attain. Then God affirmed it, saying, "I have not created a creation better than you, nor more obedient to me, nor loftier, nor nobler nor more honorable than you. Because of you I impose, I bestow, I am acknowledged as One, worshipped, called upon, hoped for, yearned for, feared and warned against. Reward is through you and punishment is through you." God gathered every good in the Intellect and that is why it is the origin of existence, divine law (*sharīʿa*) and wayfaring.

The Intellect has been created on the principle of divine unity and this is the very nature of its existence. It has not been imposed by something external to it such as the *sharīʿa*. Even though the *sharīʿa* has been designed to bring a person to divine unity, the Intellect by its very nature realizes it. Because it was the first and only creation of God, it saw nothing but God. Moreover, God looked upon it exclusively since there was nothing else in existence. It was both the object of divine gaze and the exclusive witness to divine unity. This represents the perfect union between the Creator and creation, or lover and beloved. The reality of the Intellect is now, as it always was, so that if a person returns to the original nature (*fiṭra*) of the Intellect in all its pristine luminosity, then he will be like the first creation, seeing God exclusively and being the object of God's gaze.

Through these attributes God forged destiny and established the way, the Intellect being the criterion, the principle of the law, the scale of justice, the way of truth and the straight path. The Intellect was the complete manifestation of these attributes and the medium of divine effusion. Creation reaches its potential only after receiving from it, or the entities receive from the Intellect only when they move towards it, seek it, reach for it, subsist after becoming annihilated in it. Subsistence in the Intellect must occur after annihilation in it, because there is nothing after the Intellect except the presence of God, Almighty. Thus, when a creature becomes annihilated and subsists in the Intellect, it becomes clothed and colored by it and assumes its form. By its own hands the Intellect paints it and transforms it into a new creation. The creature then assumes its characteristics and realizes its reality, becoming adorned by all of the attributes of the Intellect, in the same way that the Intellect was adorned by the divine attributes and light.

Thus, the entities are transformed into *a new creation* from the effusions of the Intellect. That is why the world cannot do without one who has reached the station of the Intellect, since the whole of creation would be in darkness without such an individual. As long as the entities have not arrived at the station of the Intellect, they are in darkness and as long as they have not been given life by the Intellect, they are considered dead. They only have meaning through the endowment of the Intellect, otherwise they are like 'words' without meaning and value. The light of the Intellect must emanate to all that is below and its spirit must flow through all things, since it has been created from its light, spirit and meaning. If creation is devoid of Intellect, it is like the picture of a person on a wall, not an actual person who is a living, breathing human being. Even if it is said that entities are like the reflections in a mirror, moving images in a mirror are not alive in themselves. The reflection in a mirror moves with its subject but it cannot be said that the reflection is alive, nor can it be conceived that the image develops on its own accord. Likewise, a person without Intellect does not develop and transform even if there is movement since movement alone is not evidence for life.

Therefore, one must strive to perceive the Intellect's light, spirit and meaning, or perceive life, light and meaning in the Intellectual, Imaginal and material worlds. The knowledge of reality, allusion and expression are the means of perception in the three worlds because each type of knowledge is founded on light. The rational mind, however, cannot grasp it because it arrives at conclusions through proofs, reasoning, experimentation or coincidence, not light. The rational mind does not have light like the Intellect. That is why when it is said that "knowledge is light," it is not referring to knowledge acquired through the rational mind. Even if one reaches the correct conclusion, it is still considered a shadow of a shadow. The rational mind has neither light nor life, which is why there is hardly any spirituality in the religious establishment.

The focus of religious training has been rational thought, discursive learning, history, legal theory, logic, etc. However, the gnostics and the saints of God do not utter a word or even a single letter devoid of spirit. The rationalists use words simply to fill the void, filling books, lectures and lessons concerning truths that can be said in a few lines. But every word and sentence of the saint contains meaning, either having received it directly from God or derived from their own luminous souls.

There is a distinction between Intellect and knowledge. One cannot perceive the realities of perfection with knowledge alone, because the Intellect is the origin. That is why Imam 'Alī says, "He whose knowledge exceeds his Intellect is doomed." The Intellect is all good and it always calls to goodness, because it is the scale of truth and justice. It can never call towards evil but it is possible that knowledge can lead towards evil. All knowledge that does not have Intellect's assent is misguidance.

The microcosmic intellect of the individual is connected to the macrocosmic Intellect but it is veiled. Thus, the ultimate end of the human being is to perceive its reality. While the entities seek the Intellect and are adorned by it, the Intellect is adorned by God alone.

The Form of the Soul

The soul is an isthmus (*barzakh*) or boundary between the immaterial and the material. It is governed by the direction it faces. If it is oriented towards the sublime then its properties will be sublime and if it is oriented towards the base, then its properties will be base. Because the soul's orientation in either direction is relative, the degrees within the soul are limitless. As mentioned, the soul becomes a new creation through the Intellect's governance, the emanation of its light, and the participation in knowledge, deed, sincerity, reflection, and of course, divine mercy and bestowal. The perfection of the soul cannot be without the Intellect's influence and cannot arrive at perfection on its own. The movement of perfection must be through light, both for the Intellect and the soul. Even the body requires light, spirit and meaning for its perfection and ascent.

The soul which commands to evil is blind and in darkness. This 'commanding soul' does not distinguish between good and evil, truth and falsehood, the lawful and the forbidden. Its only concern is what it desires and that is why it is called the animal soul. Its ultimate aim is to achieve its desire without any regard for right or wrong.

For the soul to arrive at perfection, it must receive from both the inner and outer prophets, or the existential and legislative prophets, the Intellect and the *sharīʿa*, respectively. The soul must receive from both prophets and cannot rely on one to the exclusion of the other. If the inner prophet becomes corrupted then rationality is lost and the *sharīʿa* will become ineffectual, that is, one cannot follow the *sharīʿa* without the Intellect. However, there are matters that the inner prophet cannot grasp, and therefore the *sharīʿa* is needed for guidance. It must orient itself to and obey the authority of each vicegerent in its respective world and cannot rely on imitating a religious leader without the affirmation of the Intellect's light. If one follows a doctor of law who derives his rulings through rational deduction, it is tantamount to walking in darkness, existentially and also with respect to the *sharīʿa*. This is because rational derivation of laws without the affirmation of light cannot lead one to perfection.

Thereafter, when the soul has a hint of receptivity and discipline, it disapproves of its lowers states and begins to censure itself. This is the second stage of the soul, which is called the 'reproaching soul', "I swear by the reproaching soul" (75:2). As the soul continues to develop, it starts to receive divine breezes in place of gusts from the lower desires. If it turns to the divine breeze it is called the 'inspired soul' and if it returns to its desires, then it is still at the level of the 'commanding soul'. The soul continues receiving from God to ascend through inspiration, at which point it is called the 'inspired soul', as in the verse of Qur'ān, "By the soul and the order given to it. He inspired it of its wickedness and its rectitude" (91:7-8). Its ground is further nourished by the water of the *sharīʿa*, which is the foundation of movement and ascent. If it progresses further, it arrives at the station of the 'contented soul', and thereafter the 'pleased' and 'pleasing souls'. Some place the final two stations either as stations in themselves or attributes of the contented soul, as it appears in the Qurʾān. "O tranquil soul, return to your Lord, pleased and pleasing [Him]. Enter among my servants, enter My paradise" (89:27-30).

This is a brief description of the four main stages of the soul and its development through receiving the Intellect's light. The soul cannot be guided on the straight and upright path nor move from one stage to another except through the light. It must move through the spirit, meaning and reality of the Intellect, or through the emanation of the Intellect's light. The Intellect illuminates the soul through shining its perfections on it, "Is he who was dead and We revived, having given him a light by which he walks amongst people, like one who is in inexorable darkness? Thus, the deeds of the unbelievers are made to seem alluring to them" (6:122).

The soul is the isthmus between the body and the Intellect, if it turns towards the Intellect, it emulates it and if it turns towards the material realm it acquires the properties of materiality. Since the Intellect is pure light, God's vicegerent and divine manifestation, the soul is considered the rest of humanity. When the Intellect illuminates the soul and paints it by its brush, it completely transforms it so it becomes a new creation. Just as God had bestowed upon the Intellect these properties, the Intellect assumes the role of the divine Being in relation to the soul, making knowledge its soul, understanding its spirit, abstention its head, modesty its eye, wisdom its tongue, compassion its concern and mercy its heart. It fills and strengthens it by ten things as God filled and strengthened the Intellect: certainty, faith, truthfulness, tranquillity, sincerity, gentleness, generosity, contentment, submission and thankfulness.

Just as the Intellect adorned by divine attributes is the complete manifestation of God, the soul becomes the complete manifestation of the Intellect. It acquires the attributes of the Intellect but those that correspond to its own nature become obedient to its commands just as the Intellect obeys God's commands. Not every soul is transformed but the proximate soul which has become a new creation by the pen of the Intellect. The Intellect and the soul then become a single light, multiple in manifestation. Just as the Intellect is the light of God, the soul becomes annihilated in the light of the Intellect, subsisting therein.

When the Intellect commands it, both command and the response are one reality, even if the response manifests on the plane of the soul. However, if the soul has not annihilated its selfhood in the Intellect, it would likely disobey it. The Intellect would then say to the soul what God had said to it, "By My Might and Majesty, 'I have not created anything better than you, nor more obedient to me, nor loftier, nor nobler nor more honorable than you."

If the soul is completely immersed in light, it cannot be affected by either something within itself or something external such as Satan. If the soul becomes luminous its desires cannot dominate it and likewise it is protected from outside influences.

Finally, it must be reiterated that the Intellect is reality itself and realizing the Intellect means removing the veils that cover it.

Finding and Losing

He who finds the soul, has lost it and he who has lost it, finds it. In other words, if one finds his soul, his desires, or his ego, it means that he has not arrived at its perfection. This is because its perfection is in its annihilation in the Intellect. Jesus says, "Whoever holds on to his life loses it, and whoever renounces his life in this world will keep it for eternal life." The *hadith qudsī* states, "He who seeks Me, finds Me; he who finds Me, comes to know Me; he who comes to know Me, loves

Me; he who loves Me, he is enthralled by Me; he who is enthralled by Me, I am enthralled by him; he whom I am entralled by, I kill him; he whom I kill, I owe him blood-money; he to whom I owe blood-money, I am his blood-money."[34]

34 Kāshānī, *al-Ḥaqā'iq fī maḥāsin al-akhlāq*, p. 366.

The New Creation

الخَلْقُ الجَدِيدُ

In the Name of God, The Merciful, the Compassionate

Praise be to God, Lord of the Worlds. Peace and blessings be upon the messengers of God, saints and guides among His servants.

O Turner of the hearts and eyes, confirm my heart upon Your Way, do not make my heart swerve after you have guided me and bestow on me a mercy directly from You, for You are most generous. By Your mercy, safeguard me from the fire.

My Lord, extend my life for me, expand my sustenance, and spread out Your mercy before me. If I have been [counted] among the wretched in the Mother of the Book (*umm al-kitab*), then make me among the felicitous; You erase what You will and establish what You will, for the Mother of Book belongs to You.[1]

You turn the hearts and eyes just as your alternate the night and the day. "God alternates the night and the day. Truly in that is a lesson for those possessed of sight" (24:44), to receive the signs of God by the light of insight and eyesight and not turn away from them. "How many a sign in the heavens and the earth they encounter and yet turn away from them" (12:105), so they reach where they are able to reach. "Guidance (*baṣā'ir*) has come to you from your Lord. He who sees, it is for his own sake, and he who is blinded, harms only himself; 'I am not a guardian over you'" (6:104). "The [path] has been made easy for each thing to realize its purpose."[2] God grants success.

---

1 Qummī. *Mafātiḥ al-jinān*, p. 49.

2 Muslim: *The Book of Decree*, 4, 2040; Ibn Mājjah, ch. 10, 1, 235.

بسم الله الرحمن الرحيم

الحمد لله ربِّ العالمين، والصلاة والسلام على رسل الله وأوليائه والمهديين من عباده.

اللهم مقلِّب القلوب والأبصار ثبِّت قلبي على دينك، ولا تزغ قلبي بعد إذ هديتني، وهب لي من لدنك رحمة إنك أنت الوهاب، وأجرني من النار برحمتك.

اللهم امدد لي في عمري، وأوسع علي في رزقي، وانشر عليَّ رحمتك، وإن كنتُ عندك في أُمّ الكتاب شقياً فاجعلني سعيداً، فإنك تمحو ما تشاء وتثبت وعندك أُمّ الكتاب.[1]

وبعد: يُقلِّب الله القلوب والأبصار كما يقلِّب الليل والنهار، ﴿ يُقَلِّبُ اللهُ اللَّيْلَ وَالنَّهَارَ إِنَّ فِي ذَلِكَ لَعِبْرَةً لِّأُولِي الْأَبْصَارِ ﴾ [النور:٤٤]، لتتعرض بأنوار البصيرة والأبصار لآيات الله ولا تعرض عنها، ﴿ وَكَأَيِّن مِّنْ آيَةٍ فِي السَّمَاوَاتِ وَالْأَرْضِ يَمُرُّونَ عَلَيْهَا وَهُمْ عَنْهَا مُعْرِضُونَ﴾ [يوسف:١٠٥]، فتبلغ بها ما يمكن بلوغه، ﴿ قَدْ جَاءَكُم بَصَائِرُ مِن رَّبِّكُمْ فَمَنْ أَبْصَرَ فَلِنَفْسِهِ وَمَنْ عَمِيَ فَعَلَيْهَا وَمَا أَنَا عَلَيْكُم بِحَفِيظٍ ﴾ [الأنعام:١٠٤]، و «كلٌ مُيسَّرٌ لما خُلِقَ له»[2]، والله الموفق.

---

١ - مفاتيح الجنان/ عباس القمي/ ص ٤٩.

٢ - صحيح مسلم/ كتاب القدر/ ٤/ ٢٠٤٠، ابن ماجه / باب/ ١٠/ ١/ ٢٣٥.

Chapter 1

The Path of God

In the name of God, the Light, the Light of lights, Light upon light. In the name of God, the director of affairs, the One who created light from light.

Praise be to God, who created light and made it descend on Mount Sinai in the Inscribed Book, on the Outstretched Parchment (*raqq manshūr*) determined in degree to a prophet giving glad tidings.

All praise be to God, who is celebrated by greatness, who is renowned by glory, who is thanked in trial and in ease, and bless our master Muḥammad and his pure progeny.[1]

---

1 Sayyid ibn Ṭāwūs in *Muhaj al-da'wāt* relates a hadith from Salmān at the end of which reads, "Fāṭima taught me some words taught to her by the Prophet. She used to recite them in the morning and in the evening. She said that as long as you are in this world, you will not suffer from fever, so adhere to it.

"In the name of God, the Light, the Light of lights, Light upon light. In

الباب الأول

طريق الله

بِسْمِ اللهِ النُّورِ، بِسْمِ اللهِ نُورِ النُّورِ، بِسْمِ اللهِ نُورٌ عَلى نُورٍ، بِسْمِ اللهِ الَّذي هُوَ مُدَبِّرُ الأمورِ، بِسْمِ اللهِ الَّذي خَلَقَ النُّورَ مِنَ النُّورِ.

الْحَمْدُ للهِ الَّذي خَلَقَ النُّورَ، مِنَ النُّورِ وَأَنْزَلَ النُّورَ عَلَى الطُّورِ في كِتابٍ مَسْطُورٍ في رَقٍّ مَنْشُورٍ بِقَدَرٍ مَقْدُورٍ عَلى نَبِيٍ مَحْبُورٍ.

الحَمْدُ للهِ الَّذي هُوَ بِالْعِزِّ مَذْكُورٌ، وَبِالْفَخْرِ مَشْهُورٌ، وَعَلَى السَّرَّاءِ والضَّرَّاءِ مَشْكُورٌ، وصلّى الله على سيدنا محمدٍ وآلهِ الطاهرين.[1]

---

١ - روى السيد ابن طاووس في مهج الدعوات حديثاً عن سلمان وقد ورد في آخر الحديث ما حاصله: إن فاطمة عليها السلام علمتني كلاماً كانت تعلمته من رسول الله ﷺ وكانت تقوله غدوة وعشية وقالت: إن سرك أن لا يمسك أذى الحمى ما عشت في دار الدنيا فواظب عليه وهو: بسم الله الرحمن الرحيم: بسم الله النور، بسم الله نور

The path to God is not realized through supposition, imitation, nor is it tread through darkness, nor through light and darkness, nor through shade and shadow,[2] and nor through this nor that, since it is all light from the light of its object. "God is the Light of the heavens and the earth. The parable of His Light is as if there were a niche and within it a lamp, the lamp enclosed in glass, the glass as it were a brilliant star, lit from a blessed olive tree, neither of the east nor of the west, whose oil is almost luminous, though fire scarcely touches it: Light upon Light! God guides whom He wills to His Light. God sets forth parables for men and is of all things Omniscient" (24:35), as are its people, "Is he who was dead and We revived, having given him a light by which he walks amongst people, like one who is in inexorable darkness? Thus, the deeds of the unbelievers are made to seem alluring to them" (6:122).

In the Bible,[3] "You are the salt of the earth. But if the salt loses its saltiness, how can it be made salty again? It is no longer good for

---

the name of God, the director of affairs, the One who created light from light.

Praise be God, who created light and made it descend on Mount Sinai, in the Inscribed Book, on the Outstretched Parchment, determined in degree to a prophet giving glad tidings. All praise be to God who is celebrated by greatness, who is renown by glory, who is thanked in trial and in ease, and may God bless our master Muḥammad and his pure progeny."

Salmān said, "She taught it to me then I taught it to a thousand others in Mecca and Medina who suffered from fever and were cured as a result by God's permission. *Mafātīḥ al-jinān*, p. 159.

2 *ẓill*: A shadow due to an obstruction between you and the sun. It is said that it refers specifically to the shadow that falls after high noon. *Lisān al-ʿArab*, *ẓll*.

3 *Injīl* (Gospel) is an Arabicized word originally from Greek, which means 'glad tidings' or 'good news'. Authored by various individuals, there are twenty-seven books in Greek, which was spoken at that time in the Greek Empire and the first century.

وبعد: إنَّ طريق الله تعالى لا يُدرَك بالظنِّ والتقليد، ولا يُسلك بالظلام، ولا بالنور والظلام،ولا بالظل والفي[2]،ولا من هذا وذاك. إذ هو نور كله من نور مقصده ﴿اللهُ نُورُ السَّمَاوَاتِ وَالْأَرْضِ مَثَلُ نُورِهِ كَمِشْكَاةٍ فِيهَا مِصْبَاحٌ الْمِصْبَاحُ فِي زُجَاجَةٍ الزُّجَاجَةُ كَأَنَّهَا كَوْكَبٌ دُرِّيٌّ يُوقَدُ مِن شَجَرَةٍ مُّبَارَكَةٍ زَيْتُونَةٍ لَّا شَرْقِيَّةٍ وَلَا غَرْبِيَّةٍ يَكَادُ زَيْتُهَا يُضِيءُ وَلَوْ لَمْ تَمْسَسْهُ نَارٌ نُّورٌ عَلَى نُورٍ يَهْدِي اللهُ لِنُورِهِ مَن يَشَاءُ وَيَضْرِبُ اللهُ الْأَمْثَالَ لِلنَّاسِ وَاللهُ بِكُلِّ شَيْءٍ عَلِيمٌ﴾ [النور:٣٥]، كذلك أهله، ﴿أَوَمَن كَانَ مَيْتًا فَأَحْيَيْنَاهُ وَجَعَلْنَا لَهُ نُورًا يَمْشِي بِهِ فِي النَّاسِ كَمَن مَّثَلُهُ فِي الظُّلُمَاتِ لَيْسَ بِخَارِجٍ مِّنْهَا كَذَلِكَ زُيِّنَ لِلْكَافِرِينَ مَا كَانُوا يَعْمَلُونَ﴾ [الأنعام:١٢٢].

و في الإنجيل[3]: «أَنْتُمْ مِلْحُ الأَرْضِ. فَإِذَا فَسَدَ الْمِلْحُ، فَمَاذَا يُعِيدُ إِلَيْهِ

النور، بسم الله الذي هو مدبر الأمور، بسم الله الذي خلق النور من النور.

الحمد لله الذي خلق النور من النور، وأنزل النور على الطور في كتاب مسطور في رق منشور بقدر مقدور على نبي محبور الحمد الله الذي هو بالعز مذكور وبالفخر مشهور وعلى السراء والضراء مشكور وصلى الله على سيدنا محمد وآله الطاهرين.

قال سلمان: فتعلمتهن وعلمتهن أكثر من ألف نفس من أهل المدينة ومكة ممن بهم الحُمّى فبرئوا من مرضهم بإذن الله تعالى.

مفاتيح الجنان/ الشيخ عباس القمي/ ص ١٥٩.

٢ - والظِّلُّ: الفَيْءُ الحاصل من الحاجز بينك وبين الشمس أَيَّ شيء كان، وقيل: هو مخصوص بما كان منه إلى الزوال، وما كان بعده فهو الفيء.../ لسان العرب/ ظلل.

٣ - الإنجيل: كلمة معربة من اصل يوناني بمعنى البشرى أو الخبر السار. و يوجد في الإنجيل سبعة و عشرين سفرا، دونها كتاب مختلفون باللغة اليونانية التي كانت سائدة آنذاك في الامبراطورية اليونانية، و في القرن الميلادي، و ينقسم الإنجيل (العهد الجديد) إلى أربعة أقسام:

anything, except to be thrown out and trampled underfoot.

You are the light of the world. A town built on a hill cannot be hidden. Neither do people light a lamp and put it under a bowl. Instead they put it on its stand, and it gives light to everyone in the house. In the same way, let your light shine before others, that they may see your good deeds and glorify your fathers[4] in heaven" (Matthew 5:13, 14).

Also in the Bible, "When Jesus saw the crowd around him, he gave orders to cross to the other side of the lake. Then a teacher of the law[5] came to him and said, "Master, I will follow you wherever you go." Jesus replied, "Foxes have dens and birds have nests, but the

---

The Gospels (The New Testament) are divided into four books:

1) The Gospels written by Matthew, Mark, Luke and John inform us of the biography of Jesus while he was on earth.

2) Acts of the Apostles: It is the narrative of Jesus recorded in the early years of the Church.

3) Epistles: It begins with the Epistle to the Romans ending with the Epistle to Jude and teaches how to apply the teachings of Jesus.

4) Revelation: It describes the battle between God and Satan and informs that complete and final victory lies with Jesus. The Old Testament was written beforehand and mentions creation as well as the birth of Jesus.

4 The words father and son are used to indicate a deep spiritual relationship without reference to its literal denotation of a physical relationship. For this reason, it is used in relation to the children of Adam, Jesus and other prophets. "Adam is the son of God" (Luke 38:3).

She said, "Yes, my lord. I believe that you are the Messiah, son of God, who has come to the world." This is what Martha, one of the apostles, said to Jesus, the Messiah, peace be upon him. Those who accepted him, that is believed in his name, God granted them to become the children of God. They were born not out of blood, nor passion of the body, nor the desire of any human, but they were born from God. John 12-13; See *Qirā'a ṣufiyya lil-injīl* pp. 26-27.

مُلُوحَتَهُ؟ إِنَّهُ لاَ يَعُودُ يَصْلُحُ لِشَيْءٍ إِلاَّ لأَنْ يُطْرَحَ خَارِجاً لِتَدُوسَهُ النَّاسُ! أَنْتُمْ نُورُ الْعَالَمِ. لاَ يُمْكِنُ أَنْ تُخْفَى مَدِينَةٌ مَبْنِيَّةٌ عَلَى جَبَلٍ؛ وَلاَ يُضِيءُ النَّاسُ مِصْبَاحاً ثُمَّ يَضَعُونَهُ تَحْتَ مِكْيَالٍ، بَلْ يَضَعُونَهُ فِي مَكَانٍ مُرْتَفِعٍ لِيُضِيءَ لِجَمِيعِ مَنْ فِي الْبَيْتِ. هَكَذَا، فَلْيُضِيءْ نُورُكُمْ أَمَامَ النَّاسِ، لِيَرَوْا أَعْمَالَكُمُ الْحَسَنَةَ وَيُمَجِّدُوا أَبَاكُمُ[٤] الَّذِي فِي السَّمَاوَاتِ» [إنجيل متى/ ملح الأرض وأنوار العالم/ ١٣-١٦].

و في الإنجيل أيضاً: «وَحِينَ رَأَى يَسُوعُ أَنَّ الْجُمُوعَ قَدِ احْتَشَدَتْ حَوْلَهُ، أَمَرَ تَلاَمِيذَهُ أَنْ يَعْبُرُوا إِلَى الضَّفَّةِ الْمُقَابِلَةِ. فَتَقَدَّمَ إِلَيْهِ أَحَدُ الْكَتَبَةِ[٥] وَقَالَ: «يَا

١) الأناجيل: دونها متى و مرقس و لوقا و يوحنا، و هي تخبرنا عن حياة يسوع عندما كان على الأرض.

٢) أعمال الرسل: و هو السفر الذي سجل السنوات الأولى لكنيسة يسوع المسيح.

٣) الرسائل: تبدأ من الرسالة إلى روما (رومية) حتى رسالة يهوذا، و قد كتبت لتبصرنا بكيفية تطبيق الحياة المسيحية.

٤) الرؤيا: تظهر لنا الحرب بين الله و الشيطان، كما تعلن لنا أن النصرة التامة ونهائية ستكون للمسيح.

و هناك العهد القديم الذي كتب قبله مبتدئا بذكر أحداث الخلق و حتى قبيل مولد المسيح.

٤ - أَبَاكُمُ: كلمة الأب و الابن تستخدم للدلالة على رابطة روحية عميقة دون أن تتضمن آية إشارة إلى المعنى الحرفي للعلاقة الجسدية. و هكذا تستعمل كلمة ابن في بني آدم كما تستعمل في المسيح و غيره من الأنبياء.(إن آدم ﷺ هو ابن الله) / لوقا ٣:٣٨.

أَجَابَتْهُ: «نَعَمْ يَا ربّ. إِنّي آمَنْتُ بِأَنَّكَ الْمَسِيحُ ابْنُ اللهِ الآتي إِلَى الْعَالَمِ، هكذا قالت مرثا إحدى الحواريات مخاطبة سيدنا عيسى المسيح سلامه علينا، «أَمَّا الَّذِينَ قَبِلُوهُ، أَيِ الَّذِينَ آمَنُوا بِاسْمِهِ، فَقَدْ مَنَحَهُمُ الْحَقَّ فِي أَنْ يَصِيرُوا أَوْلاَدَ اللهِ، وَهُمُ الَّذِينَ وُلِدُوا لَيْسَ مِنْ دَمٍ، وَلاَ مِنْ رَغْبَةِ جَسَدٍ، وَلاَ مِنْ رَغْبَةِ بَشَرٍ، بَلْ مِنَ اللهِ ولدوا. يوحنا/ ١٢-١٣/ قراءة صوفية لإنجيل يوحنا/ ص ٢٦-٢٧.

Son of Man has no place to lay his head." Another disciple said to him, "Lord, first let me go and bury my father." But Jesus told him, "Follow me, and let the dead bury their own dead" (Matthew 8:18-22).

We seek refuge in God from ignorance and its people, those who are described in the following verse,[6] "Or like the depths of darkness in a vast, abysmal sea covered by wave upon wave with clouds above. Layer upon layer of darkness, when he holds out his hand he can barely see it; He whom God gives no light has no light at all" (24:40).

We seek refuge from hypocrisy and its people, "They are those who have bought error for the price of guidance, so their trade yields no profit, nor are they guided. They are like those who kindle a fire, and when it casts its light around them, God takes away their light and leaves them in utter darkness, unable to see—deaf, dumb and blind, they will not return. Or like a rainstorm from the sky, wherein is darkness, thunder and lightning. They put their fingers in their ears for fear of death from the thunderclaps. God surrounds the disbelievers.

---

5 *al-kataba*: Exegetes and professional doctors of law who were strict in maintaining tradition, many of whom were among the Pharisees. They agreed with Jesus with respect to honoring the law and adhering to divine commandments but differed from him with respect to its interpretation. They denied his being the Messiah because he did not adhere to their tradition.

The Pharisees were an austere religious group who exercised literal obedience to the law and Jewish tradition. They exerted influence in society and were in agreement with Jesus with respect to honoring the law, belief in the resurrection and obedience to God, but disputed that he was the Messiah because he did not adhere to all of their traditions and associated with the wicked of ill-repute. *al-Tafsīr al-taṭbīqī li'l-Injīl* and the Gospel of Mark 21-22, p. 1986.

6 Referring to the categories of the veiled [individuals], mentioned in the beginning of the chapter, the perceptive and the wayfarers without light. The categories according to [the degrees of] light and darkness are the ignorant, the hypocrite and the misguided scholar.

مُعَلِّمُ، سَأَتْبَعُكَ حَيْثُمَا تَذْهَبُ!» فَأَجَابَهُ يَسُوعُ: «لِلثَّعَالِبِ أَوْجَارٌ، وَلِطُيُورِ السَّمَاءِ أَوْكَارٌ؛ أَمَّا ابْنُ الإِنْسَانِ، فَلَيْسَ لَهُ مَكَانٌ يُسْنِدُ إِلَيْهِ رَأْسَهُ». وَقَالَ لَهُ آخَرُ مِنْ تَلاَمِيذِهِ: «يَا سَيِّدُ، اسْمَحْ لِي أَنْ أَذْهَبَ أَوَّلاً فَأَدْفِنَ أَبِي!» فَأَجَابَهُ يَسُوعُ: «اتْبَعْنِي الآنَ، وَدَعِ الْمَوْتَى يَدْفِنُونَ مَوْتَاهُمْ!» [إنجيل متى/ ثمن إتباع يسوع/ ٢١-٢٢].

فنعوذ بالله من الجهل وأهله الذين هم من أصناف ما ذكر[٦]، ﴿ أَوْ كَظُلُمَاتٍ فِي بَحْرٍ لُّجِّيٍّ يَغْشَاهُ مَوْجٌ مِّن فَوْقِهِ مَوْجٌ مِّن فَوْقِهِ سَحَابٌ ظُلُمَاتٌ بَعْضُهَا فَوْقَ بَعْضٍ إِذَا أَخْرَجَ يَدَهُ لَمْ يَكَدْ يَرَاهَا وَمَن لَّمْ يَجْعَلِ اللهُ لَهُ نُورًا فَمَا لَهُ مِن نُّورٍ﴾ [النور: ٤٠].

ونعوذ بالله من النفاق وأهله، ﴿ أُولَئِكَ الَّذِينَ اشْتَرَوُا الضَّلَالَةَ بِالْهُدَى فَمَا رَبِحَت تِّجَارَتُهُمْ وَمَا كَانُوا مُهْتَدِينَ ۞ مَثَلُهُمْ كَمَثَلِ الَّذِي اسْتَوْقَدَ نَارًا فَلَمَّا أَضَاءَتْ مَا حَوْلَهُ ذَهَبَ اللهُ بِنُورِهِمْ وَتَرَكَهُمْ فِي ظُلُمَاتٍ لَّا يُبْصِرُونَ ۞ صُمٌّ بُكْمٌ عُمْيٌ فَهُمْ لَا يَرْجِعُونَ ۞ أَوْ كَصَيِّبٍ مِّنَ السَّمَاءِ فِيهِ ظُلُمَاتٌ وَرَعْدٌ وَبَرْقٌ يَجْعَلُونَ أَصَابِعَهُمْ فِي آذَانِهِم مِّنَ الصَّوَاعِقِ حَذَرَ الْمَوْتِ وَاللهُ مُحِيطٌ بِالْكَافِرِينَ ۞ يَكَادُ الْبَرْقُ

---

٥ - الْكَتَبَةِ: المفسرون المحترفون للشريعة، و كانوا يشددون على حفظ التقاليد، و كان الكثيرون منهم من الفريسيين، و هم يتفقون مع عيسى عليه السلام في احترام الشريعة و الالتزام بطاعة الله، و يختلفون معه في تفسيره للشريعة، و يرفضون الاعتراف بانه هو المسيح لأنه لم يطع كل تقاليدهم.

والفريسيون: جماعة دينية متزمتة، كانوا يؤدون الطاعة الحرفية للشريعة و التقاليد اليهودية، و لهم نفوذ في المجاميع، و هم يتفقون مع عيسى عليه السلام في احترام الشريعة، والإيمان بقيامة الأموات، و الالتزام بطاعة الله، و يختلفون معه في انه المسيح لأنه لم يتبع كل تقاليدهم، و كان يختلط بالأشرار ذو السمعة السيئة./ التفسير التطبيقي للكتاب المقدس/ إنجيل مرقس/ ٢١-٢٢/ ص ١٩٨٦.

٦ - أي أصناف المحجوبين الذي تقدم ذكرهم في أول الباب، المدركون، و السالكون بغير النور، فان اخص أصنافهن من حيث النور و الظلمة: جاهل و منافق و ضال على علم.

The lightning almost snatches away their sight from them. Whenever it flashes they walk on and when darkness covers them, they stand still. If God so willed, He could take away their hearing and their sight—God has power over all things" (2:16-20).

"Have you seen the person who has taken as a god his desire, whom God allows to stray in the face of knowledge, sealing his hearing and heart and covering his sight? Then who can guide him after God? Will you not take heed?" (45:23).

"When waves loom over them like canopies they cry out to God, sincere in faith. But when He delivers them safely to land, only some remain unwavering, and only a disloyal ingrate denies Our signs" (31:32).

[Jesus says] in the Bible, "Woe to you, teachers of the law and Pharisees, you hypocrites! You shut the door of the kingdom of heaven in people's faces. You yourselves do not enter, nor will you let those enter who are trying to. Woe unto you, scribes and Pharisees, hypocrites! For you devour widows' houses, and for a pretence make long prayer: therefore you shall receive a judgment[7] more severe. Woe to you, teachers of the law and Pharisees, you hypocrites! You travel over

---

[7] Judgment and execution: God is the Ruler of existence and the one who recompenses, since the ruler both sets laws and enforces them. This is the meaning of judgment or execution here in the Bible. In the Old Testament, leaders of the tribes of the Children of Israel were the judges before they had kings. Accordingly, God is the highest Judge and the Ruler of all things. The final judgment, as Jesus taught, will be the final separation between the virtuous and the wicked.

This is because God Himself is the Judge and judgement will be just. Indeed, the one who will recompense the world over must be just. God has entrusted judgment to Jesus and every man shall be recompensed according to his own knowledge. Those who have never even heard of God's written law will be recompensed according to what they know of God by virtue of His creation and that which their conscience enjoins them towards good or evil. But in reality, all of us in our lives ascend according to our knowledge

يَخْطَفُ أَبْصَارَهُمْ كُلَّمَا أَضَاءَ لَهُم مَّشَوْا فِيهِ وَإِذَا أَظْلَمَ عَلَيْهِمْ قَامُوا وَلَوْ شَاءَ اللهُ لَذَهَبَ بِسَمْعِهِمْ وَأَبْصَارِهِمْ إِنَّ اللهَ عَلَى كُلِّ شَيْءٍ قَدِيرٌ ﴾ [البقرة:١٦ - ٢٠].

ونعوذ بالله من الضلالة على علم وأهلها، ﴿ أَفَرَأَيْتَ مَنِ اتَّخَذَ إِلَٰهَهُ هَوَاهُ وَأَضَلَّهُ اللهُ عَلَى عِلْمٍ وَخَتَمَ عَلَى سَمْعِهِ وَقَلْبِهِ وَجَعَلَ عَلَى بَصَرِهِ غِشَاوَةً فَمَن يَهْدِيهِ مِن بَعْدِ اللهِ أَفَلَا تَذَكَّرُونَ ﴾ [الجاثية/ ٢٣]، ﴿ وَإِذَا غَشِيَهُم مَّوْجٌ كَالظُّلَلِ دَعَوُا اللهَ مُخْلِصِينَ لَهُ الدِّينَ فَلَمَّا نَجَّاهُمْ إِلَى الْبَرِّ فَمِنْهُم مُّقْتَصِدٌ وَمَا يَجْحَدُ بِآيَاتِنَا إِلَّا كُلُّ خَتَّارٍ كَفُورٍ ﴾ [لقمان:٣٢].

وفي الإنجيل: «لَكِنِ الْوَيْلُ لَكُمْ أَيُّهَا الْكَتَبَةُ وَالْفَرِّيسِيُّونَ الْمُرَاؤُونَ! فَإِنَّكُمْ تُغْلِقُونَ مَلَكُوتَ السَّمَاوَاتِ فِي وُجُوهِ النَّاسِ، فَلاَ أَنْتُمْ تَدْخُلُونَ، وَلاَ تَدَعُونَ الدَّاخِلِينَ يَدْخُلُونَ! الْوَيْلُ لَكُمْ أَيُّهَا الْكَتَبَةُ وَالْفَرِّيسِيُّونَ الْمُرَاؤُونَ! فَإِنَّكُمْ تَلْتَهِمُونَ بُيُوتَ الأَرَامِلِ وَتَتَذَرَّعُونَ بِإِطَالَةِ صَلَوَاتِكُمْ. لِذَلِكَ سَتَنْزِلُ بِكُمْ دَيْنُونَةٌ[٧] أَقْسَى! الْوَيْلُ لَكُمْ أَيُّهَا الْكَتَبَةُ وَالْفَرِّيسِيُّونَ الْمُرَاؤُونَ! فَإِنَّكُمْ تَطُوفُونَ

---

٧ - الدينونة و القضاء: لأن الله هو حاكم الكون، فهو أيضاً ديانه (قاضيه) فالحاكم يسن القوانين و ينفذها. و هذا هو ما يقصده الكتاب المقدس بالدينونة أو القضاء. و قد كان القضاة في العهد القديم قوادا قوميين لبني إسرائيل قبل أن يصبح عندهم ملوك. و كان الله هو القاضي الأعلى و حاكم كل شيء. و هكذا، فالدينونة الأخيرة - كما علم المسيح - ستكون آخر فصل بين الأبرار و الأشرار.

و لأن القاضي هو الله نفسه فتكون الدينونة عادلة. فحقا أن ديان كل الأرض لا بد أن يصنع عدلا. و قد أوكل الله إلى المسيح مهمة الدينونة فعلا. و سوف يدان كل إنسان بحسب معرفته. فالذين لم يسمعوا قط شرائع الله المكتوبة سيدانون بحسب ما يعرفونه عن الله من الخليقة و ما تنبههم إليه ضمائرهم من جهة ما هو خير و ما هو شر. و لكن الحقيقة هي أننا جميعا نخفق في الارتفاع بحياتنا إلى ما نعرفه عن الله و معاييره، و جميعا مدانون على أساس الحياة التي عشناها.

land and sea to win a single convert, and when you have succeeded, you make them twice as much a child of hell as you are. Woe to you, blind guides! You say, 'If anyone swears by the temple, it means nothing; but anyone who swears by the gold of the temple is bound by that oath.' You blind fools! Which is greater: the gold, or the temple that makes the gold sacred? You also say, 'If anyone swears by the altar, it means nothing; but anyone who swears by the gift on the altar is bound by that oath.' You blind men! Which is greater: the gift, or the altar that makes the gift sacred? Therefore, anyone who swears by the altar swears by it and by everything on it. And anyone who swears by the temple swears by it and by the one who dwells in it. And anyone who swears by heaven swears by God's throne and by the one who sits on it. Woe to you, teachers of the law and Pharisees, you hypocrites! You give a tenth of your spices—mint, dill and cumin.[8] But you have neglected the more important matters of the law—justice, mercy and fulfilling trusts. You should have practiced the latter, without neglecting the former. You blind guides! You strain out a gnat but

---

of God and His criteria and all of us will be judged according to the way in which we lived out our lives.

On the great Day of Judgment the whole affair will depend upon a person's individual relationship with Jesus, since God himself has taught Jesus as such. The early Christians had complete certainty in the recompense of Judgment Day and that attaining eternal life can only occur through faith in Jesus. In the Gospel of John, "He who believes in the Son has eternal life and he who does not believe in the Son will not see life but the wrath of God shall descend upon him." *Mawsū'a al-kitāb al-muqaddas*, p. 152.

8 Dill and cumin are two herbs whose seeds are used as whole or as a powder to spice food; they also have medical uses. The Pharisees gave to God a tenth of everything, even spices such as mint, dill and cumin, but as Jesus says, they neglected things far more important such as rectitude, justice and mercy. Isaiah 25:27-28, Matthew 23:23, See also, *Mawsū'a al-kitāb al-muqaddas*, p. 185.

الْبَحْرَ وَالْبَرَّ لِتَكْسَبُوا مُتَهَوِّداً وَاحِداً؛ فَإِذَا تَهَوَّدَ جَعَلْتُمُوهُ أَهْلاً لِجَهَنَّمَ ضِعْفَ مَا أَنْتُمْ عَلَيْهِ! الْوَيْلُ لَكُمْ أَيُّهَا الْقَادَةُ الْعُمْيَانُ! تَقُولُونَ: مَنْ أَقْسَمَ بِالْهَيْكَلِ، فَقَسَمُهُ غَيْرُ مُلْزِمٍ؛ أَمَّا مَنْ أَقْسَمَ بِذَهَبِ الْهَيْكَلِ، فَقَسَمُهُ مُلْزِمٌ! أَيُّهَا الْجُهَّالُ وَالْعُمْيَانُ! أَيُّ الاثْنَيْنِ أَعْظَمُ: الذَّهَبُ أَمِ الْهَيْكَلُ الَّذِي يَجْعَلُ الذَّهَبَ مُقَدَّساً؟ وَتَقُولُونَ: مَنْ أَقْسَمَ بِالْمَذْبَحِ، فَقَسَمُهُ غَيْرُ مُلْزِمٍ؛ أَمَّا مَنْ أَقْسَمَ بِالْقُرْبَانِ الَّذِي عَلَى الْمَذْبَحِ، فَقَسَمُهُ مُلْزِمٌ! أَيُّهَا الْعُمْيَانُ! أَيُّ الاثْنَيْنِ أَعْظَمُ: الْقُرْبَانِ أَمِ الْمَذْبَحُ الَّذِي يَجْعَلُ الْقُرْبَانَ مُقَدَّساً؟ فَإِنَّ مَنْ أَقْسَمَ بِالْمَذْبَحِ، فَقَدْ أَقْسَمَ بِهِ وَبِكُلِّ مَا عَلَيْهِ؛ وَمَنْ أَقْسَمَ بِالْهَيْكَلِ، فَقَدْ أَقْسَمَ بِهِ وَبِالسَّاكِنِ فِيهِ؛ وَمَنْ أَقْسَمَ بِالسَّمَاءِ، فَقَدْ أَقْسَمَ بِعَرْشِ اللهِ وَبِالْجَالِسِ عَلَيْهِ! الْوَيْلُ لَكُمْ أَيُّهَا الْكَتَبَةُ وَالْفَرِّيسِيُّونَ الْمُرَاؤُونَ! فَإِنَّكُمْ تُؤَدُّونَ حَتَّى عُشُورَ النَّعْنَعِ وَالشِّبِثِّ وَالْكَمُّونِ[٨]، وَقَدْ أَهْمَلْتُمْ أَهَمَّ مَا فِي الشَّرِيعَةِ: الْعَدْلَ وَالرَّحْمَةَ وَالأَمَانَةَ. كَانَ يَجِبُ أَنْ تَفْعَلُوا هَذِهِ وَلاَ تُغْفِلُوا تِلْكَ! أَيُّهَا الْقَادَةُ الْعُمْيَانُ! إِنَّكُمْ تُصَفُّونَ الْمَاءَ مِنَ الْبَعُوضَةِ، وَلَكِنَّكُمْ تَبْلَعُونَ الْجَمَلَ[٩]! الْوَيْلُ لَكُمْ أَيُّهَا الْكَتَبَةُ وَالْفَرِّيسِيُّونَ الْمُرَاؤُونَ! فَإِنَّكُمْ تُنَظِّفُونَ الْكَأْسَ

و في يوم الدينونة العظيم سيتعلق الأمر كله على علاقة الإنسان الشخصية بالمسيح. فالرب يسوع نفسه علّم بهذا. و قد كان المسيحون الأولون على يقين كلي بأن الأعفاء من الدينونة و نوال الحياة الأبدية لن يكونا إلا بالإيمان بالمسيح. فقد جاء في إنجيل يوحنا: «الذي يؤمن بالابن، له حياة أبدية و الذي لا يؤمن بالابن، لن يرى حياة بل يمكث عليه غضب الله»./ موسوعة الكتاب المقدس/ ص ١٥٢.

٨ - الشبث و الكمون: نبتتان تستعمل بزورهما، كاملة أو مدقوقة كمنكهات تطيب بها الأطعمة، و لها استعمال طبي أيضاً. قدم الفريسيون لله عُشرا من كل شيء حتى الأعشاب المطيبة، كالنعنع و الشبث و الكمون، لكنهم كما قال المسيح أهملوا الأمور الأكثر أهمية كالاستقامة و العدل والرحمة./ أشعياء: ٢٥:٢٨-٢٧، متى ٢٣:٢٣/ لاحظ موسوعة الكتاب المقدس/ ص ١٨٥.

swallow a camel.[9] Woe to you, teachers of the law and Pharisees, you hypocrites! You clean the outside of the cup and dish, but you swallow a camel. Blind Pharisees! First clean the inside of the cup and dish, and then the outside also will be clean. Woe to you, teachers of the law and Pharisees, you hypocrites! You are like whitewashed tombs, which look beautiful on the outside but on the inside are full of the bones of the dead and everything unclean. In the same way, on the outside you appear to people as righteous but on the inside you are full of hypocrisy and wickedness. Woe to you, teachers of the law and Pharisees, you hypocrites! You build tombs for the prophets and decorate the graves of the righteous. And you say, 'If we had lived in the days of our ancestors, we would not have taken part with them in shedding the blood of the prophets.' So you testify against yourselves that you are the descendants of those who murdered the prophets. Go ahead, then, and complete what your ancestors started! You snakes! You brood of vipers! How will you escape being condemned to hell? Therefore I am sending you prophets and sages and teachers. Some of them you will kill and crucify; others you will flog in your synagogues and pursue from town to town. And so upon you will come all the righteous blood that has been shed on earth, from the blood of righteous Abel to the blood of Zechariah son of Berekiah, whom you murdered between the temple and the altar.[10] Truly I tell you, all this will come on this generation" (Matthew 23:13).

---

9 The Pharisees used to clean their water to prevent swallowing gnats, an impure insect according to the law. It was to this extent that they were meticulous in fulfilling the minutiae of ritual purity rather than true purity. They were concerned with external ritual purity but their hearts were corrupt and impure. *Al-Tafsīr al-taṭbīqī li'l-Injīl*, p. 1947.

10 God gave Jesus a brief account of the martyrs of the Old Testament. Abel was the first and Zechariah was the last because the Hebrew Old Testament ends with the second Book of Chronicles. Zechariah exemplified the man of God because those who killed him claimed to be the partisans of God.

وَالصَّحْفَةَ مِنَ الْخَارِجِ، وَلَكِنَّهُمَا مِنَ الدَّاخِلِ مُمْتَلِئَتَانِ بِمَا كَسَبْتُمْ بِالنَّهْبِ وَالطَّمَعِ! أَيُّهَا الْفَرِّيسِيُّ الأَعْمَى، نَظِّفْ أَوَّلاً دَاخِلَ الْكَأْسِ لِيَصِيرَ خَارِجُهَا أَيْضاً نَظِيفاً! الْوَيْلُ لَكُمْ أَيُّهَا الْكَتَبَةُ وَالْفَرِّيسِيُّونَ الْمُرَاؤُونَ! فَإِنَّكُمْ كَالْقُبُورِ الْمُطْلِيَّةِ بِالْكِلْسِ: تَبْدُو جَمِيلَةً مِنَ الْخَارِجِ، وَلَكِنَّهَا مِنَ الدَّاخِلِ مُمْتَلِئَةٌ بِعِظَامِ الْمَوْتَى وَكُلِّ نَجَاسَةٍ! كَذَلِكَ أَنْتُمْ أَيْضاً، تَبْدُونَ لِلنَّاسِ أَبْرَاراً، وَلَكِنَّكُمْ مِنَ الدَّاخِلِ مُمْتَلِئُونَ بِالرِّيَاءِ وَالْفِسْقِ! «الْوَيْلُ لَكُمْ أَيُّهَا الْكَتَبَةُ وَالْفَرِّيسِيُّونَ الْمُرَاؤُونَ! فَإِنَّكُمْ تَبْنُونَ قُبُورَ الأَنْبِيَاءِ وَتُزَيِّنُونَ مَدَافِنَ الأَبْرَارِ، وَتَقُولُونَ: لَوْ عِشْنَا فِي زَمَنِ آبَائِنَا لَمَا شَارَكْنَاهُمْ فِي سَفْكِ دَمِ الأَنْبِيَاءِ. فَبِهَذَا تَشْهَدُونَ عَلَى أَنْفُسِكُمْ بِأَنَّكُمْ أَبْنَاءُ قَاتِلِي الأَنْبِيَاءِ! فَأَكْمِلُوا مَا بَدَأَهُ آبَاؤُكُمْ لِيَطْفَحَ الْكَيْلُ! أَيُّهَا الْحَيَّاتُ، أَوْلاَدَ الأَفَاعِي! كَيْفَ تُفْلِتُونَ مِنْ عِقَابِ جَهَنَّمَ؟ لِذَلِكَ: هَا أَنَا أُرْسِلُ إِلَيْكُمْ أَنْبِيَاءَ وَحُكَمَاءَ وَمُعَلِّمِينَ، فَبَعْضَهُمْ تَقْتُلُونَ وَتَصْلِبُونَ، وَبَعْضَهُمْ تَجْلِدُونَ فِي مَجَامِعِكُمْ، وَتُطَارِدُونَهُمْ مِنْ مَدِينَةٍ إِلَى أُخْرَى. وَبِهَذَا يَقَعُ عَلَيْكُمْ كُلُّ دَمٍ زَكِيٍّ سُفِكَ عَلَى الأَرْضِ: مِنْ دَمِ هَابِيلَ الْبَارِّ إِلَى دَمِ زَكَرِيَّا بْنِ بَرَخِيَّا الَّذِي قَتَلْتُمُوهُ بَيْنَ الْهَيْكَلِ وَالْمَذْبَحِ[10]. الْحَقَّ أَقُولُ لَكُمْ: إِنَّ عِقَابَ ذَلِكَ كُلِّهِ سَيَنْزِلُ بِهَذَا الْجِيلِ» [الإنجيل/ متى/ يسوع يعنف الكتبة و الفريسيون/ ص٣٦].

---

٩ - كان الفريسيون يُصفوّن مياههم حتى لا يبتلعوا بعوضة، و هي حشرة نجسة حسب الشريعة. إلى هذا الحد بلغ بهم التدقيق من تفاصيل الطهارة الطقسية دون الطهارة الحقيقة. فكانوا أتقياء طقسيا من الخارج، و لكن لهم قلوب فاسدة نجسة/ التفسير التطبيقي للكتاب المقدس/ ص ١٩٤٧.

١٠ - اعطي الرب (المسيح) موجزا صغير عن شهداء العهد القديم، فقد كان هابيل أول شهيد (تك ٤)، و كان زكريا آخر شهيد (لأن الكتاب المقدس العبري ينتهي بسفر أخبار الأيام الثاني). كان زكريا مثالا رائعا لرجل الله، إذ قتله الذي كانوا يدعون انهم شعب الله (انظر ٢ أخ ٢٤: ٢١) / المصدر السابق ص١٩٤٨ (بتصرف).

As mentioned, neither the path to God can be comprehended, nor His realities fathomed through rational deduction and analytical reasoning, even if they prove to be sound. They can only be perceived through light, as is well-known and witnessed by the people of God.

There is hardly a hadith more well-known than, "Knowledge is not extensive learning, it is but a light that God casts in the heart of whomever He wishes to guide."[11] "Knowledge is a light and a brightness that God casts in the hearts of His saints and speaks through their tongues."[12] "The heart of every servant has two eyes; they are unseen and with them the Unseen is perceived. Thus, if God desires felicity for the servant, He opens the eyes of his heart and he sees what is hidden from his [physical] eyes."[13] There are other similar hadith.

They — may God be pleased with them — hope to learn only from God, as He says in His book, "Be God-conscious and God will teach you; God is the Omniscient" (2:272). Whoever is God-conscious, He will provide him a way out and sustenance from places beyond his reckoning. Whoever relies on God, He suffices. God will certainly accomplish His purpose as He has determined a measure for all things" (65:2-3), "Whoever is God-conscious, He will facilitate his affairs" (65:4).

Divine knowledge is a proof in and of itself and does not rely on something else, since light is luminous and illuminates others. "There are people who dispute concerning God without knowledge and follow every rebellious devil" (22:3), "There are people who dispute concerning God without knowledge, guidance or an illuminating Book" (22:8).

Only light manifests in reality, allusion or expression. Those who are guided to it and by it are but a few as Imam ʿAlī says, "Do not feel alone on the path of guidance due the paucity of its followers for people have gathered around a feast whose satiation is brief and whose hunger is prolonged.[14]

---

11 *Munyat al-murīd*, p. 149.

12 *Al-Uṣūl al-aṣīla*, p. 162.

13 *Mustadrak al-wasāʾil*, p. 196.

14 *Nahj al-balāgha*, sermon 201.

وأيضاً كما لا يدرك طريق الله تعالى بما ذكر، كذلك لا تدرك حقائقه بالاستنتاجات الفكرية والقياسات العقلية، وإن صحت، وإنما تدرك بالنور و هو معروف لأهل الله تعالى، مشهود لديهم.

ولا أشهر من حديث «ليس العلم بكثرة التعلم،إنما هو نور يقذفه الله في قلب من يريد أن يهديه»[١١]، «العلم نورٌ وضياءٌ يقذفه الله في قلوب أوليائه ونطق به على لسانهم»[١٢]، «ما من عبد إلا ولقلبه عينان، وهما غيب يدرك بهما الغيب، فإذا أراد الله بعبد خيرا فتح عيني قلبه، فيرى ما هو غائب عن بصره»[١٣]، و غير ذلك من الأحاديث.

وهؤلاء رضي الله عنهم و أرضاهم لا يرجى التعلم عندهم من غير الله تعالى، وهو الذي قال في كتابه العزيز:﴿ وَاتَّقُوا اللهَ وَيُعَلِّمُكُمُ اللهُ وَ اللهُ بِكُلِّ شَيْءٍ عَلِيمٌ ﴾ [البقرة:٢٨٢]، ﴿ وَمَن يَتَّقِ اللهَ يَجْعَل لَّهُ مَخْرَجًا ۝ وَيَرْزُقْهُ مِنْ حَيْثُ لَا يَحْتَسِبُ وَمَن يَتَوَكَّلْ عَلَى اللهِ فَهُوَ حَسْبُهُ إِنَّ اللهَ بَالِغُ أَمْرِهِ قَدْ جَعَلَ اللهُ لِكُلِّ شَيْءٍ قَدْرًا ﴾ [الطلاق:٢-٣]، ﴿ وَمَن يَتَّقِ اللهَ يَجْعَل لَّهُ مِنْ أَمْرِهِ يُسْرًا ﴾ [الطلاق:٤].

والعلم الإلهي، بعينه دليل لا يتوقف على غيره، إذ النور ظاهر بنفسه مظهر لغيره. ﴿ وَمِنَ النَّاسِ مَن يُجَادِلُ فِي اللهِ بِغَيْرِ عِلْمٍ وَيَتَّبِعُ كُلَّ شَيْطَانٍ مَّرِيدٍ﴾ [الحج:٣]، ﴿ وَمِنَ النَّاسِ مَن يُجَادِلُ فِي اللهِ بِغَيْرِ عِلْمٍ وَلَا هُدًى وَلَا كِتَابٍ مُّنِيرٍ ﴾ [الحج:٨].

فليس ثم إلا النور المتجلي بالحقيقة والإشارة والعبارة. و المهتدون إليه و به قليلون. قال الإمام علي عليه السلام: «لا تَسْتَوْحِشْ في طَرِيقَ الْهُدَى لِقِلَّةِ أَهْلِه فانَّ النّاسَ قَد اجْتَمَعُوا على مَائِدَةٍ شبعها قصيرٌ و جُوعُها طَوِيلٌ»[١٤].

---

١١ - منية المريد/ ١٤٩.

١٢ - الأصول الأصيلة/ ١٦٢

١٣ - مستدرك الوسائل / ٥ / ٢٩٧

١٤ - نهج البلاغة/خ ٢٠١.

The Bible says, "Enter through the narrow gate. For wide is the gate and broad is the road that leads to destruction, and many enter through it. But small is the gate and narrow the road that leads to life, and only a few find it" (Matthew 7:13-14).

Another passage of the Bible says, "Then Jesus went through the towns and villages, teaching as he made his way to Jerusalem. Someone asked him, "Lord, are only a few people going to be saved?" He said to them, "Make every effort to enter through the narrow door, because many, I tell you, will try to enter and will not be able to. Once the owner of the house gets up and closes the door, you will stand outside knocking and pleading, 'Sir, open the door for us.' "But he will answer, 'I don't know you or where you come from.' "Then you will say, 'We ate and drank with you, and you taught in our streets.' "But he will reply, 'I don't know you or where you come from. Away from me, all you evildoers!' "There will be weeping there, and gnashing of teeth, when you see Abraham, Isaac and Jacob and all the prophets in the kingdom of God, but you yourselves thrown out. People will come from east and west and north and south, and will take their places at the feast in the kingdom of God. Indeed there are those who are last who will be first, and first who will be last" (Luke 13:22-30).

God is the guarantor of success, upon Him is all reliance and refuge. "My success is only through God, upon him I have relied, and to Him I return" (11:88). "Their final call will be, 'Praise be to God, Lord of the Worlds'" (10:10).[15]

---

15 God says, "Those who strive in us We will show them Our way" (29:69). He also says, "If you are God-conscious, He will give you a criterion" (8:29), and "If only the people of the cities had believed and had been God-conscious, We would have opened for them blessings from the sky and from the earth" (7:96).

و في الإنجيل: «اُدْخُلوا مِنَ الْبَابِ الضَّيِّقِ! فَإِنَّ الْبَابَ الْمُؤَدِّي إِلَى الْهَلاَكِ وَاسِعٌ وَطَرِيقَهُ رَحْبٌ؛ وَكَثِيرُونَ هُمُ الَّذِينَ يَدْخُلُونَ مِنْهُ. مَا أَضْيَقَ الْبَابَ وَأَعْسَرَ الطَّرِيقَ الْمُؤَدِّي إِلَى الْحَيَاةِ! وَقَلِيلُونَ هُمُ الَّذِينَ يَهْتَدُونَ إِلَيْهِ» [إنجيل متى/ ٩].

كذلك في الإنجيل: «وَاجْتَازَ فِي الْمُدُنِ وَالْقُرَى وَاحِدَةً بَعْدَ وَاحِدَةٍ، يُعَلِّمُ فِيهَا وَهُوَ مُسَافِرٌ إِلَى أُورُشَلِيمَ. وَسَأَلَهُ أَحَدُهُمْ: «يَا سَيِّدُ، أَقَلِيلٌ عَدَدُ الَّذِينَ سَيَخْلُصُونَ؟» وَلكِنَّهُ قَالَ لِلْجَمِيعِ: «ابْذِلُوا الْجَهْدَ لِلدُّخُولِ مِنَ الْبَابِ الضَّيِّقِ، فَإِنِّي أَقُولُ لَكُمْ إِنَّ كَثِيرِينَ سَيَسْعَوْنَ إِلَى الدُّخُولِ، فَلاَ يَتَمَكَّنُونَ. فَمِنْ بَعْدِ مَا يَكُونُ رَبُّ الْبَيْتِ قَدْ قَامَ وَأَغْلَقَ الْبَابَ، وَتَبْدَأُونَ بِالْوُقُوفِ خَارِجاً تَقْرَعُونَ الْبَابَ قَائِلِينَ: يَا رَبُّ افْتَحْ لَنَا! فَيُجِيبُكُمْ قَائِلاً: لاَ أَعْرِفُ مِنْ أَيْنَ أَنْتُمْ! عِنْدَئِذٍ تَبْدَأُونَ تَقُولُونَ: أَكَلْنَا وَشَرِبْنَا بِحُضُورِكَ، وَعَلَّمْتَ فِي شَوَارِعِنَا! وَسَوْفَ يَقُولُ: أَقُولُ لَكُمْ، لاَ أَعْرِفُ مِنْ أَيْنَ أَنْتُمْ؛ اغْرُبُوا مِنْ أَمَامِي يَا جَمِيعَ فَاعِلِي الإِثْمِ! هُنَاكَ سَيَكُونُ الْبُكَاءُ وَصَرِيرُ الأَسْنَانِ، عِنْدَمَا تَرَوْنَ إِبْرَاهِيمَ وَإِسْحَاقَ وَيَعْقُوبَ وَجَمِيعَ الأَنْبِيَاءِ فِي مَلَكُوتِ اللهِ وَأَنْتُمْ مَطْرُوحُونَ خَارِجاً. وَسَيَأْتِي أُنَاسٌ مِنَ الشَّرْقِ وَالْغَرْبِ، وَمِنَ الشِّمَالِ وَالْجَنُوبِ، وَيَتَّكِئُونَ فِي مَلَكُوتِ اللهِ. فَإِذاً آخِرُونَ يَصِيرُونَ أَوَّلِينَ، وَأَوَّلُونَ يَصِيرُونَ آخِرِينَ» [إنجيل لوقا/ ١٣:٢٢].

«والله الموفق، وعليه التوكل وإليه الإنابة،﴿ وَمَا تَوْفِيقِي إِلَّا بِاللهِ عَلَيْهِ تَوَكَّلْتُ وَإِلَيْهِ أُنِيبُ ﴾ [هود:٨٨]، ﴿وَآخِرُ دَعْوَاهُمْ أَنِ الْحَمْدُ لِلهِ رَبِّ الْعَالَمِينَ ﴾ [يونس:١٠] [15].

---

١٥ – وقال تعالى: ﴿ وَالَّذِينَ جَاهَدُوا فِينَا لَنَهْدِيَنَّهُمْ سُبُلَنَا ﴾. [سورة العنكبوت:٦٩].

وقال تعالى:﴿ إِن تَتَّقُوا اللهَ يَجْعَل لَّكُمْ فُرْقَانًا ﴾. [سورة الأنفال:٢٩].

وقال تعالى: ﴿ وَلَوْ أَنَّ أَهْلَ الْقُرَى آمَنُوا وَاتَّقَوْا لَفَتَحْنَا عَلَيْهِم بَرَكَاتٍ مِّنَ السَّمَاءِ وَالْأَرْضِ ﴾ [سورة الأعراف:٩٦].

The Prophet said, "He who becomes sincere for God for forty days, wellsprings of wisdom emerge from his heart onto his tongue." *Biḥār al-anwār*, v. 67, p. 249.

Imam 'Alī says, "Knowledge is not in the heavens so that it would descend upon you nor in the depths of the earth that it would emerge for you, but knowledge is forged in your hearts. So, acquire the characteristics of the spiritual and it will become manifest to you." *Qurrat al-'uyūn*, p. 183.

In another version, "Knowledge is not in the heavens that it might descend upon you nor in the depths of the earth that it may ascend to you but it is forged in your natures, so assume the divine character and it will become manifest to you." *Maḥajjat al-bayḍā'*, p. 158.

Kashānī says, "The realities of all things are inscribed on the Guarded Tablet (*lawḥ al-maḥfūẓ*) and flow upon our hearts from that world by the pen of the Intellect, which is the writer on the tablet of our souls, as God says, "He has inscribed faith upon their hearts" (58:22), and "He taught by the pen; taught man what he knew not" (96:4-5).

All knowledge can be inscribed on the human heart. It is like a mirror that is prepared to reflect every reality of Truth arising from the Guarded Tablet. It is free to receive every type of knowledge, unless there is some essential deficiency as in the case of a child's heart, which is akin to a crude image on unpolished steel.

Or, it is due to excessive sins and turbidity accumulated from desires, that prevent purity and reflectivity; this is akin to a tarnished and rusted mirror.

Or, it is due to changing its orientation from the desired reality and expending willpower for the sake of earning a livelihood, preferring bodily actions which prevent reflecting on the Lord's presence and true divine realities. Only what is directly contemplated is perceived, as if one turns a mirror away from an object.

Or, it is due to a certain veil, such as a particular belief one has blindly held since childhood or accepted on good faith, since these obstruct a person

قال ﷺ: «من أخلص لله أربعين صباحا ظهرت ينابيع الحكمة من قلبه على لسانه». / بحار الأنوار/ ٦٧ / ٢٤٩.

وقال أمير المومنين عليه السلام: «ليس العلم في السماء فينزل إليكم، ولا في تخوم الأرض فيخرج لكم، ولكن العلم مجبول في قلوبكم، تأدبوا بآداب الروحانيين يظهر لكم»./ قرة العيون/ الفيض الكاشاني/ ص ١٨٣.

و في رواية: «ليس العلم في السماء فينزل إليكم، و لا في تخوم الأرض فيصعد إليكم، و إنما جبل في جبلتكم فتخلقوا بأخلاق الله يظهر لكم./ اللمعة البيضاء/ ١٥٨.

وقال الفيض الكاشاني: إن حقائق الأشياء كلها مسطورة في لوح المحفوظ، وإنما تفيض على قلوبنا من ذلك العالم بواسطة القلم العقلي الكاتب في ألواح نفوسنا كما قال عز وجل: ﴿أُولَئِكَ كَتَبَ فِي قُلُوبِهِمُ الْإِيمَانَ﴾، [سورة المجادلة: ٢٢]، وقال سبحانه: ﴿عَلَّمَ بِالْقَلَمِ عَلَّمَ الْإِنسَانَ مَا لَمْ يَعْلَمْ﴾، [سورة العلق: ٤-٥].

وقلب الإنسان صالح لأن ينتقش فيه العلوم كلها، وهو كمرآة مستعدة لأن يتجلى فيه حقيقة الحق في الأمور كلها من اللوح المحفوظ، وإنما خلى عما خلى عنه من العلوم. أما لنقصان ذاته كقلب الصبي، وهو يشبه نقصان صورة المرآة كجوهر الحديد قبل أن يصيقل (الصقل الجلاء).

أو لكثرة المعاصي والخبث الذي تراكم عليه من كثرة الشهوات المانعة من صفائه وجلائه، وهذا يشبه خبث المرآة وصداها. (الخبث من الحديد و نحوه وسخه، و صدى الحديد صداء: إذا علاه الجَرَب.)

أو لعدوله عن جهة الحقيقة المطلوبة لاستيعاب همته بتهيئة أسباب المعيشة وتفضيل الأعمال البدنية المانعة من التأمل في الحضرة الربوبية والحقائق الحقة الإلهية، فلا ينكشف له إلا ماهو متفكر فيه، وهذا يشبه كون المرآة معدولا بها عن جهة الصورة.

أو لحجاب بينه وبين المطلوب من اعتقاد سبق إليه منذ الصبا على سبيل التقليد والقبول بحسن الظن، فان ذلك يحول بينه وبين حقائق الحق، ويمنع أن ينكشف في

from the realities of Truth and prevent the heart's realization that it should oppose blind imitation. This is like a veil which completely covers the object from the mirror.

Or, ignorance with respect to its orientation which prevents one from discovering the goal. The seeker of knowledge cannot acquire the desired type of knowledge unless he is able to recollect its related disciplines, namely, to remember and organize those principles in himself. If he does not possess the relevant disciplines he will not achieve his aim. This all relates to ignorance of the direction from which the goal is achieved; it is one of the obstacles in perceiving realities.

Furthermore, unnecessary knowledge is acquired by the heart discursively through rational deduction and learning. It is called subjective or theoretical [knowledge] held by the scholars and philosophers.

Sometimes [knowledge] rushes into the heart as if it were cast into it without notice, whether or not after seeking and yearning, and whether or not one knows the reason for receiving that knowledge. It may be from witnessing an angel in the heart or hearing its voice, or simply audition without vision, or the inspiration in the mind (*rouʿ*) without audition, like a trace in the heart. The hadith states, "If God wishes felicity for the servant he casts a trace of light in his heart." (A trace is like a speck—*al-Munjid*); or, through inspiration which may occur in sleep as it occurs in wakefulness. Witnessing that is customarily called 'revelation' is specific for Prophets and Messengers but may occur for others as well.

Just as the veil between the mirror and the form may, at times, be removed actively by the hand, and at others, by a gust of wind, man's acquiring knowledge by the divine pen may also be due to the strength of his active reflection that divests forms of their coverings and moves between forms (*ghawīshī* is the plural of *ghāshiya* which is any type of covering). The breeze of divine grace may also blow and remove veils and coverings from the eye of inner vision and disclose a part of what is inscribed on the Highest Tablet.

This may occur during sleep and reveal the future, or sometimes during

قلبه خلاف ما تلقفه من ظاهر التقليد، وهذا يشبه الحجاب المرسل بين المرآة وبين الصورة المطلوب رؤيتها.

أو لجهل بالجهة التي يقع فيها العثور على المطلوب، فان طالب العلم ليس يمكنه أن يحصل العلم المطلوب إلا بالتذكر للعلوم التي تناسب مطلوبه، حتى إذا ذكرها ورتبها في نفسه ترتيبا مخصوصا حصل له المطلوب، فإذا لم يكن عنده العلوم المناسبة لذلك لم يحصل له المطلوب، وهذا يشبه الجهل بالجهة التي فيها الصورة المطلوبة، فهذه هي الأسباب المانعة لإدراك الحقائق.

ثم إن العلوم التي ليست ضرورية إنما تحصل في القلب: تارة بالاكتساب بطريق الاستدلال والتعلم، ويسمى اعتبارا واستبصارا ويختص بالعلماء والحكماء.

وتارة بهجومه على القلب كانه القي فيه من حيث لا يدري، سواء كان عقيب طلب وشوق أو لا، وسواء كان مع الاطلاع على السبب الذي استفيد ذلك العلم أو لا.

فانه قد يكون بمشاهدة الملك الملقى في القلب وسماع حديثه، وقد يكون بمجرد السماع من غير مشاهدة، وقد يكون بنفثه في الروع من غير سماع ينكت في القلب نكتا (في الحديث: إذا أراد الله بعبد خيرا نكت في قلبه نكتة من نور. و النكتة في الشيء كالنقطة)/ المنجد، أو يلهم إلهاما، وقد يكون ذلك الهجوم في النوم كما يكون في اليقظة والمشاهدة تختص بالأنبياء والرسل عليهم السلام وخص باسم الوحي عرفا، وقد يكون لغيرهم.

وكما أن الحجاب بين المرآة والصورة يزال تارة بتعمل اليد المتصرفة، وتارة لهبوب ريح تحركه، فكذلك استفادة العلوم بالقلم الإلهي للإنسان قد تكون بقوة فكرته المتصرفة في تجريد الصور عن الغواشي (جمع الغاشية، و هي كل ما يغطي الشيء) والانتقال من بعضها إلى بعض، وقد تهب رياح الألطاف الإلهية فيكشف الحجب والغواشي عن عين بصيرته فيتجلى فيها بعض ما هو مثبت في اللوح الأعلى.

فيكون تارة عند المنام، فيظهر ما سيكون في المستقبل، وتارة بتقشع الحجاب بلطف

wakefulness, God's subtle grace dissolves the veil and illuminates certain wondrous mysteries of the world of Dominion (*malakūt*) behind the curtain of the Unseen. It may persist or flee like a flash of lightning but its persistence is extremely rare. Inspiration and speech of the angel granting knowledge do not subside with respect to place and cause but cease in the manner of unveiling and their orientation. Neither revelation, inspiration nor speech subside but only with respect to the intensity of its clarity and hiddenness and the witnessing of the angel granting him knowledge.

The common feature is that the angel, who is the divine pen, is the intermediary, as God says, "He taught by the pen" (96:4). Perhaps, God's statement alludes to these three degrees, "It is not appropriate for man to speak to God except through revelation, behind a veil, or the sending of a messenger" (42:51).

Some scholars have said that the secret in the Prophet's exclusive awareness of the angel of revelation is that when he polished his spirit with the burnish of the Intellect for consummate worship, the curtains of nature and the rust of sins were completely expunged. His sacred soul, mighty in strength, radiantly lit all that was below did not become distracted by either direction. Thus, he encompassed both directions and embraced both aspects so that his inward senses did not obscure his outward senses.

Thus, when he oriented himself to the highest horizon and received the lights of knowledge without human intermediary but from God [directly], its effects intensified to the faculties representing a form witnessed by the human spirit, having become embodied in outward existence through the outer senses, particularly for the hearing and sight which are the noblest and subtlest. Thus, he saw an individual in sensory form and heard measured and eloquent speech or a written book. The individual was an angel who descended and carried divine revelation. The speech was God's speech and the book was His book, each descending from the world of the spoken, decreed Command. It is His true Essence and His original form to the world of written and determined creation in the best form and most beautiful

خفـي مـن الله فيلمـع في القلـب من وراء سـتر الغيـب شيء مـن غرائـب أسرار الملكوت في اليقظـة، فربـما يـدوم وربـما يكـون كالـبرق الخاطـف، ودوامـه في غاية النـدور فلـم يفارق الإلهـام وحديـث الملـك الاكتسـاب في العلـم ولا في محلـه ولا في سـببه، ولكـن يفارقـه في طريقـة زوال الحجـاب وجهتـه، ولم يفـارق الوحـي والإلهـام والحديـث في شيء مـن ذلك، بـل في شـدة الوضـوح والتوريـة ومشـاهدة الملـك المفيـد للعلم.

والـكل مشـتركة في أنهـا بواسـطة الملـك الـذي هـو القلـم كـما قـال عـز وجـل: ﴿عَلَّمَ بِالْقَلَـمِ﴾، سـورة العلـق/ ٤، ولعله أشـير إلى هـذه المراتب الثـلاث في قوله سـبحانه ﴿ وَمَا كَانَ لِبَـشَرٍ أَن يُكَلِّمَـهُ الله إِلَّا وَحْيًـا أَوْ مِـن وَرَاءِ حِجَـابٍ أَوْ يُرْسِـَل رَسُـولًا ﴾، [سـورة الشـورى:٥١].

قـال بعـض العلـماء: الـسر في اطـلاع النبـي عـلى الملك الموحـي دون غـيره انه لـما صقل روحـه بصقالة العقـل للعبودية التامـة، وزالـت عنه غشـاوة الطبيعة وريـن المعصيـة بالكلية، وكانـت نفسـه قدسـية شـديدة القوى قوية الإنـارة لما تحتها، لم يشـغلها جهـة فوقها عن جهة تحتهـا فتضبـط الطرفين وتوسـع الجانبـين ولا يسـتغرقها حسـها الباطن عن حسـها الظاهر.

فـإذا توجهـت إلى الأفـق الأعـلى وتلقـت أنـوار المعلومـات بـلا تعليـم بـشري مـن الله يتعـدى تأثيرهـا إلى قويهـا ويتمثـل صـورة مـا يشـاهده لروحهـا البـشري ومنهـا إلى ظاهـر الكـون فتمثـل للحـواس الظاهرة، سـيما السـمع والبصر لكونهـما أشرف الحـواس الظاهرة وألطفهـا، فيرى شـخصا محسوسـا ويسـمع كلاما منظوما في غاية الجـودة والفصاحة أو يرى صحيفـة مكتوبـة. فالشـخص هو الملـك النـازل الحامل للوحـي الإلهي، والـكلام هو كلام الله والكتـاب كتابـه، وقـد نـزل كل منهـما مـن عالم الأمـر القـولي القضائـي وذاتـه الحقيقية وصورتـه الأصليـة إلى عـالم الخلـق الكتابي القدري في أحسـن صـورة وأجمل كسـوة كتمثل جبرئيـل عليه السلام لنبينـا ﷺ في صـورة دحيـة بـن الخليفـة الكلبـي الـذي كان أجمل أهـل زمانه.

ويقـال ماراه في صورته الحقيقية إلا مرتين وذلك أنه ﷺ سـاله أن يريه نفسـه على صورته فواعـده ذلـك بحِـراء (حِـراء: بالكـسر و المـد، جبـل بمكة/ المنجـد) فطلع لـه جبرئيل عليه السلام

raiment, the angel Gabriel personified for our Prophet in the form of Diḥyā ibn al-Khalīfa al-Kalbī, who was the most beautiful person of his time.

It is said that what he saw of his true form occurred only twice because the Prophet requested that he show himself in his real form. So he promised him at Mount Ḥirā' (Ḥirā', with *kasra* on the *yā'* is the name of a mountain in Mecca, *al-Munjid*). Gabriel then came forth and showed himself, filling the horizon from east to west. *Biḥār al-anwār*, v. 9, p. 240. In another hadith, he had six hundred wings. The Prophet saw him once again on the Night of the Ascension (*mi'rāj*) at the farthest Lote Tree. *Qurrat al-'uyūn*, p. 125.

فسـد الأفق مـن المـشرق إلى المغرب/ بحار الأنـوار/ ٩/ ٢٤٠.

وفي روايـة: كان لـه سـتمائة جنـاح. الخصـال/ ١٥٣. ورآه مرة أخـرى على صورتـه ليلة المعـراج عنـد سـدرة المنتهـى. / قـرة العيـون/ ص١٢٥.

Chapter 2

The Knowledge of Reality

The language of the world of Intellect, which emanates from a hidden, treasured light in the ancient knowledge of God is the station of the people of Reality who do not engage in interpretation. They utter what they witness, either in wakefulness, drowsiness or sleep, in the sensory, imaginal or intellectual [realms], as was the case of Abraham when he took one look at the stars, "He took one look at the stars and said, 'I am ill'" (37:88-89). He discerned its meaning and discovered reality; he did not interpret it in a form or express it as something tangible. He spoke in the language of the world of meanings and its reality insofar as he perceived illness from his look.

He saw a dream and considered it a true vision not needing interpretation or expression, "When the boy was old enough to walk with his father, Abraham said, 'My son, I have seen myself sacrificing you in a dream. What do you think? He said, 'Father, do as you have

الباب الثاني

علم الحقيقة

لسان العالم العقلي، المفاض عن نورٍ مخزونٍ مكنونٍ في سابقِ علمِ الله، هو مقام أهل الحقيقة، الذين لا تأويل عندهم. وإنما ينطقون بما يشهدون، يقظة أو سنة أو نوما، محسوسا كان أو متخيلا أو معقولا، كالذي للخليل عليه السلام، حين نظر نظرة في النجوم: ﴿ فَنَظَرَ نَظْرَةً فِي النُّجُومِ ۞ فَقَالَ إِنِّي سَقِيمٌ ﴾ [الصافات:٨٨-٨٩]، فأفاد المعنى وأصاب الحقيقة، ولم يؤول لصورة أو يعبر لمحسوس. وإنما نطق بلسان عالم المعاني وحقيقته، حيث أدرك حقيقة السقم فيما نظر إليه.

و رأى في المنام فصدق الرؤيا كما رأى فما أوّل ولا عبّر ﴿ فَلَمَّا بَلَغَ مَعَهُ السَّعْيَ قَالَ يَا بُنَيَّ إِنِّي أَرَىٰ فِي الْمَنَامِ أَنِّي أَذْبَحُكَ فَانظُرْ مَاذَا تَرَىٰ قَالَ يَا أَبَتِ

been commanded, and God willing, you will find me steadfast.' When they had both surrendered to God, and he had laid his son down on the side of his face, We called out to him, 'Abraham, You have already fulfilled the dream.' This is how we reward the virtuous. It was a clear test. Then We ransomed him with a tremendous sacrifice, and let him be praised by successive generations: Peace be upon Abraham! This is how We reward the virtuous. Truly he was one of Our faithful servants" (37:102-111).

The world of meaning is the world of Intellect which governed the speech of Abraham and his vision after he had been given guidance. "We gave Abraham sound judgement from before, and We were aware when he said to his father and his people, 'What are these images to which you are devoted? They said, 'We found our fathers worshipping them. He said, 'You and your fathers have clearly gone astray.' They asked, 'Have you brought us the truth or are you playing around?' He said, 'Your true Lord is the Lord of the heavens and the earth, who created them, and to which I am a witness. By God, I shall certainly plot against your idols as soon as you have turned your backs!' He broke them all into pieces, but left the biggest one for them so that they would return to it. They said, 'Who has done this to our gods? How wicked he must be!' Some said, 'We heard a youth called Abraham talking about them.' They said,'Bring him before the people, so that they may witness [his trial].' They asked, 'Was it you, O Abraham, who did this to our gods?' He said, 'No, it was done by the biggest of them– this one. Ask them, if they can talk.' They turned to one another, saying, 'It is you who are in the wrong,' but then they lapsed again and said,'You know very well these gods cannot speak.' Abraham said, 'How can you worship what can neither benefit nor harm you, instead of God? Shame on you and on the things you worship instead of God. Have you no sense?'" (21:51-67).

افْعَلْ مَا تُؤْمَرُ سَتَجِدُنِي إِن شَاءَ اللهُ مِنَ الصَّابِرِينَ ۞ فَلَمَّا أَسْلَمَا وَتَلَّهُ لِلْجَبِينِ ۞ وَنَادَيْنَاهُ أَن يَا إِبْرَاهِيمُ ۞ قَدْ صَدَّقْتَ الرُّؤْيَا إِنَّا كَذَٰلِكَ نَجْزِي الْمُحْسِنِينَ ۞ إِنَّ هَٰذَا لَهُوَ الْبَلَاءُ الْمُبِينُ ۞ وَفَدَيْنَاهُ بِذِبْحٍ عَظِيمٍ ۞ وَتَرَكْنَا عَلَيْهِ فِي الْآخِرِينَ ۞ سَلَامٌ عَلَىٰ إِبْرَاهِيمَ ۞ كَذَٰلِكَ نَجْزِي الْمُحْسِنِينَ ۞ إِنَّهُ مِنْ عِبَادِنَا الْمُؤْمِنِينَ ﴾ [الصافات:١٠٢-١١١].

وعالم المعاني، هو عالم العقل الذي غلب على خطاب إبراهيم ومشهده من بعد أن أوتي رشده: ﴿وَلَقَدْ آتَيْنَا إِبْرَاهِيمَ رُشْدَهُ مِن قَبْلُ وَكُنَّا بِهِ عَالِمِينَ ۞ إِذْ قَالَ لِأَبِيهِ وَقَوْمِهِ مَا هَٰذِهِ التَّمَاثِيلُ الَّتِي أَنتُمْ لَهَا عَاكِفُونَ ۞ قَالُوا وَجَدْنَا آبَاءَنَا لَهَا عَابِدِينَ ۞ قَالَ لَقَدْ كُنتُمْ أَنتُمْ وَآبَاؤُكُمْ فِي ضَلَالٍ مُّبِينٍ ۞ قَالُوا أَجِئْتَنَا بِالْحَقِّ أَمْ أَنتَ مِنَ اللَّاعِبِينَ ۞ قَالَ بَل رَّبُّكُمْ رَبُّ السَّمَاوَاتِ وَالْأَرْضِ الَّذِي فَطَرَهُنَّ وَأَنَا عَلَىٰ ذَٰلِكُم مِّنَ الشَّاهِدِينَ ۞ وَتَاللَّهِ لَأَكِيدَنَّ أَصْنَامَكُم بَعْدَ أَن تُوَلُّوا مُدْبِرِينَ ۞ فَجَعَلَهُمْ جُذَاذًا إِلَّا كَبِيرًا لَّهُمْ لَعَلَّهُمْ إِلَيْهِ يَرْجِعُونَ ۞ قَالُوا مَن فَعَلَ هَٰذَا بِآلِهَتِنَا إِنَّهُ لَمِنَ الظَّالِمِينَ ۞ قَالُوا سَمِعْنَا فَتًى يَذْكُرُهُمْ يُقَالُ لَهُ إِبْرَاهِيمُ ۞ قَالُوا فَأْتُوا بِهِ عَلَىٰ أَعْيُنِ النَّاسِ لَعَلَّهُمْ يَشْهَدُونَ ۞ قَالُوا أَأَنتَ فَعَلْتَ هَٰذَا بِآلِهَتِنَا يَا إِبْرَاهِيمُ ۞ قَالَ بَلْ فَعَلَهُ كَبِيرُهُمْ هَٰذَا فَاسْأَلُوهُمْ إِن كَانُوا يَنطِقُونَ ۞ فَرَجَعُوا إِلَىٰ أَنفُسِهِمْ فَقَالُوا إِنَّكُمْ أَنتُمُ الظَّالِمُونَ ۞ ثُمَّ نُكِسُوا عَلَىٰ رُءُوسِهِمْ لَقَدْ عَلِمْتَ مَا هَٰؤُلَاءِ يَنطِقُونَ ۞ قَالَ أَفَتَعْبُدُونَ مِن دُونِ اللَّهِ مَا لَا يَنفَعُكُمْ شَيْئًا وَلَا يَضُرُّكُمْ ۞ أُفٍّ لَّكُمْ وَلِمَا تَعْبُدُونَ مِن دُونِ اللَّهِ أَفَلَا تَعْقِلُونَ ﴾ [الأنبياء :٥١ - ٦٧].

This is the speech of the divine Intellect whose words originate from the lights of Reality. It contains hidden premises that the rational mind normally produces through reflection, not illumination, since the divine Intellect is light and the rational mind is a veil and a trace. It is related that a certain group of Jews came to test the Master of the Faithful ('Alī) while he was speaking to a group of people. "O son of Abū Ṭālib, had you learnt philosophy you would have occupied a great position amongst us.

He replied, "What do you mean by philosophy? Can it not be expressed in the following: He whose nature is harmonized his disposition becomes pure; he whose disposition becomes pure the effects of the soul within him become strong; He in whom the effects of the soul are strong elevates to where it ascends. He who elevates to where it ascends has exemplified the qualities of the soul. He who exemplifies the qualities of the soul becomes an existent qua human and not an existent qua animal. He thus enters the door of becoming an angel in form and there is nothing that can remove him from this summit."[1]

The Jewish man exclaimed, "God is great, O Ibn Abī Ṭālib! You have uttered the whole of philosophy in these words, may God be pleased with you.[2]

This is how the Jewish man had understood it, although the Imam words originated from the heart's lights spoken to a person who was veiled by philosophy.

The world of the Intellect is the source of proof and evidence, an argument and rebuttal. For one who possesses it, it is a sublime word and an utterance, commensurate to its station and rank like the station of Abraham. Accordingly the misguidance Abraham's nation was also manifest. "He said, 'You and your fathers have clearly gone astray' (21:54). His trial was also manifest, "This is indeed a manifest

---

1 *Ṣirāt al-mustaqīm*, v. 1, p. 214; *Mustadrak safīnat al-biḥār*, v. 8, p. 311.

2 *Qurrat al-'uyūn*, p. 72.

فهذا لسان العقل الإلهي الناطق بأنوار الحقيقة، من وراء مقدمات مطوية تظهرها العقول الكسبية بالتفكير عادة لا التنوير، إذ العقل الإلهي أنوار، والعقل الكسبي أستار و آثار.

روي أن بعض اليهود اجتاز أمير المؤمنين ﷺ، وهو يتكلم مع جماعة فقال له: «يا ابن أبي طالب لو انك تعلمت الفلسفة لكان يكون منك شانا من الشان.

فقال ﷺ: وما تعني بالفلسفة؟ أليس من اعتدل طباعه صفا مزاجه، ومن صفا مزاجه قوى اثر النفس فيه، ومن قوى اثر النفس فيه سمى إلى ما يرتقيه، ومن سمى إلى ما يرتقيه فقد تخلق بالأخلاق النفسانية، ومن تخلق بالأخلاق النفسانية فقد صار موجودا بما هو إنسان دون أن يكون موجودا بما هو حيوان، فقد دخل في الباب الملكي الصوري وليس له من هذه الغاية مغير[1].

فقال اليهودي : الله اكبر يا ابن أبي طالب لقد نطقت بالفلسفة جميعا في هذه الكلمات رضي الله عنك»[2].

هكذا فهم اليهودي و لكن الإمام نطق بأنوار القلوب مما هو عن الفلسفة محجوب.

وعالم العقل كيف ما كان، منبع الحجة والدليل، والقال والقيل، ولصاحبه الكلمة العليا والبيان المناسب لمقامه ومنزلته، كمقام إبراهيم سلام الله عليه. ولأجل ذلك أيضاً كان ضلال قومه مبين للمناسبه، ﴿قَالَ لَقَدْ كُنتُمْ أَنتُمْ وَآبَاؤُكُمْ فِي ضَلَالٍ مُّبِينٍ﴾ [الأنبياء:٥٤]، وكان بلاؤه مبين كذلك، ﴿إِنَّ هَٰذَا لَهُوَ الْبَلَاءُ الْمُبِينُ﴾ [الصافات:١٠٦]، وأيضاً من ذريته محسن وظالم لنفسه مبين، ﴿وَبَارَكْنَا عَلَيْهِ وَعَلَىٰ إِسْحَاقَ وَمِن ذُرِّيَّتِهِمَا مُحْسِنٌ وَظَالِمٌ

١ - الصراط المستقيم/ ١ / ٢١٤، و مستدرك سفينة البحار/ ٨ / ٣١١، و في (خ) معبر.

٢ - قرة العيون/ الفيض الكاشاني/ ص ٧٢.

trial" (37:6), as it was for his progeny, the righteous and one who has wronged himself, "We gave Abraham the good news of Isaac—a prophet and a righteous man—and blessed him and Isaac too: some of their offspring were good, but some clearly wronged themselves" (37:112-113).

The source of all of these meanings and their instantiations is the knowledge of Reality and its world. They occur as they truly are, without interpretation or expression, and are neither confused dreams, nor vain imaginings which must be annulled.

The world of Intellect is the world of lights, as was Abraham's place of witnessing, "When the night covered him he saw a star and said, 'This is my Lord,' but when it set, he said, 'I do not like things that set.' And when he saw the moon rising he said, 'This is my Lord,' but when it too set, he said, 'If my Lord does not guide me, I shall be one of those who have gone astray.' Then he saw the sun rising and cried, 'This is my Lord! This is greater.' But when the sun set, he said, 'My people, I disavow all that you worship besides God'"(6:76-78).

The world of lights is the world of spirits, as was Abraham's place of witnessing. "When Abraham said, 'My Lord, show me how You give life to the dead.' He said, 'Do you not believe?' He said, 'Yes, but only so my heart is put to rest.' God said, 'Take four birds and train them to come back to you. Then place them on separate hilltops, call them back, and they will come flying to you: know that God is all powerful and wise'" (2:260).

The world of spirits is the world of life. That is why when Abraham offered the four birds and sacrificed his son, God ransomed it with "a mighty sacrifice." Abraham disputed with him concerning his Lord, solely on the basis of realization of the divine names determined for him, realizing the verses vis-à-vis his vision, as evidenced in other identically phrased verses or those of similar import, or those that correspond with the unequivocal and sound vision. Abraham's vision and his dreams emerged from the kernel of Truth, Reality, existence and witnessing.

لِّنَفْسِهِ مُبِينٌ ﴾ [الصافات:١١٣].

فمرجع هذه المعاني كلها، وأمثالها علم الحقيقة وعالمها، تقع كما هي، وتظهر من حيث عينها لا تأويل فيها، ولا تعبير، ولا هي أضغاث أحلام و أباطيل توجب التعطيل.

وعالم العقل هو عالم الأنوار، كذلك مشهد إبراهيم عليه السلام، ﴿ فَلَمَّا جَنَّ عَلَيْهِ اللَّيْلُ رَأَىٰ كَوْكَبًا قَالَ هذَا رَبِّي فَلَمَّا أَفَلَ قَالَ لَا أُحِبُّ الْآفِلِينَ ۝ فَلَمَّا رَأَى الْقَمَرَ بَازِغًا قَالَ هذَا رَبِّي فَلَمَّا أَفَلَ قَالَ لَئِن لَّمْ يَهْدِنِي رَبِّي لَأَكُونَنَّ مِنَ الْقَوْمِ الضَّالِّينَ ۝ فَلَمَّا رَأَى الشَّمْسَ بَازِغَةً قَالَ هذَا رَبِّي هذَا أَكْبَرُ فَلَمَّا أَفَلَتْ قَالَ يَا قَوْمِ إِنِّي بَرِيءٌ مِّمَّا تُشْرِكُونَ ﴾ [الأنعام:٧٦-٧٩].

وعالم الأنوار هو عالم الأرواح، كذلك مشهد إبراهيم عليه السلام، ﴿ وَإِذْ قَالَ إِبْرَاهِيمُ رَبِّ أَرِنِي كَيْفَ تُحْيِي الْمَوْتَىٰ قَالَ أَوَلَمْ تُؤْمِن قَالَ بَلَى وَلكِن لِّيَطْمَئِنَّ قَلْبِي قَالَ فَخُذْ أَرْبَعَةً مِّنَ الطَّيْرِ فَصُرْهُنَّ إِلَيْكَ ثُمَّ اجْعَلْ عَلَىٰ كُلِّ جَبَلٍ مِّنْهُنَّ جُزْءًا ثُمَّ ادْعُهُنَّ يَأْتِينَكَ سَعْيًا وَاعْلَمْ أَنَّ اللهَ عَزِيزٌ حَكِيمٌ ﴾ [البقرة:٢٦٠].

وعالم الأرواح هو عالم الحياة، كذلك كان لإبراهيم عليه السلام، لما تقدم في أربعة من الطير، وذبح ابنه، ففداه الله بذبح عظيم. والذي حاج إبراهيم عليه السلام في ربه، فما حاجه عليه السلام إلا من عين التحقق الاسمي الثابت له، وعليه جاءت جمعية التحقق في الآية المباركة التالية، رؤية عين كما جاءت في غيرها من الآيات الناطقة باللفظ نفسه، أو المفيدة لمعناه، أو ما يعطي ذلك من مناسبة للرؤية والشهود الصريح والصحيح. فله عليه السلام تمام الرؤية والرؤيا من عين الحق والحقيقة، والوجود والشهود.

Complete realization of the following verses is the sublime word, the supreme evidence and the sufficient discourse, all of which originate from the station and world which is represented by the Intellect, light, life and so forth, as you have come to know. For this reason you find his speech, arguments in this and other instances governed by this principle; Herein lies an abundance for one with vision and insight!

"Have you not seen the one who disputed with Abraham about his Lord because God had given him kingship? When Abraham said, 'My Lord is the one who gives life and death,' he said, 'I too give life and cause death.' Abraham said, 'God brings the sun from the east, so bring it up from the west.' So the disbeliever was dumbfounded, and God does not guide the wicked" (2:258).

All praise be to God, the Lord of the worlds, and peace and blessings be upon our father Abraham.[3]

---

3 It is worth pondering the words of Ibn 'Arabī in *Fuṣūṣ al-ḥikam*. It is cited here with Jāmī's commentary in order to clarify his meaning. (May God assist you and us, know that...) In order to perceive realities as they truly are (Abraham, the friend of God) according to our prophet, upon him be peace and blessings (said to his son, Isaac) "I saw in a dream that I am sacrificing you" (37:102) (and the dream is the [limited] Imaginal world), whose nature is to express forms representing their intended meanings. (Abraham did not interpret it), that is, he did not exceed the intent of the perceived form because he was accustomed to receiving [knowledge] from the Absolute Imaginal world. Whatever he received from it was necessarily true and corresponded to reality and did not require interpretation. Thus, when he saw the image of himself sacrificing his own son he assumed that he was commanded to do it without interpretation and explanation, so he began to carry it out (in the dream the sheep manifested in the form of Abraham's son) because of the corresponding qualities between the two such as submission and obedience. But God intended the sheep not Abraham's son (Abraham acceded to the dream), that is, he actualized the form of the vision and making it truly correspond to the external physical form by moving

ومن جمعية التحقق في الآية المباركة التالية،كلمته العليا و حجته البالغة، وبيانه الوافي. كل ذلك وأمثاله جاء من حيث المقام والعالم الذي تمثل بالعقل، والنور، والحياة، وغيرها كما علمت. ولذا تجد خطابه واحتجاجه في هذا وغيره يغلب عليه ويحكمه ما ذكرنا، وفيه الأكثر و الكثير للباصر و البصير.

﴿ أَلَمْ تَرَ إِلَى الَّذِي حَاجَّ إِبْرَاهِيمَ فِي رَبِّهِ أَنْ آتَاهُ اللهُ الْمُلْكَ إِذْ قَالَ إِبْرَاهِيمُ رَبِّيَ الَّذِي يُحْيِي وَيُمِيتُ قَالَ أَنَا أُحْيِي وَأُمِيتُ قَالَ إِبْرَاهِيمُ فَإِنَّ اللهَ يَأْتِي بِالشَّمْسِ مِنَ الْمَشْرِقِ فَأْتِ بِهَا مِنَ الْمَغْرِبِ فَبُهِتَ الَّذِي كَفَرَ وَ اللهُ لَا يَهْدِي الْقَوْمَ الظَّالِمِينَ ﴾ [البقرة:٢٥٨].

والحمد لله رب العالمين، والصلاة والسلام على أبينا إبراهيم.[٣]

---

٣ - و في فصوص الحكم للشيخ محي الدين ابن عربي كلام يقتضي التأمل - ننقله مع شرح الجامي ليتضح مراده - حيث يقول: (اعلم أيدنا الله و إياك) لإدراك الحقائق على ما هي عليه (إن إبراهيم الخليل) على نبينا و عليه الصلاة و السلام (قال لابنه إسحاق) عليه السلام ﴿ إِنِّي أَرَى فِي الْمَنَامِ أَنِّي أَذْبَحُكَ ﴾ [الصافات:١٠٢] (و المنام حضرة الخيال) المقيد الذي من شأنه أن تعبر عن الصورة الممثلة فيها إلى المعاني المقصودة منها (فلم يعبرها) إبراهيم عليه السلام، أي لم يتجاوزها إلى لمقصود من الصور المرئية فيها لما تعوّد به من الأخذ عن عالم المثال المطلق، و كلما أخذ منه لا بد أن يكون حقا مطابقا للواقع من غير تعبير. فلما شاهد عليه السلام صورة ذبح ابنه فيه ظن انه مأمور به من غير تعبير و تأويل فتصدى له (و كان كبش ظهر في صورة ابن إبراهيم في المنام)، لمناسبة واقعة بينهما و هي الاستسلام و الانقياد فكان مراد الله سبحانه به الكبش لا ابن إبراهيم (فصدق إبراهيم الرؤيا)، أي قق الصورة المرئية و جعلها صادقة مطابقة للصورة الحسية الخارجية بالأقدام على الذبح و التعرض لمقدماته (ففداه)، أي ابن إبراهيم (ربه) لينقذه من الذبح. و ذكر الفداء ههنا إنما هو من جهة وهم إبراهيم و ظنه و إلا لم يكن فداء حقيقة (بذبح العظيم الذي هو

towards and preparing for the slaughtering. (So He ransomed), Abraham's son to save him from being killed. Some people state that this sacrifice was from Abraham's supposition and conjecture otherwise it would not have been ransomed (for the great sacrifice which was the interpretation of the dream with God). Abraham was unaware of its interpretation as God kept it hidden for a certain wise purpose. What is specifically understood from the Shaykh's words and the words of his commentators is that Abraham, the friend [of God] was accustomed to receiving [knowledge] directly from the Imaginal world, whose nature is to correspond a visionary form with the external sensory form without any discrepancy; thus there is no need for interpretation. Therefore, when complete annihilation in God was attained and necessitated that this locus of witnessing became the highest station in the Imaginal world or the soul and heart, without intermediary, God desired to externally manifest a form which is the realization of annihilation, slaughtering the sheep, and to make him transcend this place of witnessing. Thus, he showed him that he was slaughtering the sheep but in the form of his son and concealed the intent therein. He then made him imagine that his son was intended, based on his habit of receiving from the Imaginal World. Thus, what occurred to him in his imagination he believed to be true, namely, slaughtering his son so he embarked upon it and his son submitted to him. Thereafter, the secret of the perfection of their submission and obedience became manifest when God ransomed the sheep instead of his son and delivered him from the slaughter. God's intent in the dream was not to slaughter the sheep having realization externally and for Abraham to become annihilated in it and ascend from his habitual place of witnessing. But the witnessed form was not from the Imaginal world but its meaning emerged from another plane above the Imaginal. It sprang up from his heart and the form of his imagination as such. He knew of its transcendence when the slaughtering of the sheep occurred and not his son. It is no secret to the author that this is a prime example of God's sound method of instructing Abraham and furthermore, the Shaykh's explanation does not show any discourtesy to Abraham. Other respected individuals have handwritten footnotes on this subject [included below]:

تعبير رؤياه عند الله و هو)، أي إبراهيم عليه السلام (لا يشعر) بذلك التعبير لما أخفاه الله سبحانه عليه لحكمة تقتضيه. و التفصيل في هذا المقام على ما يفهم من كلام الشيخ رضي الله عنه و شارحي كلامه، أن إبراهيم الخليل صلوات الله عليه كان قبل هذا المقام معوّدا بالأخذ عن عالم المثال الذي من شأنه أن تطابق الصور المرئية فيه الصور الظاهرة في الحس من غير اختلال، فلا حاجة فيه إلى التعبير، فلما تحقق الفناء في الله بالكلية و اقتضى ذلك الفناء في الله عن هذا المشهد بأن يشاهد الأمور في مراتب هي أعلا مراتب المثال أو في نفسه و قلبه من الوجه الخاص من غير توسط أمر آخر، أراد الله سبحانه أن يظهر في الحس صورة ليحققه بالفناء هي ذبح الكبش و أن يرقيه عن هذا المشهد فاراه في المنام أن أذبح الكبش و لكن في صورة ظبح ابنه وستر عليه المقصود منه، و أوقع في وهمه أن ابنه هو المقصود بعينه بناء على ما اعتاده من الأخذ عن عالم المثال، فاعتقد صدق ما وقع في وهمه من ظبح ابنه فتصدى له و انقاد له ابنه، فظهر سر كمال استسلامهما و انقيادهما لله تعالى، فجعل سبحانه الذبح العظيم فداء لابنه، وانقذه من الذبح، و ما كان مراد الله من منامه و هو ذبح الكبش لتكون صورة حسية لتحقق إبراهيم بالفناء فيه و حصل له الترقي عن مشهده المعتاد، فان الصورة المرئية لم تكم من عالم المثال بل فاض هذا المعنى عليه من مرتبة أخرى فوق عالم المثال، و انبعث من قلبه و صورته متخيلة بتلك الصورة، و علم ذلك الترقي أيضاً حيث وقع منه ذبح الكبش لا ذبح ابنه. و لا يخفى على المصنف أن ذلك بيان لحسن تربية الله سبحانه إبراهيم الخليل عليه السلام و ليس شائبة سوء أدب من الشيخ رضي الله عنه بالنسبة إلى إبراهيم عليه السلام، و كتب بعض من اشتهر بالفضل بخطه على الهامش في المقام.

"The Shaykh has embellished on this and I do not see it as correct since it shows discourtesy. The best we can say is that Ibn 'Arabī was overcome [by a certain state]. The truth is, and God knows best, that Abraham saw in his dream that he was prepared to sacrifice, namely he lay his son down and took placing the knife on his throat to cut it but did not. This is the meaning of, 'I see in my dream that I am sacrificing you,' that is, I saw that I was engaged in the acts of sacrifice. This does not necessitate its fulfillment. What he saw in his dream may have occurred to him in his wakefulness and he and his son made up their minds to fulfill it. When their resolve became firm and met the prerequisites of the sacrifice the purpose of the test was achieved and God intervened with His mercy and ransomed it with another sacrifice that they performed before their very eyes. His dream was not imaginary or supposition. Far be the station of divine companionship (*khilla*) from such an error! God is the author of success." It is remarkable that this accomplished scholar and others would criticise the Shaykh regarding this book even though in the introduction the Shaykh comentions whatever he included in the book was specified by the Prophet, without emendations in a vision. If they acknowledge this then there is no room for criticism because then it would all refer back to the Prophet. If however, they do not accept it and believe that it is fabricated, a lie, an omission or a mistake, then the criticism would be directed towards that, not what is written here. How can one who recognizes his states, stations, and visions, all of which have been detailed in his books and his other works, not acknowledge it? (The theophany of form in the limited Imagination) requires another type of knowledge called the knowledge of expression, through which one perceives the divine intent within the form, outwardly [expressed] in the Imaginal plane. It entails the knowledge of the correspondence between the form and its meaning and the knowledge of the mirror of the souls which manifest these forms in their imaginations. It also entails the knowledge of the times and other contextual factors which also have an effect in dream interpretation because the meaning of a particular image may have different meanings according to individuals of differing degrees, or a single person in two different times or planes. The perfection of this knowledge or lack

هـذا الـكلام زخرفـه الشيـخ و لا أراه حقـا بل كلـه صادر عن سـوء أدب أحسـن محامله أن يقـال انـه صـدر عنـه في حـال كونه مغلوبـا، و الحق في ذلـك و الله أعلـم أن إبراهيم عليه السلام رأى في المنـام أنـه مبـاشر للذبـح بمعنـى أنه أضجـع ابنه أخـذ المديـة و أمرّها عـلى حلقومه ليقطعـه، و لكـن لم يحصـل القطع و هذا هـو المراد بقولـه ﴿إِنِّي أَرَي فِي الْمَنَـامِ أَنِّي أَذْبَحُكَ﴾، أي رأيـت أني مشـتغل بأفعـال الذبـح و لا يلـزم منـه تمامـه، و قد وقع منـه في اليقظـة ما رآه في المنـام و وطّـن هـو و ابنـه للانقيـاد لذلك، فلما تـم العزم و وجـد مقدمـات الذبح حصل المقصـود مـن الابتـلاء فتداركـه الله برحمته بإعطـاء الذبح ليذبح فـداء له فوقع مـا رآه بعينه، و لم تكـن رؤيـاه وهما و خيالا حاشـا المنصـب الخلة عن مثل هذا الخطـأ و الله ولي التوفيق. و العجـب مـن هـذا الفاضل، بل مـن كل معترض على الشـيخ رضي الله عنه في هـذا الكتاب، فـان مـا ذكره الشـيخ من مفتتـح الكتاب من مبشـرة أريها و إن مـا أورده في هـذا الكتاب ما حـده رسـول الله ﷺ مـن غـير زيـادة و لا نقصـان إن كان مسـلما عنده فلا مجـال للاعتراض فـإن ذلـك يعـود إلى النبـي ﷺ، و إن لم يكـن مسـلما عنـده بل أعتقـد أن ذلك افـتراء و كذب أو سـهو و خطـأ فالأعـراض عليـه ذاك لا هـذا وكيف لا يسـلم ذلك من اطلع عـلى أحواله و مقاماتـه و مكاشـفاته ممـا أدرجـه في هذا الكتـال و سـائر مصنفاته (و التجلي الصوري في حـضرة الخيـال) المقيـد (محتـاج إلى علـم آخـر) يسـمى علـم التعبـير (يـدرك به مـا أراد الله تعـالى بتلـك الصـورة) الظاهـرة في حـضرة الخيـال بأرائـه، و هـو معرفـة المناسـبة التي بين الصـور و معانيهـا، و معرفـة مـرآة النفوس التـي تظهر تلـك الصور في خيالاتهـم، و معرفة الأزمنـة و غيرهـا مما لـه مدخل في التعبـير، فانه قـد ينقلب حكـم الصـورة الواحدة بالنسـبة إلى أشـخاص مختلفـة المراتـب بـل بالنسـبة إلى شـخص واحد في زمانـين و مكانـين و بكمال هـذه المعرفـة و نقصانهـا يتفـاوت حـال المعبريـن في الإصابـة و الخطـأ في التعبـير (إلا تـري كيـف قال رسـول الله ﷺ لابي بكـر في تعبير الرؤيا: أصبـت بعضا وأخطأت بعضا فسـأله)، أي رسـول الله ﷺ (أبـو بكـر أن يعرفـه ما أصـاب فيه و مـا اخطأ فلـم يفعل ﷺ.

عن ابن عباس رضي الله عنهما.

thereof determines the degree of correctness of the interpretation. Do you not see what the Prophet said to Abū Bakr regarding the interpretation of the dream, "Some of it is correct and some of it is not," so Abū Bakr asked the Prophet to inform him which part did he interpret correctly but he did not."

Abū Ḥurayra narrates that a man came to the Apostle of God and said, "I saw (in my dream) a piece of cloud from which fat and honey were dripping. I saw the people spreading their hands. Some of them took much and some a little. I also saw a rope hanging from Heaven to the earth. I saw you, O Messenger of God, catch hold of it and ascend by it. Then another man caught hold of it and ascended it. Then another man caught hold of it and ascended it. Then another man caught hold of it, but it broke, and then it was joined and he ascended it." Abū Bakr said, "May my parents be sacrificed for you, if you allow, I shall interpret it."

The Prophet said, "Interpret it." Then Abū Bakr said, "The piece of cloud is the cloud of Islam; the fat and honey that were dropping from it are the Qur'ān, which contains softness and sweetness. Those who received much or little of it are those who learn much or little of the Qur'ān. The rope hanging from Heaven to the earth is the truth which you are following. You catch hold of it and then God will raise you to Him. Then another man will catch hold of it and ascend it, then another man will catch hold of it and it will break. But it will be joined and he will ascend it. Tell me Apostle of Allah, whether I am right or wrong. He said: You are partly right and partly wrong. He said: I swear on my father and mother that you, O Messenger of God, should tell me where I am wrong." The Prophet said, "Do not swear." There is consensus that this hadith is reliable.

God said to Abraham when He called out to him. "O Abraham, you have fulfilled the vision" (37:104-105), that is, you have made its outward aspect conform to reality by proceeding with its preliminaries. God did not say to Abraham, "You have fulfilled [part] of your vision" in the lesser sense, that is, you have fulfilled part of your vision whereby you deemed that what you saw was truly your son. This is on account of Abraham not interpreting his dream but taking it at face value, although dreams

قـال: كان أبـو هريـرة يحـدث أن رجـلا اتى رسـول الله ﷺ فقـال: إني رأيت ظُلَّـة ينظف منهـا السـمن والعسـل ورأيت النـاس يسـتقون بأيديهم فالمسـتكثر والمسـتقل ورأيت سـببا واصـلا مـن السـماء إلى الأرض فـأراك يا رسـول الله أخـذت به فعلـوت، ثم أخـذ به رجل مـن بعـد فعـلا ثـم أخذه بـه رجل آخـر فعلا ثم أخـذ به رجـل آخـر فانقطع به ثـم وصل له فعـلا فقـال: أبو بكر أي رسـول الله بأبي أنـت وأمـي والله لتدعني أعبرها، فقـال: «اعبرها» فقـال: أمـا الظلـة فظلـة الإسـلام وأمـا مـا ينطـف مـن السـمن والعسـل فهـو القـرآن لينه وحلاوتـه وأمـا المسـتكثر والمستقل فهـو المسـتكثر مـن القـرآن والمستقل منه وأما السـبب الواصـل مـن السـماء إلى الأرض فهـو الحـق الـذي أنت بـه تاخـذ بـه فيعليك الله ثـم يأخذ بـه بعـدك رجـلٌ آخـر فيعلـو بـه ثـم يأخذ بـه رجلٌ آخـر فيعلـو به ثـم يأخـذ به رجـلٌ آخر بعـده فينقطـع بـه ثم يوصـل فيعلو بـه أي رسـول الله ﷺ لتحدثـني أصبـت أم أخطأت قال النبـي ﷺ «أصبـت بعضـا وأخطـأت بعضـا»، فقال أقسـمت بأبي أنـت وأمي يا رسـول الله لتخـبرني مـا الـذي أخطـأت فقـال النبـي ﷺ «لا تقسـم» هذا حديـث متفق عـلى صحته.

(وقـال الله لإبراهيـم عليه السلام حـين نـاده ﴿ أَن يَـا إِبْرَاهِيمُ قَـدْ صَدَّقْـتَ الرُّؤْيَـا ﴾ [الصافـات: ١٠٤-١٠٥]، أي جعلـت ظاهرهـا مطابقـا للواقـع بالإقـدام عـلى مقدماته.

(و مـا قـال) الله تعـالى (لـه) أي لإبراهيـم عليه السلام (قـد صدقـت في الرؤيـا) بالتخفيـف، أي ما قـال لـه: صدقـت في رؤياك حيـث حكمت (انـه)، أي المرئي فيهـا هو (ابنـك) حقيقة (لأنه مـا عبرهـا) بالتخفيـف أو التشـديد (بل أخـذ بظاهر مـا رأى)، أي من غير تعبـير (و الرؤيا تطلـب التعبـير) في اكثـر الصـور، فـلا ينبغـي أن تحمـل على سـبيل القطـع (و لذلـك)، أي طلـب الرؤيـا بالتعبـير (قـال عزيـز: إن كنتـم للرؤيـا تعـبرون و معنـى التعبـير)، بـل معنى العبـور الـلازم لـه (الجـواز من صـورة مـا رأى إلى أمر آخر) هـو المراد بهـا (فكانـت البقر) العجـاف التـي رآهـا العزيـز في منامـه (سـنين في المحـل)، أي القحـط (و) الغـلاء و البقـر السـمان سـنين (في فاحصـب)، أي السـعة (فلـو صدق في الرؤيـا)، أي لـو كان إبراهيم عليه السلام صادقـا فيـما حكـم بـه أن المرئـي في رؤياه ابنـه (لذبح ابنـه) لأنه رأى انـه كان يذبحـه (وإنما

in most cases require interpretation, so it is not appropriate to take a dream decisively at face value but seek its interpretation as the king said, "[Interpret it for me] if you are indeed interpreters of visions." The meaning of interpretation is the transference from the witnessed form to another, namely, its meaning, as the lean cows in the king's dream meant years of scarcity and fat cows meant years of plenty. If Abraham had fulfilled his vision exactly as he had seen it he would have actually sacrificed his son. He did indeed fulfill his vision since what he saw was precisely his son so he went forward with the act but in the sight of God what Abraham saw was the Great Sacrifice represented in the form of his ransomed son. God called it a ransom for what occurred in the mind of Abraham, namely the vision of his son being sacrificed, but for God, this was not a ransom in reality. Sensory perception conceived the sacrifice and the imagination conceived it as Abraham's son. If he had seen the ram in his imagination he would have interpreted as his son or something else. Then God said, "This, indeed was a clear trial" (37:106), a clear test of outward [meaning], or a test of knowledge, namely whether or not he possessed the knowledge required to interpret the domain of dreams. God knows that the domain of imagination requires interpretation but Abraham neglected this and did not fulfill the rights of this domain, for which reason he deemed the dream to be true, as did Taqī ibn Mukhallad, the *imām* and author of *al-Musnad*.

He heard a well-founded narration that the Prophet said, "Whoever sees me in a dream has seen me in wakefulness for Satan cannot assume my form" (Muslim 42:12). Satan cannot assume his form because he is the manifestation of the name, the Guide, one who is sent for guidance, and Satan is the manifestation of the name the Misguider (*al-Muḍill*) and has been created to misguide. If he had the power to assume his form it would undermine the nature of guidance. If it is said that this does not entail Satan's inability to assume his form since his Imaginal form can assume the likeness of the Prophet's imaginal form just as it is possible for him to assume the form of a king, spirit, human, or a meaning regarding the law and Sunna, etc., insofar as he has a correspondence with guidance or something else.

صدق الرؤيا)، أي جعل صادقة (في أن ذلك المرئي عين ولده) فتصدى لذبح (و ما كان) ذلك المرئي (عند الله إلا الذبح العظيم) متمثلا (في صورة ولده ففداه)، أي الحق سبحانه ولده بالذبح العظيم، وإنما سماه فداه (لما و قع في ذهن إبراهيم عليه السلام)، من أن المرئي هو ابنه (ما هو)، أي ليس هو (فداء في نفس الأمر عند الله فصور الحس)، أي أدرك الحس (الذبح) بالكسر أي صورته المحسوسة حين ذبحه أو صور الحس، أي حاسة البصر الذبح في الحس المشترك (و صور الخيال لعبر) الكبش غالبا (بابنه أو بأمر آخر) يكون مرادا بتلك الصورة (ثم قال الله تعالى إن هذا)، أي تصوير الكبش بصورة ابنه (﴿ لَهُوَ الْبَلَاءُ الْمُبِينُ ﴾ أي الاختبار الظاهر) يقال: بلوته، أي اختبرته (تعين الاختبار في العلم)،فان الحق سبحانه اختبر إبراهيم عليه السلام (هل يعلم ما يقتضيه) غالبا (موطن التعبير) من الرؤيا (أم لا) يعلم وإنما اختبره (لأنه تعالى يعلم أن موطن الخيال) إذ تمثل فيه معنى (يطلب التعبير) غالبا (فغفل) إبراهيم عليه السلام عما تستحقه مواطن الخيال (فما و في الموطن حقه و صدق الرؤيا لهذا السبب، كما فعل تقي بن مخلد الإمام صاحب المسند) في الحديث.

(سمع في الخبر الذي ثبت عنده انه عليه السلام قال من رآني) على ما انا عليه من الحلية (في النوم) حقيقة (فقد رآني في اليقظة)، أي حكما أي لرؤيتي في النوم حكم رؤيتي في اليقظة فيما سيأتي (فان الشيطان لا يتمثل على صورتي) وإنما لم يتمثل الشيطان بصورته عليه السلام، لأنه مظهر للاسم الهادي و مبعوث للهداية و الشيطان مظهر للاسم المضل و مخلوق للأضلال فلو كان له تمكن من التمثل بصورته عليه الصلاة و السلام لاختل أمر الهداية فان قلت: لا يلزم من عدم تمكن الشيطان من التمثل بصورته عليه السلام أن تكون صورته المثالية عينه عليه السلام لا غيره لجواز أن يتمثل بصورته ملك أو روح أو إنسان أو معنى من المعاني كشرعه و سننه و غير ذلك مما له نسبة إليه في معنى الهداية و غيرها.

قلت: يمكن أن تكون سنة الله تعالى جارية بأن لا يتمثل بصورته و حليته عليه السلام شيء أصلا تعظيما لشأنه و يكون تخصيص الشطان بالذكر للاهتمام بنفي تمكنه من التمثل

I say that perhaps it is God's way to not allow Satan to assume the Prophet's form and appearance out of respect for his stature which is specifically emphasized for Satan. So Taqī ibn Mukhallad saw the Prophet in a dream in which the Prophet gave him milk to drink. Taqī ibn Mukhallad believed his dream, but when he awoke he induced vomiting and threw up the milk. If he had interpreted the dream, he would have known that milk meant knowledge, equal to the quantity that he drank. Just as milk nourishes the body from its inception until its end, similarly, knowledge nourishes the spirit in every state. Thus, great knowledge was forbidden to Taqī ibn Mukhallad except for the amount that he drunk; he then vomited the rest. He would have been wiser to interpret it as knowledge and not vomit it, taking assurance in the soundness of the following narration, "Do you not see that the Messenger of God, may Allah bless him and grant him peace, received a goblet of milk in a dream and he said, "I drank it until satiety came out of my nails, and then I gave the surplus to 'Umar." It was asked, "O Messenger of God, what do you interpret it as?" He replied, "Knowledge." He did not leave it as milk in its dream form since he had knowledge of the state of dreams and how they must be interpreted.

Since the discussion on seeing the Prophet in dreams has been brought up, [the Shaykh] says that it is known that the form of the Prophet that he had during his life, which the senses see, is buried in Madina. [The Shaykh] writes *inna* with the *kasra* so that it is attached to its subject and predicate because the *fatḥa* would be repetitive because of the distance between it and its predicate. It is known his spirit and his spiritual subtlety have never been seen by anyone nor by himself. It is among the immaterial beings whose very nature precludes it from being seen by the senses. Rather, the Intellect perceives it based on its effects as is the case for every spirit. Its nature does not allow for it to be seen by the senses so the Prophet's spirit becomes corporeal for the perceiver, that is, it assumes an imaginal form in the form of his pure and noble body as he was when he died without anything missing from it. He is as he was buried without any deficiency, so it is Muḥammad, peace be upon him, who appears in dreams by virtue of his spirit manifesting in bodily form, that is, an imaginal form since the body often refers to

بصورته ﷺ لما لا يخفى و جهه (فرآه)، أي النبي ﷺ (تقي بن مخلد و سقاه النبي ﷺ لبنا فصدق تقي بن مخلد رؤياه) بعدما استيقظ (فاستقاء فقاء لبنا، و لو عبر رؤياه لكان ذلك اللبن علما) تمثل بصورة اللبن فان اللبن كما انه يغذي الأبدان و يربها من أول الفطرة إلى آخرها كذلك العلم يغذي الأرواح في جميع أحوالها (فحرمه) إليه، أي تقي بن مخلد (علما كثيرا على قدر ما شرب) ثم قاء من اللبن فكان الأحرى بحاله أن يعبر اللبن بالعلم و لا يستقيئ و أن أورث له ذلك زيادة طمأنينة بصدق ذلك الخبر (ألا تري أن رسول الله ﷺ أتى في المنام بقدح لبن قال: «فشربته حتى خرج الري من أظافيري ثم أعطيت فضلي عمر قيل: ما أولته لا رسول الله قال: أولته العلم» و ما تركه لبنا على صورة ما رآه لعلمه بموطن الرؤيا و ما تقتضي من التعبير).

و لما انحر الكلام إلى ذكر رؤية النبي ﷺ في المنام أراد أن يحقق أن المرئي حينئذ ما هو، فقال: (و قد علم أن صورة النبي ﷺ التي شاهدها الحس) عند حياته ﷺ (أنها في المدينة مدفونة) فقوله: إنها بكسر الهمزة على أن تكون مع اسمها و خبرها خبرا لأن المفتوحة أو بفتحها على أن تكون تكرار لها لبعد وقع بينها و بين خبرها (و) علم أيضاً (أن صورة روحه)، أي ورح النبي ﷺ (و لطيفته) الروحانية (ما شاهدها احد) بل شاهد احد الصورة الروحانية مطلقا (من احد و لا من نفسه) فإنها من المجردات التي ليس من شأنها أن تشاهد بالحس بل إنما يدركها العقل بآثارها (كل روح) من الأرواح (بهذه المثابة)، أي ليس من شأنه أن يشاهد الحس (فيتجسد)، أي يتمثل (له)،أي للرائي (روح النبي ﷺ) في المنام (بصورة جسده) المطهر المكرم حال كون تلك الصورة (كما مات عليها)، أي مماثلة للصورة التي مات عليها النبي ﷺ (لا يخرم) بالخاء المعجمة و الراء فمهملة من الخرم و هو القطع، أي لا يقطع (منه)، أي مما مات عليه (شيئا فهو)، أي ما رآه في المنام (محمد المرئي من حيث روحه) الظاهر (في صورة جسدية)، أي مثالية فان الجسد في اصطلاح هذه الطائفة يطلق غالبا على الصورة المثالية (تشبه) الصورة (المدفونة) في البدنية (لا يتمكن الشيطان أن يتصور)، أي يتمثل (بصورة جسده) المثالي

the imaginal body in the terminology of the group. It resembles his buried body, for Satan cannot assume his bodily form, that is, the form of his imaginal body which represents his pure physical body; this is a protection from God for the one who sees him lest he become confused. Thus, whoever sees this bodily form resembling the interred body in Medina takes from it all that he commands, prohibits, gives good news of, just as he would take judgements from him in this worldly life, according to what they indicate from text, explicit or implicit, or it may be something spoken that is does not require expression or interpretation. If the Prophet gives something in the dream, in some cases it requires interpretation but if it manifests in the sensory realm exactly as it occurred in the imagination, then it does not require interpretation. Both Abraham and Taqī ibn Mukhallad both relied on the latter type." *Sharḥ Jāmī*, pp. 180-186.

المماثـل لجسـمه المطهـر (ﷺ عصمـة مـن الله) تعـالى (في حـق الرائـي) أن يتلبـس الأمـر (و لهـذا مـن رآه بهـذه الصـورة) الجسـدية المشـابهة لصورتـه المدفونـة في المدينة (يأخـذ جميع ما يأمـره بـه أو ينهـاه عنه أو يخبره كما كان يأخـذ عنه) عليه السلام (في الحيـاة الدنيا مـن الأحكام على حسـب مـا يكـون)، أي يوجب (منـه اللفظ الـدال عليه)، أي عـلى ما يأخذه منـه (من نص أو ظاهـر أو مجمل ما كان)، أي أو أي شيء كان من أقسـام اللفـظ بلا تعبير و لا تأويل (كان أعطـاه)، أي النبـي ﷺ الرائـي (شـيئا) في المنـام (فـان ذلك الـشيء) المعطى (هـو في الخيال) بعينـه (فتلـك الرؤيـا لا تعبـير لهـا و بهـذا القدر) الـذي هو قسـم مـن الرؤيا حـرم (و عليه اعتمـد إبراهيـم الخليـل عليه السلام و تقي بـن مخلد...الخ)./ شرح الجامـي/ ص ١٨٠-١٨٦.

Chapter 3

The Manifestations of Reality

Know that Reality is the unveiling of a phenomenon as it truly is. It is a luminous unveiling in any world irrespective of language, corporeal, imaginal, intellectual, or [occurring] in wakefulness, drowsiness or sleep. Accordingly, the people of reality do not see a dream except see a reality therein, and when they see a vision it is [clear] like the break of dawn and holds true just as it was seen, requiring no interpretation, or perplexing the one who sees it. It is not a confused dream but a firm sign and a clear token. Other than this, even if it is a luminous reality, it is subject to interpretation and is an ambiguous sign that becomes true and realized outwardly. It has a luminous reality which is its mystery, and for every truth there is a reality which is its mystery and inscription.[1]

---

1 The Prophet asked Hārith ibn Mālik, "How are you? " He replied, "Imbued with faith, O Prophet of God." He asked, "Are you truly imbued with faith?"

الباب الثالث

مجالي الحقيقة

اعلم أن الحقيقة، هي كشف الواقع كما هو، كشفا نوريا في أي عالم، وبأي لسان: حسيا كان، أو مثاليا، أو عقليا. يقظة كان، أو سنة، أو نوما. وعلى هذا أهلها لا يرون رؤية إلا و فيها حقيقة ما يرون، و لا يرون رؤيا إلا وقعت كفلق الصبح، وصدقت كما رؤيت، لا يطلب لها تأويل، ولا تشبَّه على رائيها، ولا هي من الأضغاث. بل هي آية محكمة وعلامة بينة. بخلاف غيرها مع كونها حقيقة نورية، إلا أنها تأويلية وآية متشابهة تجعل حقا فتتحقق واقعا، ولها حقيقة نورية هي سرها. فان لكل حق حقيقة هي سِرُّه و نَقشُه[١].

---

١ إن رسـول الله ﷺ وسـلم قال لحارث بن مالك: كيف أنت يا حارث ؟

قال: مؤمن يا رسـول الله، قال مؤمن حقا؟ قال: مؤمن حقا.

He said, "Indeed!" The Prophet said, "For every truth there is a reality so what is the reality of [your faith]?" He replied, "I have abstained from the world and kept vigil during my nights and remained thirsty during my days. It is as if I am witnessing the Throne of my Lord, the Mighty and Magnificent. It is as if I see the people of paradise visiting each other and hear the wailing of the people of hell." The Prophet then said, "He is a believer whose heart God has illuminated." *Mufradāt alfāẓ al-Qur'ān*, p. 247.

In al-Kāfī, Imām al-Ṣādiq relates that the Prophet performed the morning prayer with the people then saw a young man in the mosque who was trembling with head hung low. He was sallow and emaciated with sunken eyes so the Prophet asked, "What has become of your state?" He replied, "O Prophet, I have become certain." The Prophet surprised at his answer said, "For every certainty there is a reality, so what is the reality of your certainty?" He replied, "O Prophet, my certainty has grieved me and kept me up at night. I have abstained from the world and kept vigil during my nights and remained thirsty during my days. It is as if I am witnessing the Throne of my Lord, the Mighty and Magnificent. It is as if I see the people of paradise visiting each other and hear the wailing of the people of hell." The Prophet then said, "He is a believer whose heart God has illuminated." Then he added, "Hold fast to what you have attained." The young man said, "O Prophet, pray to God for me that I am martyred by your side." The Prophet had no sooner prayed for him than he set off for battle with one of the legions and became martyred along with nine others; he was the tenth. *al-Kāfī*, v. 2, p. 53.

Fayḍ Kashānī writes in *al-Wāfī*, "*al-khafaqa* means motion of the head caused by sleepiness. *al-hājira* means the intensity of afternoon heat. *'Uzūf* means abstention and *iṣṭirākh* means calling for help.

The illumination to which the hadith refers is superlative faith and intense certainty. Their result is that one gains awareness of realities, both tangible and intellectual. Veils and curtains are removed and one comes to know things as they truly are with the eye of certainty and without being marred by uncertainty or the blemish of doubt. Thus, his heart becomes tranquil and his spirit quieted. This is the true wisdom referred to in the statement, "He who has been given wisdom has been given a great good."

قال: لكل حق حقيقة، فما حقيقة ذلك؟

قال: عزفت نفسي عن الدنيا، فأسهرت ليلي، وأظمأت نهاري، وكأني أنظر إلى عرش ربي عز وجل، وكأني أنظر إلى أهل الجنة يتزاورون فيها، وكأني أسمع عواء أهل النار، فقال رسول الله: مؤمن نور الله قلبه. مفردات ألفاظ القرآن/ الراغب الاصفهاني/ ص٢٤٧.

وفي الكافي عن الصادق عليه السلام: إن رسول الله صلى الله عليه وآله صلى بالناس الصبح فنظر إلى شاب في المسجد، و هو يخفق و يهوي برأسه مصفرا لونه قد نحف جسمه، و غارت عيناه في راسه، فقال له رسول الله صلى الله عليه وآله: كيف أصبحت يا فلان ؟

قال أصبحت يا رسول الله موقنا، فعجب رسول الله من قوله، وقال: إن لكل يقين حقيقة فما حقيقة يقينك؟ فقال: إن يقيني يا رسول الله هو الذي احزنني واسهر ليلي واظما هواجري، فعزفت نفسي عن الدنيا وما فيها حتى كأني انظر إلى عرش ربي وقد نصب للحساب وحشر الخلائق لذلك وأنا فيهم، وكأني انظر إلى أهل الجنة يتنعمون في الجنة، ويتعارفون على الأرائك متكئون، وكأني انظر إلى أهل النار وهم فيها معذبون مصطرخون، وكأني الآن اسمع زفير النار يدور في مسامعي.

فقال رسول الله صلى الله عليه وآله لأصحابه: هذا عبد نور الله قلبه بالإيمان، ثم قال له: الزم ما أنت عليه. فقال الشاب: ادع الله لي يا رسول الله أن ارزق الشهادة معك، فدعى رسول الله صلى الله عليه وآله، فلم يلبث أن خرج في بعض غزوات النبي صلى الله عليه وآله، فاستشهد بعد تسعة نفر وكان هو العاشر. الكافي/ ج٢/ ٥٣.

قال الفيض الكاشاني في الوافي: الخفقة: تحريك الرأس بسبب النعاس. والهاجرة: اشتداد الحر نصف النهار. والعزوف عن الشي: الزهد فيه. والاصطراخ: الاستغاثة.

وهذا التنوير الذي أشير به في الحديث، إنما يحصل بزيادة الإيمان وشدة اليقين، فإنما ينتهيان بصاحبهما إلى أن يطلع على حقائق الأشياء محسوساتها ومعقولاتها، فينكشف له حجبها وأستارها فيعرفها بعين اليقين على ما هي عليه من غير وصمة ريب أو شائبة شك، فيطمئن لها قلبه ويستريح بها روحه، وهذه هي الحكمة الحقيقية التي من أوتيها فقد أوتي خيرا كثيرا.

A sound dream is divided according to the world in which it occurs, Intellectual, Imaginal and material. One may see a reality[2] and an intellectual, transcendent, spiritual, luminous phenomenon is unveiled, along with the names that correspond to the named or inform it.[3]

One may see a reality and an Imaginal, formal, intermediary and shadowy phenomenon is unveiled, along with the names that correspond to the named or inform it.

One may see a reality and a sensory, corporeal, manifest and opaque phenomenon is unveiled, along with the names that correspond to the named or inform it.

In each of these worlds the vision occurs in and for that very world. That is, one sees a reality in a particular world and that reality belongs to that world without being interpreted in any other world. If it is interpreted from the Intellectual to the Imaginal or the Intellectual to the material, or the Imaginal to the material, it is expressed as it is witnessed without interpretation, otherwise it would be the manifestation of that world. This is because the reality of the Intel-

---

Majlisī writes in *Biḥar*, "The Prophet became surprised either due to the scarcity of such a person or that he felt happiness because of him.

"My nights are sleepless" due to the grief of the hereafter, or in preparation for it, or for the love of worshipping God and His communion, or wondering at how a lover can sleep. This metaphor means, "I pass the nights in vigil" and "my days are thirsty" means that I am thirsty during the day due to the intensity of heat while keeping fast in the summertime. *Biḥār al-anwār*, v. 67, p. 160.

2 From the perspective that the Intellectual world is the first and the primary, although reality subsists in every world, in fact, every world is reality.

3 The names that refer to the named, such as the Intellectual world referring to the world of lights, the world of Imagination to the world of shadows and the material world to the world of darkness. Similarly, there are also corresponding names for realities not mentioned here.

والرؤية المحكمة بالنسبة إلى العوالم بحسبها: عقلية، ومثالية، وحسية.

فمنهم: من يرى حقيقة[2]، وينكشف له واقع عقلي معنوي روحي نوري وما اليها من الأسماء المطابقة لمسماها أو الحاكية عنه[3].

ومنهم من يرى حقيقة، وينكشف له واقع مثالي صوري برزخي ظلي، وما اليها من الأسماء المطابقة لمسماها أو الحاكية عنه.

ومنهم من يرى حقيقة، وينكشف له واقع حسي جسماني شهادي ظلماني، وما اليها من الأسماء المطابقة لمسماها أو الحاكية عنه.

وفي كل من هذه العوالم له رؤية في نفسه لنفسه، أي يرى حقيقة في عالم ما، هي حقيقة في نفس العالم المعين لنفسه لا تَعْبُر إلى غيره من العوالم. فان عَبُرتْ من عقل لمثال، أو عقل لحس، أو مثال لحس، فإنما تَعْبُر بالحقيقة كما رؤيت من غير تأويل. إذ ليس هي إلا تجلي عالم لآخر،

وقال المجلسي في البحار: فعجب رسول الله ﷺ، أي تعجب منه لندرة مثل ذلك أو أعجبه وسر به.

اسهر ليلي: لحزن الآخرة أو الاستعداد لها أو لحب عبادة الله ومناجاته، عجبا للمحب كيف ينام، والاستناد مجازي أي اسهرني في ليلي، وكذا اظمأ هواجري، أي أظمأني عند الهاجرة وشدة الحر للصوم في الصيف/ البحار/ ج٦٧/ ١٦٠.

٢ - باعتبار أن العالم العقلي هو الأول و الأولى، و إلا الحقيقة في كل العوالم؛ بل كل العوالم حقيقة.

٣ - الأسماء المطابقة لمسماها، كتسمية العالم العقلي بعالم الأنوار، و تسمية العالم المثالي بعالم الظلال، و تسمية العالم الحس بعالم الظلام، و هكذا تطلق أسماء غير ما ذكر مطابقة لمسماها.

lectual, Imaginal and material worlds is one that is represented in some plane or another and assumes the colors and properties of any given plane. There is a descent[4]—of that reality—from one plane to the next, according to the vertical or horizontal unity of the worlds. This is true even for something Imaginal or in form, for example, if one believes that the worlds are like a images in a mirror that do not have external reality, or are mirages that a thirsty person imagines to be water.

It also has an ascending vision, so that one sees the sensory as a reality in the Intellectual world and sees the sensory as a reality in the Imaginal, and the Imaginal as a reality in the Intellectual. Each witnessed reality becomes colored by the world in which it is manifested, assuming its properties and presenting it in its own manifestation, without interpretation, shadow or suspension, so that its luminosity is witnessed by the inner vision of its people. This is also the case for visions.

As for dreams, the witnessed reality is a dream seen in its true form, which is true and occurs in reality without interpretation. Or, it may be a dream within a dream, namely, a dream that discloses its reality on the same plane as the dream and does not transfer to another world. There are true Imaginal dreams and an Imaginal sensory dreams, which are realized in the sensory realm. The sensory dream is a dream within a dream. It is a dream that discloses its reality in the dream and is not transferred elsewhere, even when it is perceptible in the sensory. This is because people are asleep and when they die they awaken. This includes everyone, even those who have attained reality and have established themselves in it, so long as there are other manifestations and sensory Imaginal dreams, since the sensory is a dream which

---

4 The terms 'descent' and 'ascent' do not apply to all views concerning existence. For this reason we say 'descent' or an explanatory term which refers to the witnessed reality.

وحقيقة عقلية مثالية حسية واحدة تمثلت في هذا العالم وذاك، وتلونت بلونه وانصبغت بصبغته، وهذا لها - أي للحقيقة المذكورة - نزولا[٤] من عالم إلى ما دونه بناءا على طولية العوالم، أو عرضيتها أو وحدتها. بل حتى مع كونها خيالا أو صورة، لمن يعتقد أن العوالم كصورة المرآة ليس لها واقع من وجه، أو كسراب يحسبه الضمان ماءا.

ولها رؤية أخرى صعودا فترى الحس حقيقة في العقل، وترى الحس حقيقة في المثال، وترى المثال حقيقة في العقل. كل ذلك وهي تتلون بلون العالم المتجلية فيه، وتنصبغ بصبغته، فتعطي حقيقتها المَرْئِيَّة وواقعها من عين مجلاها، بلا تأويل ولا تظليل ولا تعطيل. لتشهد نورانيتها بنور بصائر أهلها. هذا للرؤية.

وأما للرؤيا فالحقيقة المَرْئِيَّة مناما ترى مناما كما هي، فتقع حقا وحقيقة من غير تأويل، وهي منام في منام، أي منام يعطي حقيقته مناما لا يَعْبُر لغيره من العوالم، وبعبارة: رؤيا حقيقية مثالية فحسب. ورؤيا مثالية حسية، أي منام يتحقق في حس، ورؤيا حسية، وهي منام في منام، أي منام يعطي حقيقته مناما لا يعبر إلى غيره، وان كان محسوس وفي عالم الحس، لأن الناس نيام إذا ماتوا انتبهوا، وهذا سار على الجميع حتى لمن تحقق بالحقيقة نفسها، وأقام فيها ما دام له مجلى في ما سواها،

---

٤ - كلمة نزولا و صعودا لا تتناسب مع كل النظريات حول العالم، و لذا نقول نزولا أو ما يفسر المعنى المعبر عن الحقيقة المشهودة.

takes place on the Imaginal plane. The same reciprocal relationships exists between the Imaginal and the Intellectual and the Intellectual and the Imaginal, and between the sensory and the Intellectual and the Intellectual and the sensory; each is either sleep or wakefulness in relation to the other. Just as a dream is realized in wakefulness from one perspective, wakefulness is a dream that is realized in the Imaginal plane, which is wakefulness and actuality from another perspective. Similarly, the intelligible in the Intellectual world is a dream which is realized in the Imaginal world, which is wakefulness, from one perspective, and the Imaginal world is a dream that is realized in the Intellectual world which is wakefulness and actuality from another perspective. The same relationship of dream and wakefulness holds true between the sensory and Intellectual worlds.

Furthermore, there is one reality even in *sina* (hypnagogic state), which is *sina* within *sina*. That is, one sees the reality of *sina* on the plane of *sina* and it is not interpreted to another plane or transferred to the dream or to wakefulness. If it transfers, it is done so according to the unveiled phenomenon and witnessed reality, which does not have interpretation. It crosses to the sensory after having witnessed it in *sina*, just as it was witnessed in *sina* after having assumed two-fold colorations and properties according to the two worlds. It is nonetheless a single reality that remains as is irrespective of which realm it becomes manifest, and is not subject to interpretation. It is thus a firm sign, a clear reality, witnessed in its places of witnessing at their appropriate moments, without interpretation, even if it possible to do so.

What has been said concerning sleep and wakefulness with respect to the previous worlds, sensory, Imaginal and Intellectual is also true of *sina* and its changing of roles. *Sina* is like the dream which is realized in wakefulness, from one perspective, and wakefulness is the dream which is realized in *sina*. It is wakefulness from another perspective given that people are asleep and when they die they awaken. Awakening

ورؤيا حسية مثالية، لكون الحس منام يتحقق في واقع المثال. وهكذا الأمر بين المثال والعقل، وبين العقل والمثال، وبين الحس والعقل، وبين العقل والحس، كل منهم نوما ويقظة. فكما أن المنام في عالم المثال يتحقق في اليقظة من وجه، واليقظة مناما تتحقق في عالم المثال الذي هو اليقظة و الواقع من وجه، فكذلك المعقول في عالم العقل منام يتحقق في عالم المثال الذي هو اليقظة من وجه، وعالم المثال مناما يتحقق في عالم العقل الذي هو اليقظة والواقع من وجه، والأمر كذلك بين الحس والعقل يقظة ونوما.

وأيضاً الحقيقة واحدة في السِّنة، وهي سِنة في سِنة، أي يرى حقيقة السِنة في نفس السِنة لا يأولها ولا يَعْبُر لغيرها من اليقظة والنوم. وان عَبَرَ فإنما يَعْبُر من حيث الواقع المكشوف، والحقيقة المشهودة لا تأويل معها، فيتعدى من بعد رؤية السِنة إلى شهودها حسا، كما رأها سنة مع تغاير اللونين واختلاف الصبغتين بحسب العالمين، ولكن الحقيقة واحدة تحفظ نفسها، بأي عالم تجلت، غير قابلة للتأويل، فهي آية محكمة وحقيقة بينة تشهد في مشهودها من حينه بلا تأويل و إن كان لها ذلك.

ويجري للسنة مع اليقظة والنوم ما جرى سابقا للعوالم المتقدمة - حسية، ومثالية، وعقلية - من تبادل الأدوار. فالسنة كالمنام له تحقق في اليقظة من وجه، واليقظة منام له تحقق في السنة التي هي اليقظة من وجه. لكون الناس نيام إذا ماتوا انتبهوا، والانتباهة هنا تكون في السنة،

here occurs in *sina* given that it is more revelatory than the sensory. The more each plane is rarefied the more it becomes clear. Thus, the people of insight witness what others do not. However, all will witness what is inescapable to witness in their own world. "You were certainly unmindful of this, and We have removed from you your covering, so your sight this Day is sharp" (50:22).

Praise be to God, Lord of the Worlds.

لكونها اكشف من الحس فان العوالم كلما لطفت اتضحت في نفسها فيشهد أهل البصائر ما لا يشهده غيرهم ، ويشهد الجميع ما لا بد من شهوده في عالمهم ﴿لَّقَدْ كُنتَ فِي غَفْلَةٍ مِّنْ هذَا فَكَشَفْنَا عَنكَ غِطَاءَكَ فَبَصُرُكَ الْيَوْمَ حَدِيدٌ﴾ [ق:٢٢].

والحمد لله رب العالمين.

Chapter 4

The Station of Reality

The station of reality is the Intellectual world, as it ought to be, originating from His hidden, treasured light. The manifold darkness of nature does not obfuscate it, nor does the intermediary world cast a shadow upon it, neither shade nor suspension.[1] "God is the Light of the heavens and the earth. The example of His light is like a niche within which is a lamp, the lamp is within glass, the glass as

---

[1] Shade is more general than darkness and shadow. The gnosis of [one whose station is of Intellect] is not affected by the darkness of nature which necessitates obstruction and veiling, nor does the shade of the intermediary world (*barzakh*) causes confusion and conjecture.

Suspension: What he sees is not like the confused dream, which is false or suspended. Or it may be said that [his vision] is not 'shade' with respect to shadows of the intermediary world, suspension with respect to the darkness of nature, or a confused dream.

الباب الرابع

مقام الحقيقة

مقام الحقيقة هو العالم العقلي كما ينبغي له أن يكون بنوره المخزون المكنون، لا تظلمه ظلمات الطبيعة، ولا تظله ظلل البرزخ، فلا يقتضي التظليل ولا التعطيل[1]، لكونه نور كله تبعا لأصله الذي خلق منه، وهو أجلى مظهر من مظاهر خالقه. ﴿الله نُورُ السَّمَاوَاتِ وَالْأَرْضِ مَثَلُ نُورِهِ كَمِشْكَاةٍ فِيهَا مِصْبَاحٌ الْمِصْبَاحُ فِي زُجَاجَةٍ الزُّجَاجَةُ كَأَنَّهَا كَوْكَبٌ دُرِّيٌّ يُوقَدُ مِن شَجَرَةٍ مُّبَارَكَةٍ

---

١ - التظليل: اعم من الظلمة و الظل أي لا تُؤثِّر ظلمة الطبيعة على معرفة مشهوده فيلزم منها المنع و الحجب، و لا يؤثر ظل البرزخ فيلزم اللبس و التخمين.

التعطيل: أي لا يكون مشهوده من قبيل أضغاث الأحلام فيقتضي البطلان و التعطيل أو نقول: لا يقتضي التظليل من حيث ظلل البرزخ و ما يلزم منه، و لا يقتضي التعطيل من حيث ظلمة الطبيعة، و ما يلزم منها و كون مشهوده أضغاث أحلام.

if it were a glittering star lit from a blessed olive tree, neither of the east nor of the west, whose oil would almost glow even if untouched by fire. Light upon light. God guides to His light whom He wills. God teaches mankind through parables and He is the Omniscient" (24:35). Such is the case for its people and their path, "Is he who was dead and We revived, having given him a light with which he walks amongst people, like one who is in inexorable darkness? Thus, the deeds of the unbelievers are made to seem alluring to them" (6:122). Based on this, their visions and dreams are true and real and occur exactly as they are seen, without interpretation, as is the case for the intermediary world, which needs interpretation and is governed by 'shade'. They are not false and confused dreams, as in the case of the soul veiled by darkness and governed by suspension, for these do not occur and are not realized. In fact, perceptions from the world of Intellect occur like the crack of dawn, without the slightest covering and obfuscation, in whichever plane they occur, whether as vision or dream. Such is the case for the Intellectual world and its people. This is because it emanates from the divine names of original Being, the Light, the Giver of Life, the Originator, the Creator, and others, according to the embodying and realizing of these [names] by its people.

Each one of them has [names] that dominate his state and govern his material, imaginal or spiritual existence; it is one reality that manifests through it. It is witnessed in his very existence, manifesting through light, spirit, meaning, etc., and its individuals and its people are the chosen, the *imāms*, and those endowed with whatever the station of the Intellect's reality bestows to each individual.

Likewise, they possess the conclusive argument, an exaltedly truthful tongue, clear speech, an upright intellect and a sound heart. They have embodied or realized the original divine names according to degrees and nobility of rank. They are perfect monotheists, witnessing none other than God to whom they pay complete obeisance. They

زَيْتُونَةٍ لَّا شَرْقِيَّةٍ وَلَا غَرْبِيَّةٍ يَكَادُ زَيْتُهَا يُضِيءُ وَلَوْ لَمْ تَمْسَسْهُ نَارٌ نُّورٌ عَلَىٰ نُورٍ يَهْدِي اللهُ لِنُورِهِ مَن يَشَاءُ وَيَضْرِبُ اللهُ الْأَمْثَالَ لِلنَّاسِ واللهُ بِكُلِّ شَيْءٍ عَلِيمٌ ﴾ [النور:٣٥]. كذلك أهله وطريقهم، ﴿ أَوَمَن كَانَ مَيْتًا فَأَحْيَيْنَاهُ وَجَعَلْنَا لَهُ نُورًا يَمْشِي بِهِ فِي النَّاسِ كَمَن مَّثَلُهُ فِي الظُّلُمَاتِ لَيْسَ بِخَارِجٍ مِّنْهَا كَذَٰلِكَ زُيِّنَ لِلْكَافِرِينَ مَا كَانُوا يَعْمَلُونَ ﴾ [الأنعام:١٢٢]، وعلى ذلك لا يكون لهم رؤية أو رؤيا إلا تقع حقا وحقيقة أي تتحقق مثلما رؤيت بلا تأويل، كما هو شأن عالم البرزخ المقتضي للتأويل والمحكوم بالتظليل، ولا هي باطلة وأضغاث أحلام كما هو شأن النفس المحجوبة بالظلمات والمحكومة بالتعطيل لعدم واقعيتها وتحققها. بل إدراكات العالم العقلي تقع كفلق الصبح دون أدنى غشاوة ولبس في أي عالم حصلت، ومن أي نوع كانت رؤية أو رؤيا. وإنما يكون العالم العقلي كذلك ولأهله ما ذكر، لأنه من أسماء النشأ الأول كالنور، والمحيي،و الفاطر، والخالق، وغيرها بحسب تخلق وتحقق أصحابه،

فكل منهم له ما يغلب على حاله ويحكم وجوده جسمانيا كان أو مثاليا أو روحانيا، والحقيقة واحدة لا يظهر إلا بها، وهي الشهود كما هو موجود، فيظهر بالنور، والروح، والمعنى، وأمثالها ولأهله مقام الاصطفاء والإمامة، وغير ذلك مما تعطيه حقيقة المقام العقلي الكائنة في كل واحد بحسبه.

كذلك عندهم الحجة البالغة، ولسان صدق عليا، والكلام المبين، والعقل الصحيح، والقلب السليم. وهم متخلقون أو محققون بأسماء النشأ الأول على تفاضلهم ورفعت درجاتهم. موحدون تمام التوحيد، لا يشهدون إلا الله، ومطيعون تمام الطاعة لا يعصون الله ما أمرهم ويفعلون ما يؤمرون. ناصحون صادقون صديقون. هذا شأن العقل و العقلاء حقا وحقيقة. كذلك

do not disobey God's commands and perform what they have been enjoined. They are the truthful, veracious and sincere. This is truly the nature of the Intellect, the intelligent and the state of Abraham, "Peace be upon Abraham" (37:109). "Who is better in religion than one who submits himself to God, does good deeds and follows the religion of Abraham, inclining toward truth? God took Abraham as an intimate friend" (4:125).

As for light, which is the reality of the Intellect and its source, as mentioned in the hadith, "God created the Intellect from a hidden, treasured light, in His ancient knowledge, of which neither a messenger nor proximate angel had any awareness..."[2] This is the language of the world of Intellect which speaks the language of reality and emanates from the hidden, treasured light in God's ancient knowledge, as evidenced in Abraham's vision, argument and defense. It was not the deduction and argument of the rationalist, even if it is the same outwardly, the deduction appearing identical or equivalent in content.

This is because the distinction between the rationalist and those who assume and realize the divine names of original Being and the station of the Intellect is like the difference between divine spiritual insight (*firāsa*) and speculative insight, whereby one sees with the light of God in the former, "Be wary of the believer's spiritual insight for he sees with the light of God."[3] "Had we wished, we could have shown them to you and you would have known them by their marks, but

---

2 *Biḥār al-anwār: The signs of Intellect and Ignorance*, ch. 4, v. 3 p. 94. It adds: "So the Intellect fell in prostration and remained there for a thousand years. God said, 'Raise your head, ask and you shall receive, intercede and it will be granted.' So Intellect raised its head and said, 'My Lord, intercede on my behalf for the one whom I have been created.' God said to the angels, 'Bear witness that I have interceded for the one whom I have created the Intellect.'"

3 *Kanz al-ʿummāl*, hadith no. 30730 and "Be wary of the believer's spiritual insight for he sees with the light of God." *Kanz al-ʿummāl*, hadith no. 30731.

لإبراهيم، ﴿سَلَامٌ عَلَى إِبْرَاهِيمَ﴾ [الصافات:١٠٩]. ﴿وَمَنْ أَحْسَنُ دِينًا مِّمَّنْ أَسْلَمَ وَجْهَهُ لِلهِ وَهُوَ مُحْسِنٌ وَاتَّبَعَ مِلَّةَ إِبْرَاهِيمَ حَنِيفًا وَاتَّخَذَ اللهُ إِبْرَاهِيمَ خَلِيلًا﴾ [النساء:١٢٥].

فأما النور - الذي هو حقيقة العقل ومصدره كما جاء في الحديث: «إنَّ الله خلق العقل من نور مخزون مكنون في سابق علمه الذي لم يطلع عليه نبي مرسل ولا ملك مقرب فجعل...»[٢] - هو لسان العالم العقلي المفاض عن نورٍ مخزونٍ مكنونٍ في سابقِ علمٍ ينطق بالحقيقة، وبذلك كانت رؤيته واستدلاله واحتجاجه. وما هو حقيقة استدلال واحتجاج أهل النظر، وان كان المظهر واحد، وصورة القياس هي بعينها أو ما ينطوي عليها كلامه.

وذلك لاختلاف ما يفيده لسان المتخلقين والمتحققين بأسماء النشأ الأول، ومقام العقل، كالاختلاف بين الفراسة الإلهية والكسبية، حيث أن الأول ناظر بنور الله، «اتقوا فراسة المؤمن فانه ينظر بنور الله عز وجل»[٣]، ﴿وَلَوْ نَشَاءُ لَأَرَيْنَاكَهُمْ فَلَعَرَفْتَهُم بِسِيمَاهُمْ وَلَتَعْرِفَنَّهُمْ فِي لَحْنِ الْقَوْلِ وَاللهُ يَعْلَمُ أَعْمَالَكُمْ﴾ [محمد:٣٠].فالمتفرس هو المصيب بأول مرماه إلى مقصده، ولا يعرج على تأويل وظن وحسبان، ولا يصحبه سهو و نسيان. بل هو حكم حق

---

٢ - بحار الأنوار/ المجلسي/ باب ٤، علامات العقل و الجهل/ ٣/ ص ٩٤. و فيها أضافه: (فخر العقل عند ذلك ساجدا، فكان في سجوده ألف عام، فقال الله تبارك و تعالى: ارفع راسك، و سل تعط، و اشفع تشفع، فرفع العقل راسه فقال: الهي أسالك أن تشفعني فيمن خلقتني فيه، فقال الله جل جلاله لملائكته: أشهدكم أني قد شفعته فيمن خلقته فيه.

٣ - كنز العمال / ح ٣٠٧٣٠، وأيضا: احذروا فراسة المؤمن فانه ينظر بنور الله وينطق بتوفيق الله./ المصدر السابق ح ٣٠٧٣١

you will certainly recognize them by the tone of their speech. God knows your deeds" (47:30). One endowed with spiritual insight hits the mark at the very first instance and does not resort to interpretation, supposition and calculation. He neither experiences neglect nor forgetfulness rather it is God's judgement spoken on the tongue of the servant,[4] unlike speculative insight which relies on knowledge and study, which at best, is speculative.

The hadith states, "Knowledge is not extensive learning but a light that God casts in whomever He wishes to guide."[5] Things are seen through this light so let not the singularity of manifestation and deduction deceive you. "Can they be compared to those who have clear proof from their Lord, recited by a witness from Him" (11:17). Thus, Abraham's place of witnessing was from two luminosities and lights because he had realized the divine name, the Light (*al-Nūr*). "When the night grew dark over him he saw a star and said, 'This is my Lord,' but when it set, he said, 'I do not like things that set.' And when he saw the moon rising he said, 'This is my Lord,' but when it too set, he said, 'If my Lord does not guide me, I shall be one of those who have gone astray.' Then he saw the sun rising and cried, 'This is my Lord! This is greater.' But when the sun set, he said, 'My people, I disavow all that you worship beside God'"(6:76-78).

Because he is one who has realized the divine names of original Being, such as the Originator, he says, "I have turned my face as a true believer towards Him who created the heavens and the earth. I am not one of the polytheists'" (6:79). He can never be a polytheist because the Intellect is the first creation, the best, most obedient, sublime, noble, majestic, and chosen by its Lord. God created it on the principle of divine unity, worship, obedience, supplication, hope, yearning, fear, caution, reward and chastisement.

---

4 See *Risāla Qushayriyya*, pp. 266-268.

5 *Munyat al-murīd*, p. 149.

جرى على لسان عبد[٤]، بخلاف الفراسة الكسبية المعتمدة على العلم والتعلم الكسبي المفيدة للظن أحيانا.

وقد جاء في الحديث: «ليس العلم بكثرة التعلم، إنما هو نور يقذفه الله في قلب من يريد أن يهديه»[٥]، فبهذا النور تنظر الأمور، ولا يغرك وحدة المظهر، وصورة القياس ﴿ أَفَمَن كَانَ عَلى بَيِّنَةٍ مِّن رَّبِّهِ وَيَتْلُوهُ شَاهِدٌ مِّنْهُ ﴾ [هود:١٧]. كذلك كان مشهد إبراهيم، وإنما كان ناظرا للنيرين والأنوار لأنه ممن تحقق باسم الله النور، ﴿ فَلَمَّا جَنَّ عَلَيْهِ اللَّيْلُ رَأَىٰ كَوْكَبًا قَالَ هذَا رَبِّي فَلَمَّا أَفَلَ قَالَ لَا أُحِبُّ الْآفِلِينَ ۞ فَلَمَّا رَأَى الْقَمَرَ بَازِغًا قَالَ هذَا رَبِّي فَلَمَّا أَفَلَ قَالَ لَئِن لَّمْ يَهْدِنِي رَبِّي لَأَكُونَنَّ مِنَ الْقَوْمِ الضَّالِّينَ ۞ فَلَمَّا رَأَى الشَّمْسَ بَازِغَةً قَالَ هذَا رَبِّي هذَا أَكْبَرُ فَلَمَّا أَفَلَتْ قَالَ يَا قَوْمِ إِنِّي بَرِيءٌ مِّمَّا تُشْرِكُونَ ﴾ [الأنعام:٧٦-٧٨].

ولكونه ممن تحقق بأسماء النشأ الأول والتي منها الفاطر، قال: ﴿ إِنِّي وَجَّهْتُ وَجْهِيَ لِلَّذِي فَطَرَ السَّمَاوَاتِ وَالْأَرْضَ حَنِيفًا وَمَا أَنَا مِنَ الْمُشْرِكِينَ ﴾ [الأنعام:٧٩]، ولا يقتضي الشرك أبداً. إذ العقل أول الخلق واحسنه وأطوعه وارفعه وأشرفه واعزه، واحد بخالقه. خلق على التوحيد والعبادة وامتثال الأمر. ومنه الدعاء والرجاء والابتغاء والخوف والحذر. وعليه ترتب الثواب والعقاب.

---

٤ - لاحظ الرسالة القشيرية/ ص ٢٦٦-٢٦٨

٥ - منية المريد / ١٤٩.

One who has realized its station can only bring forth these qualities, as God says, "By My honor and majesty, I have not created a creation greater than you, nor more obedient to Me than you, nor higher, nor nobler, nor majestic. I give and take through you, through you My unity is recognized, through you I am worshipped, supplicated, yearned for, hoped for, feared and cautioned against. By you I reward and punish."[6]

As for the Spirit, since the world of the Intellect is the world of spirits, when the manifestation reaches the complete and perfected station of the Spirit, the divine name, the Living becomes realized and one gains the power of life. This occurs when the Intellect governs the entirety of the human kingdom and is the wellspring of all things manifest and hidden in the human being, such as the spirit's governance of the body and the source of physical life and the human faculties. In correspondence with light and darkness, life and death, God says, "Is he who was dead and We revived, having given him a light by which he walks amongst people, like one who is in inexorable darkness? Thus, the deeds of the unbelievers are made to seem alluring to them" (6:122). The following station is for one who has realized this.

"Have you not seen the one who disputed with Abraham about his Lord because God had given him kingship? When Abraham said, 'My Lord is the one who gives life and death,' he said, 'I too give life and cause death' Abraham said, 'God brings the sun from the east, so bring it up from the west.' So the disbeliever was dumbfounded, and God does not guide the wicked" (2:258). These acts which accorded with his creation and station were easy for him to perform, "He said, 'How can you worship things you carve with your own hands, when it is God who has created you and all your handiwork?'" (37:95-96). He whom God has chosen He has chosen his Intellect, and God is aware of this. "We gave Abraham right guidance beforehand, and We were well-aware of him" (21:51).

---

6 Cited earlier in the hadith of Imam ʿAlī's concerning the Intellect.

فمن تحقق بمقامه لا يأتي إلا به، قال الرب تبارك وتعالى: «وعزتي وجلالي ما خلقت خلقا أحسن منك، ولا أطوع لي منك، ولا أرفع منك، ولا أشرف منك، ولا أعزّ منك، بك أُؤخذ، وبك أعطي، وبك أُوحّد، وبك أُعبد، وبك أُدعى، وبك أُرتجى، وبك أُبتغى، وبك أُخاف، وبك أُحذر، وبك الثواب، وبك العقاب»[٦].

وأما الروح، فلان عالم العقل هو عالم الأرواح، فان بلغ المظهر كمال مقام الروح وتمامه، وتحقق بالاسم المحيي، جرى على يديه الأحياء. وإنما يكون له ذلك لتدبير العقل تمام المملكة الإنسانية، وكونه مصدر حكم الشهادة والغيب الإنساني، كتدبير الروح للبدن وكونها مصدر الحياة الحسية، والقوى الأنفسية . ولتناسب النور والظلام والموت والحياة قال تعالى: ﴿ أَوَمَن كَانَ مَيْتًا فَأَحْيَيْنَاهُ وَجَعَلْنَا لَهُ نُورًا يَمْشِي بِهِ فِي النَّاسِ كَمَن مَّثَلُهُ فِي الظُّلُمَاتِ لَيْسَ بِخَارِجٍ مِّنْهَا كذلِكَ زُيِّنَ لِلْكَافِرِينَ مَا كَانُوا يَعْمَلُونَ ﴾ [الأنعام:١٢٢]، فهذا مقام ما بعده مقام، يقوله من تحقق به، وكان أهله.

﴿ أَلَمْ تَرَ إِلَى الَّذِي حَاجَّ إِبْرَاهِيمَ فِي رَبِّهِ أَنْ آتَاهُ اللهُ الْمُلْكَ إِذْ قَالَ إِبْرَاهِيمُ رَبِّيَ الَّذِي يُحْيِي وَيُمِيتُ قَالَ أَنَا أُحْيِي وَأُمِيتُ قَالَ إِبْرَاهِيمُ فَإِنَّ اللهَ يَأْتِي بِالشَّمْسِ مِنَ الْمَشْرِقِ فَأْتِ بِهَا مِنَ الْمَغْرِبِ فَبُهِتَ الَّذِي كَفَرَ وَاللهُ لَا يَهْدِي الْقَوْمَ الظَّالِمِينَ ﴾ [البقرة:٢٥٨]. وصار عمله على وفق خلقه ومن مقامه الميسر له، ﴿ قَالَ أَتَعْبُدُونَ مَا تَنْحِتُونَ ۞ وَاللهُ خَلَقَكُمْ وَمَا تَعْمَلُونَ ﴾ [الصافات:٩٥-٩٦]، وممن اصطفاه ربه اصطفاء العقل، وكان اعلم به ﴿ وَلَقَدْ آتَيْنَا إِبْرَاهِيمَ رُشْدَهُ مِن قَبْلُ وَكُنَّا بِهِ عَالِمِينَ ﴾ [الأنبياء:٥١]،

---

٦ - المصدر السابق حديث العقل المروي عن أمير المؤمنين علي ابن أبي طالب عليه السلام.

"Who but a fool would forsake the religion of Abraham? We have chosen him in this world and he will rank among the righteous in the Hereafter" (2:130).

God made Abraham an *imām*, in its entire meaning, and called him a 'nation', God said, "When Abraham's Lord tested him with certain commandments, which he fulfilled, He said, 'I am going to make you a leader of mankind.' Abraham asked, 'Will You make leaders from my descendants as well?' God answered, 'My pledge is not binding for the evildoers'" (2:124). "Abraham was a nation, devoted to God, sincere in faith, and he was not among the idolaters" (16:120). God gave him the decisive argument stemming from the Intellect's nature and lofty station. For this reason there is nothing higher than it, "Such was the argument We gave to Abraham against his people– We raise in rank whoever We will– your Lord is all wise, all knowing" (6:83).

We raised his speech in truthfulness, so that his speech would prevail and his message become clear, "We granted Our grace to all of them and gave them a noble reputation" (19:50).

God gave him a rightly guided Intellect to make his argument reach and make his guidance predominate, "We gave Abraham sound judgement from before of which We were aware. When he said to his father and his people, 'What are these images to which you are devoted?' They said, 'We found our fathers worshipping them.' He said, 'You and your fathers have clearly gone astray.' They asked, 'Have you brought us the truth or are you playing around?' He said, 'Your true Lord is the Lord of the heavens and the earth, He who created them, and I am a witness to this. By God, I shall certainly plot against your idols as soon as you have turned your backs!' He broke them all into pieces, but left the biggest one for them so that they would return to it. They said, 'Who has done this to our gods? How wicked he must be!' Some said, 'We heard a youth called Abraham talking about them.' They said, 'Bring him before the people, so that they may witness [his trial].'

﴿ وَمَن يَرْغَبُ عَن مِّلَّةِ إِبْرَاهِيمَ إِلَّا مَن سَفِهَ نَفْسَهُ وَلَقَدِ اصْطَفَيْنَاهُ فِي الدُّنْيَا وَإِنَّهُ فِي الْآخِرَةِ لَمِنَ الصَّالِحِينَ ﴾ [البقرة:١٣٠].

وجعله إماما لتمام مقامه، وكان أمة، ﴿ وَإِذِ ابْتَلَى إِبْرَاهِيمَ رَبُّهُ بِكَلِمَاتٍ فَأَتَمَّهُنَّ قَالَ إِنِّي جَاعِلُكَ لِلنَّاسِ إِمَامًا قَالَ وَمِن ذُرِّيَّتِي قَالَ لَا يَنَالُ عَهْدِي الظَّالِمِينَ ﴾ [البقرة:١٢٤]، ﴿ إِنَّ إِبْرَاهِيمَ كَانَ أُمَّةً قَانِتًا لِلَّهِ حَنِيفًا وَلَمْ يَكُ مِنَ الْمُشْرِكِينَ ﴾ [النحل:١٢٠]، وأتاه الحجة وهي من شؤون العقل ومقامه لرفعته، فانه ما خلق خلقا أرفع منه، ﴿ وَتِلْكَ حُجَّتُنَا آتَيْنَاهَا إِبْرَاهِيمَ عَلَىٰ قَوْمِهِ نَرْفَعُ دَرَجَاتٍ مَّن نَّشَاءُ إِنَّ رَبَّكَ حَكِيمٌ عَلِيمٌ ﴾ [الأنعام:٨٣].

وجعل له لسان صدق عليا، لتعلو كلمته ويظهر بيانه، ﴿ وَوَهَبْنَا لَهُم مِّن رَّحْمَتِنَا وَجَعَلْنَا لَهُمْ لِسَانَ صِدْقٍ عَلِيًّا ﴾ [مريم:٥٠]. وأتاه عقلا رشيدا لتبلغ حجته، ويغلب هديه، ﴿ وَلَقَدْ آتَيْنَا إِبْرَاهِيمَ رُشْدَهُ مِن قَبْلُ وَكُنَّا بِهِ عَالِمِينَ ۞ إِذْ قَالَ لِأَبِيهِ وَقَوْمِهِ مَا هَٰذِهِ التَّمَاثِيلُ الَّتِي أَنتُمْ لَهَا عَاكِفُونَ ۞ قَالُوا وَجَدْنَا آبَاءَنَا لَهَا عَابِدِينَ ۞ قَالَ لَقَدْ كُنتُمْ أَنتُمْ وَآبَاؤُكُمْ فِي ضَلَالٍ مُّبِينٍ ۞ قَالُوا أَجِئْتَنَا بِالْحَقِّ أَمْ أَنتَ مِنَ اللَّاعِبِينَ ۞ قَالَ بَل رَّبُّكُمْ رَبُّ السَّمَاوَاتِ وَالْأَرْضِ الَّذِي فَطَرَهُنَّ وَأَنَا عَلَىٰ ذَٰلِكُم مِّنَ الشَّاهِدِينَ ۞ وَتَاللَّهِ لَأَكِيدَنَّ أَصْنَامَكُم بَعْدَ أَن تُوَلُّوا مُدْبِرِينَ ۞ فَجَعَلَهُمْ جُذَاذًا إِلَّا كَبِيرًا لَّهُمْ لَعَلَّهُمْ إِلَيْهِ يَرْجِعُونَ ۞ قَالُوا مَن فَعَلَ هَٰذَا بِآلِهَتِنَا إِنَّهُ لَمِنَ الظَّالِمِينَ ۞ قَالُوا سَمِعْنَا فَتًى يَذْكُرُهُمْ يُقَالُ لَهُ إِبْرَاهِيمُ ۞ قَالُوا فَأْتُوا بِهِ عَلَىٰ أَعْيُنِ النَّاسِ لَعَلَّهُمْ يَشْهَدُونَ ۞ قَالُوا أَأَنتَ فَعَلْتَ هَٰذَا بِآلِهَتِنَا يَا إِبْرَاهِيمُ ۞ قَالَ بَلْ فَعَلَهُ كَبِيرُهُمْ هَٰذَا فَاسْأَلُوهُمْ إِن كَانُوا يَنطِقُونَ ۞ فَرَجَعُوا إِلَىٰ أَنفُسِهِمْ فَقَالُوا إِنَّكُمْ أَنتُمُ الظَّالِمُونَ ۞ ثُمَّ نُكِسُوا عَلَىٰ رُءُوسِهِمْ لَقَدْ عَلِمْتَ مَا هَٰؤُلَاءِ يَنطِقُونَ ۞ قَالَ أَفَتَعْبُدُونَ مِن دُونِ اللَّهِ مَا لَا يَنفَعُكُمْ شَيْئًا وَلَا يَضُرُّكُمْ ۞ أُفٍّ

They asked, 'Was it you, Abraham, who did this to our gods?' He said, 'No, it was done by the biggest of them – this one. Ask them, if they can talk.' They turned to one another, saying, 'It is you who are in the wrong,' but then they lapsed again and said,'You know very well these gods cannot speak.' Abraham said, 'How can you worship what can neither benefit nor harm you, instead of God? Shame on you and on the things you worship instead of God. Have you no sense?'" (21:51-67).

As such, Abrahamic speech originates from the inspiration of the Intellect, "Then We revealed to you 'Follow the creed of Abraham, a man of pure faith who was not a polytheists' (16:123). Perhaps God will inspire us and you to follow the creed of truth and reality so we can follow in his footsteps and his way to attain what we can of his station, "The path is made easy for that which you have been created."[7] God says, "He said, 'Our Lord is He Who gave everything its nature, then guided it aright'" (20:50). So let us be the most worthy of it and work towards that station.

"Indeed, the most worthy of Abraham among the people are those who followed him and this prophet, and those who believe, God is the ally of the believers" (3:68). Let us be careful not to waste what is left of our lives, because what has passed will never return.

Imam 'Alī said, "Be careful of wasting what remains of your lives for what has passed will not return."[8] He also said, "You are but a certain number of days, each day that passes a part of you is gone. So lessen your desires and beautify your attainments."[9]

"My success is only with God, upon whom I have relied and to whom I return" (11:88), "Their final call will be, 'Praise to God, Lord of the worlds'" (10:10). Praise be to God, Lord of the worlds.

---

7 Cited in the introduction.

8 *Ghurar al-ḥikam*, p. 92, hadith no. 39.

9 *Ghurar al-ḥikam*, p. 129, hadith no. 3028.

لَّكُمْ وَلِمَا تَعْبُدُونَ مِن دُونِ اللَّهِ أَفَلَا تَعْقِلُونَ ﴾ [الأنبياء:٥١-٦٧].

وهكذا تجد الخطاب الإبراهيمي من وحي العقل، ﴿ ثُمَّ أَوْحَيْنَا إِلَيْكَ أَنِ اتَّبِعْ مِلَّةَ إِبْرَاهِيمَ حَنِيفًا وَمَا كَانَ مِنَ الْمُشْرِكِينَ ﴾ [النحل:١٢٣]. فعسى الله يوحي إلينا وإياك باتباع ملته حقا وحقيقة. فنتبع اثره ونسير على خطاه وندرك ما يسر لنا من مقامه «كل ميسر لما خلق له»[٧]، فان الله تعالى ﴿ قَالَ رَبُّنَا الَّذِي أَعْطَىٰ كُلَّ شَيْءٍ خَلْقَهُ ثُمَّ هَدَىٰ ﴾ [طه:٥٠]، فنكون أولى الناس به واشغل لمنزله، والله ولينا ﴿ إِنَّ أَوْلَى النَّاسِ بِإِبْرَاهِيمَ لَلَّذِينَ اتَّبَعُوهُ وَهَذَا النَّبِيُّ وَالَّذِينَ آمَنُوا وَاللهُ وَلِيُّ الْمُؤْمِنِينَ ﴾ [آل‌عمران:٦٨]، ولنحذر ضياع الأعمار فيما لا يبقى لنا، ففائتها ل ايعود.

قال سيد الأوصياء ﵇: «احذروا ضياع الأعمار فيما لا يبقى لكم، ففائتها لا يعود»[٨].

وقال ﵇: «إنما أنت عدد أيام، فكل يوم يمضي عليك، يمضي ببعضك فخفف في الطلب، واجمل في المكسب»[٩] ﴿ وَمَا تَوْفِيقِي إِلَّا بِاللَّهِ عَلَيْهِ تَوَكَّلْتُ وَإِلَيْهِ أُنِيبُ ﴾ [هود:٨٨]، ﴿ وَآخِرُ دَعْوَاهُمْ أَنِ الْحَمْدُ لِلهِ رَبِّ الْعَالَمِينَ ﴾ [يونس:١٠].

والحمد لله رب العالمين.

---

٧ - سبق تخريجه في المقدمة.

٨ - غرر الحكم، ٩٢/ ٣٩.

٩ - غرر الحكم، ١٢٩/ ٣٠٢٨

Chapter 5

The Knowledge of Allusion

The knowledge of allusion is one of the properties of the Imaginal world, which is an isthmus between the Intellectual and material worlds, whose speech is the language of both the Connected and Discrete Imagination, from a treasured, hidden light in God's ancient knowledge. This type of knowledge is interpreted, whether it occurs in dreams or visions.

"Your Lord has chosen you and will teach you the interpretation of events, completing His blessing upon you and the family of Jacob, as He completed it for your fathers before, Abraham and Isaac. Indeed, your Lord is Omniscient and Wise" (12:6). "Thus, We established Joseph in the land that We might teach him the interpretation of events. God always prevails in His purpose, but most people do not realize" (12:21). "My Lord, You have given me some sovereignty and taught me dream interpretation. Creator of the heavens and earth, You are my protector

الباب الخامس

علم الإشارة

علم الإشارة من شؤون عالم المثال، برزخ بين العالمين العقلي والمادي، ينطق بلسان الخيال المتصل والمنفصل عن نورٍ مخزونٍ مكنونٍ في سابقِ علمِ الله، وهو الذي يؤول سواء وقع رؤيا أو رؤية.

﴿ وَكَذلِكَ يَجْتَبِيكَ رَبُّكَ وَيُعَلِّمُكَ مِن تَأْوِيلِ الْأَحَادِيثِ وَيُتِمُّ نِعْمَتَهُ عَلَيْكَ وَعَلَى آلِ يَعْقُوبَ كَمَا أَتَمَّهَا عَلى أَبَوَيْكَ مِن قَبْلُ إِبْرَاهِيمَ وَإِسْحَاقَ إِنَّ رَبَّكَ عَلِيمٌ حَكِيمٌ ﴾ [يوسف:٦]، ﴿ وَكَذلِكَ مَكَّنَّا لِيُوسُفَ فِي الْأَرْضِ وَلِنُعَلِّمَهُ مِن تَأْوِيلِ الْأَحَادِيثِ وَ الله غَالِبٌ عَلَى أَمْرِهِ وَلَكِنَّ أَكْثَرَ النَّاسِ لَا يَعْلَمُونَ ﴾ [يوسف:٢١]، ﴿ رَبِّ قَدْ آتَيْتَنِي مِنَ الْمُلْكِ وَعَلَّمْتَنِي مِن تَأْوِيلِ الْأَحَادِيثِ فَاطِرَ السَّمَاوَاتِ وَالْأَرْضِ أَنتَ وَلِيِّي فِي الدُّنْيَا وَالْآخِرَةِ تَوَفَّنِي مُسْلِماً وَأَلْحِقْنِي بِالصَّالِحِين ﴾

in this world and in the Hereafter. Cause me to die in submission and join me with the righteous" (12:101).

For one who has realized the Imaginal world, interpretation applies to [physical] vision as it applies to dreams. "He said, 'I can tell you what this means before any meal arrives. This is part of what my Lord has taught me. I reject the faith of those who disbelieve in God and deny the life to come'" (12:37). This differs from one who has realized the Intellect, the spirit and the names of original Being, like Abraham, as mentioned, and similarly Jesus. "In God's eyes Jesus is just like Adam. He created Him from dust; then He said to him, 'Be,' and he was" (3:59). What manifested with Jesus corresponded to his world and the dominant and governing property, namely, creation, breath [spirit], healing, reviving, and the informing of realities without interpretation. "He will send him as a messenger to the Children of Israel: 'I have come to you with a sign from your Lord: I will make the shape of a bird for you out of clay, then breathe into it and, with God's permission, it will become a real bird; I will heal the blind and the leper, and bring the dead back to life with God's permission; I will tell you what you may eat and what you may store up in your houses. There truly is a sign for you in this, if you are believers.'" (3:49).

The same can be said of Abraham's dream which came to pass just as he saw it, without interpretation, "When the boy was old enough to walk with his father, Abraham said, 'My son, I have seen myself sacrificing you in a dream. What do you think?' He said, 'Father, do as you have been commanded, and God willing, you will find me steadfast.' When they had both surrendered to God, and he had laid his son down on the side of his face, We called out to him, 'Abraham, You have already fulfilled the dream.' This is how we reward the virtuous" (37:102-105).

This dream occurred in the Imaginal world, whose place of witnessing is knowledge of reality, the true knowledge of phenomena, like

[يوسف:١٠١].

وله في الروية مثلما للرؤيا من تأويل ، ذلك شأن من تحقق في عالم المثال ﴿ قَالَ لَا يَأْتِيكُمَا طَعَامٌ تُرْزَقَانِهِ إِلَّا نَبَّأْتُكُمَا بِتَأْوِيلِهِ قَبْلَ أَن يَأْتِيَكُمَا ذَلِكُمَا مِمَّا عَلَّمَنِي رَبِّي إِنِّي تَرَكْتُ مِلَّةَ قَوْمٍ لَّا يُؤْمِنُونَ بِاللَّهِ وَهُم بِالْآخِرَةِ هُمْ كَافِرُونَ ﴾ [يوسف:٣٧] ، وهو غير من تحقق في عالم العقل والروح وأسماء النشأ الأول كما تقدم في إبراهيم ومثله عيسى عليهما السلام ،﴿ إِنَّ مَثَلَ عِيسَى عِندَ اللَّهِ كَمَثَلِ آدَمَ خَلَقَهُ مِن تُرَابٍ ثُمَّ قَالَ لَهُ كُن فَيَكُونُ ﴾ [آل عمران:٥٩] ، ولذا ما ظهر إلا من حيث عالمه ، وما عليه من حكم وغلبة ، فكان منه الخلق، والنفخ ، والإبراء ، والإحياء ، والإنباء عن حقيقة دون تأويل ﴿ وَرَسُولًا إِلَى بَنِي إِسْرَائِيلَ أَنِّي قَدْ جِئْتُكُم بِآيَةٍ مِّن رَّبِّكُمْ أَنِّي أَخْلُقُ لَكُم مِّنَ الطِّينِ كَهَيْئَةِ الطَّيْرِ فَأَنفُخُ فِيهِ فَيَكُونُ طَيْرًا بِإِذْنِ اللهِ وَأُبْرِئُ الْأَكْمَهَ وَالْأَبْرَصَ وَأُحْيِي الْمَوْتَى بِإِذْنِ اللهِ وَأُنَبِّئُكُم بِمَا تَأْكُلُونَ وَمَا تَدَّخِرُونَ فِي بُيُوتِكُمْ إِنَّ فِي ذَلِكَ لَآيَةً لَّكُمْ إِن كُنتُم مُّؤْمِنِينَ ﴾ [آل عمران:٤٩].

ومثله رؤيا إبراهيم عليه السلام وقعت كما رأى دون تأويل ﴿ فَلَمَّا بَلَغَ مَعَهُ السَّعْيَ قَالَ يَا بُنَيَّ إِنِّي أَرَى فِي الْمَنَامِ أَنِّي أَذْبَحُكَ فَانظُرْ مَاذَا تَرَى قَالَ يَا أَبَتِ افْعَلْ مَا تُؤْمَرُ سَتَجِدُنِي إِن شَاءَ اللهُ مِنَ الصَّابِرِينَ ۞ فَلَمَّا أَسْلَمَا وَتَلَّهُ لِلْجَبِينِ ۞ وَنَادَيْنَاهُ أَن يَا إِبْرَاهِيمُ ۞ قَدْ صَدَّقْتَ الرُّؤْيَا إِنَّا كَذَلِكَ نَجْزِي الْمُحْسِنِينَ ﴾ [الصافات:١٠٢ - ١٠٥].

the dreams of Prophet Muḥammad which occurred like the break of dawn. "The advent of revelation was a true dream. He never saw a dream except that it came like the break of dawn."[1]

Nābulsī says, "It occurred in the sensory world exactly as it was seen, which does not need interpretation or explanation"[2] Some dreams or visions that the Prophet saw did require interpretation.

"[O Muḥammad], when We told you that your Lord has encompassed the people. The dream We showed you was only a test for people, as was the accursed tree [mentioned] in the Qur'an; we frighten them, but it only increases them in transgression" (17:60). God informed the Prophet that what he saw in his dream was true. "God has truly fulfilled His Messenger's vision, that God willing, you will certainly enter the Sacred Mosque in safety, heads shaven or hair cut short, without fear. God knew what you did not know and He has granted

---

1 Rayshahrī, *Mīzan al-ḥikma*, v. 4, p. 8; Bukhārī, *Ṣaḥīḥ*: The Advent of Revelation, hadith no. 3 (1/4); Muslim, *Ṣaḥiḥ*: The Advent of Revelation, hadith no. 160 (1/139); and others.

2 Nābulsī adds, "It does not need interpretation or explanation. It is permissible for the prophets to err with respect to dreams and this has indeed occurred. However, they are protected from erring consistently and to confuse it with wakefulness. For example, it is related that when the Prophet saw in a dream that he placed his hand in a shield, he said, 'I have interpreted this as entering the city.' However, the imagination erred in the dream and when he awoke he then realized its true interpretation. Prophetic dreams come from God through the angel of dreams who descends upon their hearts, by God's command. What is disclosed to the imagination is exactly what [the prophets] see, either its like or a correspondence. Thus, dream interpretation is permissible in the same way that Qur'ānic exegesis and interpretation is permissible. There are sound dreams and ambiguous dreams just as it applies to the Qur'ān. Furthermore, it is related in the hadith that dreams are a part of prophecy, "Prophecy has ended but visions remain." The believer sees or is shown sound dreams. Nābulsī, *Jawāhir al-fuṣūṣ*, v. 1, p. 286.

فهذه رؤيا عالم المثال، مشهدها علم الحقيقة، وهو علم حقيقة الأحاديث الواقع كما هو. كذلك كانت بعض رؤيا النبي محمد ﷺ، تقع كفلق الصبح كما روي: «أول ما بدئ به النبي ﷺ من الوحي الرؤيا الصادقة، فكان لا يرى رؤيا إلا جاءت مثل فلق الصبح»[1].

قال النابلسي: «إلا وقعت بعينها في عالم الحس، و مثل هذه الرؤيا لا تحتاج إلى التأويل و التعبير...»[2] وبعضها يقع بالتأويل، كالرؤيا أو الرؤية التي راها الرسول ﷺ على وجه كونها تأويل. ﴿ وَإِذْ قُلْنَا لَكَ إِنَّ رَبَّكَ أَحَاطَ بِالنَّاسِ وَمَا جَعَلْنَا الرُّؤْيَا الَّتِي أَرَيْنَاكَ إِلَّا فِتْنَةً لِّلنَّاسِ وَالشَّجَرَةَ الْمَلْعُونَةَ فِي الْقُرْآنِ وَنُخَوِّفُهُمْ فَمَا يَزِيدُهُمْ إِلَّا طُغْيَانًا كَبِيرًا ﴾ [الإسراء:٦٠]، فاخبر الله رسوله بانه رأي الصدق في منامه، ﴿ لَّقَدْ صَدَقَ اللهُ رَسُولَهُ الرُّؤْيَا بِالْحَقِّ لَتَدْخُلُنَّ

١ - ميزان الحكمة للريشهري ج٤ ص٨ ورواه البخاري في صحيحه في أبواب عدة منها: باب كيف بدء الوحي إلى...حديث رقم (٣) (١/ ٤)، و رواه مسلم في صحيحه، باب بدء الوحي إلى...حديث رقم (١٦٠) (/ ١٣٩)، و رواه غيرهما.

٢ - و أضاف النابلسي إلى قوله: لا تحتاج إلى التأويل و التعبير، و خطأ الخيال في عالم الرؤيا المنامية جائز في حق الأنبياء عليهم السلام و واقع لهم أيضا، و لكنهم محفوظة من دوام الخطأ و التباسه عليهم في اليقظة. ولهذا ورد انه ﷺ رأى في المنام انه ادخل يده في درع، فقال: أولته بدخول المدينة، فقد اخطأ خياله في المنام فلما استيقظ أصاب في هذا التعبير، و رؤيا الأنبياء عليهم السلام و هي من الله تعالى لهم بملك الرؤيا ينزل على قلوبهم بأمر الله، فكشف عن ذلك خيالهم بعين ما رأوا و بمثله و مناسبة، و لهذا شرع تعبير المنام و تأويله كما تفسير القرآن و تأويله. و في الرؤيا المحكم، و المتشابه كما شرع في القرآن و ورد في الحديث أن الرؤيا الصادقة جزء من أجزاء النبوة. و في رواية: ذهبت النبوة، و بقيت المبشرات: الرؤيا الصادقة يراها المؤمن أو ترى له./ جواهر الفصوص/ النابلسي/ ج ١/ ص ٢٨٦.

you a swift victory" (48:27).

These types of dreams are of the Imaginal world whose place of witnessing is the knowledge of allusion. It consists of the knowledge of interpretation of events. They can only be understood through the use of interpretation as it occurred for prophet Joseph. "He raised his parents upon the throne, and they bowed to him in prostration, and he said, "Father, this is the interpretation of my dream I had before. My Lord has made it come true and has been gracious to me when He released me from prison and brought you [here] from the desert after Satan had sowed discord between me and my brothers. My Lord is most subtle in achieving what He wills. He is the Omniscient, the Wise" (12:100).

Joseph relates his dream to his father, Jacob, "When Joseph said to his father, 'Father, I saw in a dream eleven stars, and the sun and the moon all prostrating before me.' He replied, 'My son, do not relate your dream to your brothers for they may plot against you—Satan is man's sworn enemy. Thus, your Lord will choose you, teach you to interpret events, and complete His blessing upon you and the House of Jacob, just as He had completed it upon your forefathers Abraham and Isaac; your Lord is Omniscient, Wise'" (12:4-6).

All praise be to God, the Lord of the worlds.

الْمَسْجِدَ الْحَرَامَ إِن شَاءَ اللهُ آمِنِينَ مُحَلِّقِينَ رُءُوسَكُمْ وَمُقَصِّرِينَ لَا تَخَافُونَ فَعَلِمَ مَا لَمْ تَعْلَمُوا فَجَعَلَ مِن دُونِ ذَلِكَ فَتْحًا قَرِيبًا﴾ [الفتح:٢٧]

فهذه وأمثالها رؤيا عالم المثال مشهدها علم الإشارة، وهو علم تأويل الأحاديث يعبر فيه إلى الحق بالتأويل ليس إلا، كما هو للنبي العزيز يوسف عليه السلام، ﴿وَرَفَعَ أَبَوَيْهِ عَلَى الْعَرْشِ وَخَرُّوا لَهُ سُجَّدًا وَقَالَ يَا أَبَتِ هَذَا تَأْوِيلُ رُؤْيَايَ مِن قَبْلُ قَدْ جَعَلَهَا رَبِّي حَقًّا وَقَدْ أَحْسَنَ بِي إِذْ أَخْرَجَنِي مِنَ السِّجْنِ وَجَاءَ بِكُم مِّنَ الْبَدْوِ مِن بَعْدِ أَن نَّزَغَ الشَّيْطَانُ بَيْنِي وَبَيْنَ إِخْوَتِي إِنَّ رَبِّي لَطِيفٌ لِّمَا يَشَاءُ إِنَّهُ هُوَ الْعَلِيمُ الْحَكِيمُ﴾ [يوسف:١٠٠]، في الرؤيا التي قصها على أبية يعقوب عليهما السلام،﴿ إِذْ قَالَ يُوسُفُ لِأَبِيهِ يَا أَبَتِ إِنِّي رَأَيْتُ أَحَدَ عَشَرَ كَوْكَبًا وَالشَّمْسَ وَالْقَمَرَ رَأَيْتُهُمْ لِي سَاجِدِينَ قَالَ يَا بُنَيَّ لَا تَقْصُصْ رُؤْيَاكَ عَلَى إِخْوَتِكَ فَيَكِيدُوا لَكَ كَيْدًا إِنَّ الشَّيْطَانَ لِلْإِنسَانِ عَدُوٌّ مُّبِينٌ وَكَذَلِكَ يَجْتَبِيكَ رَبُّكَ وَيُعَلِّمُكَ مِن تَأْوِيلِ الْأَحَادِيثِ وَيُتِمُّ نِعْمَتَهُ عَلَيْكَ وَعَلَى آلِ يَعْقُوبَ كَمَا أَتَمَّهَا عَلَى أَبَوَيْكَ مِن قَبْلُ إِبْرَاهِيمَ وَإِسْحَاقَ إِنَّ رَبَّكَ عَلِيمٌ حَكِيمٌ﴾ [يوسف:٤-٦].

والحمد لله رب العالميـن.

Chapter 6

The Knowledge of Expression

The knowledge of expression relates to the material world and unveils its mysteries which emanate from the hidden, treasured light. "Moses said to him, 'May I follow you so that you can teach me some of the right guidance you have been taught?' He said, 'You will not be able to bear with me patiently. How could you be patient in matters beyond your knowledge?' Moses said, 'God willing, you will find me patient. I will not disobey you in any way.' He said, 'If you follow me then, do not ask about anything I do before I mention it to you myself.' They travelled on. Later, when they got into a boat, and he made a hole in it, Moses said, 'How could you make a hole in it? Do you want to drown its passengers? What a strange thing to do!' He replied, 'Did I not tell you that you would never be able to bear with me patiently?' Moses said, 'Forgive me for forgetting. Do not make it too hard for me to follow you.' And so they travelled on. Then, when

الباب السادس

علم العبارة

علم العبارة شأن العالم المادي، يفاض عن نور مخزون مكنون يكشف أسرار الحس، ﴿ قَالَ لَهُ مُوسَى هَلْ أَتَّبِعُكَ عَلَى أَن تُعَلِّمَنِ مِمَّا عُلِّمْتَ رُشْدًا ۞ قَالَ إِنَّكَ لَن تَسْتَطِيعَ مَعِيَ صَبْرًا ۞ وَكَيْفَ تَصْبِرُ عَلَى مَا لَمْ تُحِطْ بِهِ خُبْرًا ۞ قَالَ سَتَجِدُنِي إِن شَاءَ اللهُ صَابِرًا وَلَا أَعْصِي لَكَ أَمْرًا ۞ قَالَ فَإِنِ اتَّبَعْتَنِي فَلَا تَسْأَلْنِي عَن شَيْءٍ حَتَّى أُحْدِثَ لَكَ مِنْهُ ذِكْرًا ۞ فَانطَلَقَا حَتَّى إِذَا رَكِبَا فِي السَّفِينَةِ خَرَقَهَا قَالَ أَخَرَقْتَهَا لِتُغْرِقَ أَهْلَهَا لَقَدْ جِئْتَ شَيْئًا إِمْرًا ۞ قَالَ أَلَمْ أَقُلْ إِنَّكَ لَن تَسْتَطِيعَ مَعِيَ صَبْرًا ۞ قَالَ لَا تُؤَاخِذْنِي بِمَا نَسِيتُ وَلَا تُرْهِقْنِي مِنْ أَمْرِي عُسْرًا ۞ فَانطَلَقَا حَتَّى إِذَا لَقِيَا غُلَامًا فَقَتَلَهُ قَالَ أَقَتَلْتَ نَفْسًا زَكِيَّةً بِغَيْرِ نَفْسٍ لَّقَدْ جِئْتَ شَيْئًا نُّكْرًا ۞ قَالَ أَلَمْ أَقُل لَّكَ إِنَّكَ لَن تَسْتَطِيعَ مَعِيَ صَبْرًا ۞ قَالَ

they met a young boy and the man killed him, Moses said,'How could you kill an innocent person? He has not killed anyone! What a terrible thing to do!' He replied, 'Did I not tell you that you would never be able to bear with me patiently?' Moses said, 'From now on, if I ask anything you do, banish me from your company–you have put up with enough from me.' And so they travelled on. Then, when they came to a town and asked the inhabitants for food but were refused hospitality, they saw a wall there that was on the point of collapse and the man repaired it. Moses said, 'But if you had wished you could have taken payment for doing that.' He said, 'This is where you and I part company. I will tell you the meaning of the things you could not bear with patiently: the boat belonged to some needy people who made their living from the sea and I damaged it because I knew that coming after them was a king who was seizing every [serviceable] boat by force. The young boy had parents who were people of faith, and so, fearing he would trouble them through wickedness and disbelief, we wished that their Lord should give them another child– purer and more compassionate–in his place. The wall belonged to two young orphans in the town and there was buried treasure beneath it belonging to them. Their father had been a righteous man, so your Lord intended them to reach maturity and then dig up their treasure as a mercy from your Lord. I did not do [these things] of my own accord: these are the explanations for those things you could not bear with patience.' (18:66-82).

This interpretation did not go as far as unveiling mysteries but was directed only at the material world, even if it emanated from a hidden, treasured light in God's ancient knowledge. It does, however, raise the question as to the reality of Intellect and Imaginal form. Still, it is not the unveiling of mysteries in the natural world but can be obtained through reflection, experience and coincidence. Perception of the material world stemming from light, spirit, or meaning is considered the knowledge of reality.

إن سَأَلْتُكَ عَن شَيْءٍ بَعْدَهَا فَلَا تُصَاحِبْنِي قَدْ بَلَغْتَ مِن لَّدُنِّي عُذْرًا ۞ فَانطَلَقَا حَتَّى إِذَا أَتَيَا أَهْلَ قَرْيَةٍ اسْتَطْعَمَا أَهْلَهَا فَأَبَوْا أَن يُضَيِّفُوهُمَا فَوَجَدَا فِيهَا جِدَارًا يُرِيدُ أَن يَنقَضَّ فَأَقَامَهُ قَالَ لَوْ شِئْتَ لَاتَّخَذْتَ عَلَيْهِ أَجْرًا ۞ قَالَ هَذَا فِرَاقُ بَيْنِي وَبَيْنِكَ سَأُنَبِّئُكَ بِتَأْوِيلِ مَا لَمْ تَسْتَطِع عَّلَيْهِ صَبْرًا ۞ أَمَّا السَّفِينَةُ فَكَانَتْ لِمَسَاكِينَ يَعْمَلُونَ فِي الْبَحْرِ فَأَرَدتُّ أَنْ أَعِيبَهَا وَكَانَ وَرَاءَهُم مَّلِكٌ يَأْخُذُ كُلَّ سَفِينَةٍ غَصْبًا ۞ وَأَمَّا الْغُلَامُ فَكَانَ أَبَوَاهُ مُؤْمِنَيْنِ فَخَشِينَا أَن يُرْهِقَهُمَا طُغْيَانًا وَكُفْرًا ۞ فَأَرَدْنَا أَن يُبْدِلَهُمَا رَبُّهُمَا خَيْرًا مِّنْهُ زَكَاةً وَأَقْرَبَ رُحْمًا ۞ وَأَمَّا الْجِدَارُ فَكَانَ لِغُلَامَيْنِ يَتِيمَيْنِ فِي الْمَدِينَةِ وَكَانَ تَحْتَهُ كَنزٌ لَّهُمَا وَكَانَ أَبُوهُمَا صَالِحًا فَأَرَادَ رَبُّكَ أَن يَبْلُغَا أَشُدَّهُمَا وَيَسْتَخْرِجَا كَنزَهُمَا رَحْمَةً مِّن رَّبِّكَ وَمَا فَعَلْتُهُ عَنْ أَمْرِي ذَلِكَ تَأْوِيلُ مَا لَمْ تَسْطِع عَّلَيْهِ صَبْرًا ﴾ [الكهف:٦٦-٨٢]. فهذا تأويل لا يتعدى كشف أسرار هي لعالم المادة نفسه، لكنها مفاضة عن نورٍ مخزونٍ مكنونٍ في سابقِ علم الله، ويبقى السؤال ما حقيقته العقلية وصورته المثالية؟ ومع ذلك هو غير كشف أسرار الطبيعة وفق العلوم الكسبية الحاصلة بالتفكير والتجربة والاتفاق. وأما ما يقع من إدراك لعالم الحس مفاده النورية أو الروحية أو المعنوية وما إليها فهو من علم الحقيقة.

As it was for the 'friend' (Abraham), "He cast a glance at the stars and said, 'I am ill'" (37:88-89). This glance signified a meaning and heralded a reality. Were it not the case, then how could one explain the relationship between the stars and illness. Given that he is truthful in speech how did he read illness? Normally, if illness is discovered from a mystery in nature, it is discovered through a natural cause, whether it is through a divine or a rational science. However, this case goes beyond normal mysteries found in nature insofar as he found the reality of his illness in the form of the stars through the light of the station of his Intellect—arising from the treasured, hidden knowledge of God.

Furthermore, whatever perception of the material world that occurs is subject to Imaginal interpretation and is therefore the knowledge of allusion, as it occurred for the truthful one, Joseph. "He said, 'I can tell you what this means before any meal arrives. This is part of what my Lord has taught me. I reject the faith of those who disbelieve in God and deny the life to come" (12:37). The interpretation for the material transfers to the Imaginal, or as the hadith states, "People are asleep and when they die they awaken."[1] Some of its forms require interpretation, as you have come to know concerning the dreams which indicate reality in other forms, according to the people who know the language of that world.

If you have come to know this then know that some mysteries of the material world are interpretations, as mentioned, and others are explanations that unveil the mask of the thing witnessed.

If it calls for explanation or interpretation, insofar as it does not reveal a mystery, it is the knowledge of expression and the material world, irrespective of the fact that the true station of the saint is

---

1 Most transmitters of hadith attribute this statement to Imām 'Alī. See Majlisī, *Biḥār al-anwār*, v. 4, p. 43; Mazandarānī, *Sharḥ Uṣūl al-kāfī*, v. 2, p. 192; 'Irāqī, *Takhrīj aḥadīth iḥyā 'ulūm al-dīn*, v. 4, p. 28; Suyūtī, *al-Durr al-manthūr*, p. 133.

كالذي للخليل عليه السلام: ﴿ فَنَظَرَ نَظْرَةً فِي النُّجُومِ * فَقَالَ إِنِّي سَقِيمٌ ﴾ [الصافات:٨٨-٨٩]، فهذه نظرة أفادت معنى وبينت حقيقة. وإلا فما علاقة النجوم بالسقم؟ وهو الصادق في قوله بأي نحو أخذ السقم. والعادة أن السقم إن كشف عن سر طبيعي إنما يكشف عن سببه الطبيعي، سواء بالعلوم الإلهية أو الكسبية، ولكنه هنا تعدى أسرار الطبيعة المعتادة ليشهد حقيقة سقمه في صورة النجم بأنوار مقامه العقلي المفاضة عن علم الله المخزون المكنون.

وأيضاً ما يقع من إدراك لعالم الحس مفاده التأويل المثالي فهو من علم الإشارة، كالذي للصديق يوسف عليه السلام ﴿ قَالَ لَا يَأْتِيكُمَا طَعَامٌ تُرْزَقَانِهِ إِلَّا نَبَّأْتُكُمَا بِتَأْوِيلِهِ قَبْلَ أَن يَأْتِيَكُمَا ذَلِكُمَا مِمَّا عَلَّمَنِي رَبِّي إِنِّي تَرَكْتُ مِلَّةَ قَوْمٍ لَّا يُؤْمِنُونَ بِاللَّهِ وَهُم بِالْآخِرَةِ هُمْ كَافِرُونَ ﴾ [يوسف:٣٧]، فهذا تأويل لمحسوس يعبر إلى صورة مثالية. أو كما جاء في الحديث: «الناس نيامٌ فإذا ماتوا انتبهوا»[1]، فانه في بعض صوره يقتضي التأويل، لما علمت من المنام الذي يقتضي الحقيقة كما هي في بعض صورها الأخرى، وعلى حسب مقام أهله و ما ينطقون به.

وإذا علمت هذا فاعلم أن من أسرار العالم المادي بعضها تأويل كما تقدم، وبعضها تفسير يتولى كشف القناع عن وجه مشهوده فحسب.

فإن أفاد التفسير المذكور أو التأويل بها لا يتعدى كشف السر، فهو علم العبارة وعالم المادة، بقطع النظر عن حقيقة مقام الولي في مقام آخر غير مقام الظاهر وعلم العبارة، أو مقام الظاهر التفسيري أو باطن الظاهر التأويلي[2].

وإن أفاد التأويل إلى صورة مثالية، أو رمز يؤول إلى أمر ما، خارج عن

---

١ - روي أكثر من محدث عن علي إبن طالب عليه السلام، راجع تخريج أحاديث إحياء علوم الدين/ العراقي/ ٤/ ٢٨/ و الدر المنثور/ السيوطي/ ١٣٣.

٢ -أي كشف السر الظاهر.

elsewhere. It is not the station of the outward, nor the knowledge of expression, nor the station of outward explanation, nor the inward of outward interpretation.[2]

If it entails interpretation of an Imaginal form or a symbol that indicates something short of unveiling among the mysteries in nature, it is called the knowledge of allusion and the Imaginal world. However, if it entails reality itself, describing a phenomenon as it truly is, it is called the knowledge of reality and the world of Intellect.

Praise be to God, Lord of the Worlds

---

2 Unveiling an outward mystery.

مجرد كشف الأسرار الطبيعية، فهو علم الإشارة وعالم المثال.

وإن أفاد الحقيقة نفسها، وعبر إلى واقع تحققها كما هي، فهو علم الحقيقة وعالم العقل.

والحمد لله رب العالمين.

Chapter 7

The Universal Worlds and the Five Presences

You have come to know that divine paths are a single luminous reality but multiple in manifestation, according to the language of its people as they would express it.

He who speaks concerning the material world, speaks [the language of] expression, which emanates from a hidden, treasured light in the ancient knowledge of God.

He who speaks concerning the Imaginal world, speaks [the language of] allusion, which emanates from a hidden, treasured light in the ancient knowledge of God.

He who speaks concerning the Intellectual world, speaks [the language of] reality, which emanates from a hidden, treasured light in the ancient knowledge of God.

If you have come to know this, then know that the aforementioned types of knowledge relate to creation and not divinity since the

الباب السابع

العوالم الكلية والحضرات الخمسة

قد علمتَ أن الطرق الإلهية حقيقة نورية واحدة متعددة المظاهر على لسان أهلها، وما ينطقون به: فمنهم: من ينطق لسانه بالعالم المادي يفاض عن نورٍ مخزونٍ مكنونٍ في سابقِ علمٍ ينطق بالعبارة ومنهم: من ينطق لسانه بالعالم المثالي يفاض عن نورٍ مخزونٍ مكنونٍ في سابقِ علمٍ ينطق بالإشارة. ومنهم: من ينطق لسانه بالعالم العقلي يفاض عن نورٍ مخزونٍ مكنونٍ في سابقِ علمٍ ينطق بالحقيقة.

إذا علمت هذا فاعلم أن ما ذكرناه من العلوم المذكورة إنما يتعلق بالشؤون الكونية دون الشؤون الإلهية وإلا العوالم الكلية والحضرات خمس أو ست على ما ستعلم، مثلها مثل الشجرة في الحبة، التي تجليها وتعينها لنفسها - أي الحبة - من دون لحاظ الجذر والساق والغصن والورق وغير

universal worlds and divine planes are five or six, as you will realize. It is like a tree in the seed manifesting in and of itself, without taking into consideration its roots, trunk, branches, leaves and so forth. Since it is undifferentiated, possessing neither rational division or existential multiplicity, it is the first individuation.

The seed then manifests in the form of a root, trunk, branch, leaf and so forth so that you see the part within the whole. There exists a rational division even though there is no multiplicity in existence itself; this is the second individuation.

The first degree which is devoid of any relative rational division, outward existential multiplicity, annihilated in the singularity of the Essence relates to the Essence, which is the unseen of the Unseen, the first Unseen and the first individuation. It is called the Singular Essence for it is pure singularity and there is no distinction between the Kingdom and Dominion nor between the Dominion and the Invincibility, nor between the Invincibility and the divine degree which is the degree of the Singular Essence.

The second degree is called the Permanent Archetypes (*al-aʿyān al-thābita*) in the terminology of the gnostics, quiddities in the terminology of the philosophers. It is the second Unseen, the second individuation and the degree of Unity. The Archetypes at this degree do not manifest in themselves nor to their likes. This is why it is called the second Unseen, except that is has an Intellectual existence so it manifests as relative multiplicity, which is a mental construct, whereas the first degree is completely absorbed and obliterated in the Essence.

The third degree is the manifestation of immaterial, simple realities, the universal, immaterial, intellects and souls. It is the degree of the spirits and is also called the relative Unseen. Realities in this degree are perceptible and distinct with respect to their essences and their likes.

The fourth degree is the Imaginal realm, the absolute Imagination and the discontinuous Imagination, the intermediary realm and

ذلك، فليس للأشياء هناك تميز علمي ولا تعدد وجودي. وهو التعين الأول.

وتتجلى الحبة لنفسها على شكل جذر وساق وغصن وورق وغير ذلك لتشاهد المفصل في المجمل، فيكون لها تميز علمي وإن لم يكن له تعدد وجودي عيني، وهو التعين الثاني.

فالمرتبة الأولى الخالية من التميز العلمي النسبي والتعدد الوجودي العيني الخارجي واستهلاكها في أحدية الذات، هي الشؤون الذاتية، وهي غيب الغيب و الغيب الأول والتعين الأول، وتسمى بأحدية الذات، فهي وحدة صرفة، لا يتميز فيها الملك عن الملكوت، ولا الملكوت عن الجبروت، ولا الجبروت عن اللاهوت الذي هو مرتبة أحدية الذات

والمرتبة الثانية تسمى بالأعيان الثابتة باصطلاح العرفاء، والماهيات باصطلاح الفلاسفة، وهي الغيب الثاني، والتعين الثاني، ومرتبة الواحدية. والأعيان في هذه المرتبة لا تظهر لنفسها ولا لأمثالها، ولهذا سميت بالغيب الثاني إلا أن لها وجودا علميا فتظهر الكثرة النسبية التي هي كثرة اعتبارية، غير المرتبة الأولى التي تكون فيها مندرجة ومندكة في الذات.

أما المرتبة الثالثة: فهي مرتبة ظهور الحقائق المجردة البسيطة أي العقول والنفوس الكلية المجردة، وهي مرتبة الأرواح، وتسمى بالغيب المضاف أيضاً. والحقائق في هذه المرتبة مدركة ومميزة لا عيانها وأمثالها.

وأما المرتبة الرابعة: وهي مرتبة المثال والخيال المطلق والخيال المنفصل و البرزخ ولاحد الاعتبارات الغيب المضاف، وهي مرتبة ظهور المعاني في قوالب محسوسة كظهور العلم في صورة اللبن، والثبات في الدين في صورة القيد وغير ذلك. فهذه الصور رغم تميزها ببعض خصوصيات الأجسام إلا أنها

is one of perspectives of the relative Unseen. It is the degree of the manifestation of meaning in a perceptible vessels, such as knowledge appearing in the form of milk and steadfastness in religion in the form of a prison, and so forth. Even if these forms have some of the properties of physical bodies, they are not susceptible to division, separation, perforation, or cohesion, because they exist in meaning in subtle worlds.

The fifth degree is the degree of the sensory and the visible, the existence of bodies, and dense worlds, which is capable of division and partition.

The sixth degree is the comprehensive degree that contains every other degree and is the reality of the perfect human.

The first and second degrees are considered one. Thus the degrees are limited to five and are called five [divine] planes, each of which contains a world:

The plane of the absolute Unseen: Its world is the Permanent Archetypes.

The absolute Visible: Its world is the Kingdom.

The relative Unseen which is proximate to the absolute Unseen. Its world is the world of spirits of the Invincible and the Dominion, that is, the world of Intellects and souls.

The relative Unseen which is proximate to the absolute Visible, whose world is the Imaginal and the absolute and disconnected Imagination, is the intermediary world between that of the spirits and bodies.

The comprehensive plane which includes all that has preceded is the human world.

Jāmī writes in *Naqd al-nuṣūṣ*, "There is nothing in Being except a single individuation, which is the existence of God, the Absolute and His reality. He is the only witnessed existent. However, this singular Reality and unified Essence has degrees of manifestation whose distinctions and individuations never cease. The universals of

غير قابلة للتجزئة والتبعيض والخرق والالتئام كما أنها في المعنى أكوان لطيفة.

المرتبة الخامسة: مرتبة الحس والشهادة، وهي مرتبة وجود الأجسام والأكوان الكثيفة، والتي هي قابلة للتجزئة والتبعيض.

المرتبة السادسة: وهي المرتبة الجامعة لجميع المراتب، التي هي حقيقة الإنسان الكامل.

وتعتبر المرتبة الأولى والثانية مرتبة واحدة، فتنحصر المراتب في خمسة تدعى بالحضرات الخمس لكل حضرة عالم وهي:

- حضرة الغيب المطلق، وعالمها عالم الأعيان الثابتة.

- حضرة الشهادة المطلقة، وعالمها عالم الملك.

- حضرة الغيب المضاف، القريب من الغيب المطلق، وعالمها عالم الأرواح الجبروتية والملكوتية، أي عالم العقول والنفوس.

- حضرة الغيب المضاف، القريب من الشهادة المطلقة، وعالمها عالم المثال والخيال المطلق والمنفصل، وهو عالم البرزخ المتوسط بين عالم الأرواح وعالم الاجسام

- الحضرة الجامعة، وهي الجامعة لما تقدم، وعالمها العالم الإنساني.

قال الجامي في نقد النصوص: ما في الوجود إلا عين واحدة، هي عين الوجود الحق المطلق وحقيقته، وهو الموجود المشهود لا غير. ولكن هذه الحقيقة الواحدة والعين الأحدية لها مراتب ظهور لا تتناهى أبداً في التعين والتشخص. ولكن كليات هذه المراتب منحصرة في خمس، اثنان منها منسوبتان إلى الحق سبحانه، وثلاث منسوبة إلى الكون، وسادسها هي الحضرة الجامعة بينها.

وذلك لأن هذه المراتب لما كانت مظاهر ومجالي، فلا تخلو: إما أن تكون

these degrees are limited to five, two of which are affiliated with the divine and three of which are affiliated with creation, and the sixth is the comprehensive degree. That is because these degrees, being theophanies and manifestations, are either a locus of theophany and manifestation for God alone, and not for the entities in creation, or a locus for both God and creation.

The former is called the degree of the Unseen since every existing thing is hidden in it from itself and from others. It has no [outward] manifestation except for God Himself.

Entities cease manifesting in two instances: their Archetypes cease entirely, indicated by, 'There was God and nothing else was with Him.' Their manifestation ceases in knowledge and reality by the cessation of their Archetype. This theophany is called the first individuation and the first degree of the Unseen.

The second instance is when the qualities of manifestation no longer exist even though the Archetypes themselves subsist and are distinct in the eternal divine knowledge, as is the case for images existing in our minds. This theophany and manifestation is the second individuation, the world of meaning, the second degree which is generally called the Unseen, as mentioned earlier.

There are three types of theophany and manifestation that occur for creation, in knowledge and reality: Either for entities simple in essence, called the degree of spirits, or for compound entities. Compound entities are either subtle and not susceptible to division, separation, perforation and cohesion, called the degree of the Imagination, or they are compound and dense relatively, and susceptible to division, separation, perforation and cohesion, called the visible and world of bodies. The true complete human being encompasses all of them. We have now summarized the division of the universal degrees, with God's help."[1]

---

1 Jāmī, *Naqd al-nuṣūṣ*, p. 43.

مجلى ومظهرا يظهر فيه ما يظهر للحق سبحانه وحده، لا للأشياء الكونية، أو تكون مظهرا يظهر فيه ما يظهر للحق وللأشياء الكونية أيضاً.

فالأول يسمى مرتبة الغيب، لغيبة كل شيء كوني فيها عن نفسه وعن مثله. فلا ظهور لشي فيها إلا للحق تعالى.

وانتفاء الظهور للأشياء يكون بأحد وجهين: أحدهما: بانتفاء أعيانها بالكلية - حيث كان الله ولا شيء معه - فينتفي الظهور لها علما ووجدانا لانتفاء أعيانها بالكلية. وذلك المجلى هو التعين الأول والمرتبة الأولى من الغيب.

والوجه الثاني: بانتفاء صفة الظهور للأشياء عن أعيان الأشياء مع تحققها وتميزها وثبوتها في العلم الأزلي وظهورها للعالم بها - لا لأنفسها وأمثالها -كما هو الأمر في الصور الثابتة في أذهاننا. وهذا المجلى والمظهر هو التعين الثاني وعالم المعاني والمرتبة الثانية ويعمها اسم الغيب كما ذكرنا.

وإما ما يكون مجلى يظهر فيه ما يظهر للأشياء الكونية أيضاً علما ووجدانا فهو ثلاثة أقسام: فانه إما أن يكون مظهرا ومجلى يظهر فيه ما يظهر للأشياء الكونية الموجودة البسيطة في ذاتها، فذلك يسمى مرتبة الأرواح، أو مظهرا ومجلى يظهر فيه ما يظهر للأشياء الموجودة المركبة، فتلك الأشياء الموجودة المركبة: إما أن تكون لطيفة - بحيث لا تقبل التجزئة والتبعيض والخرق والالتئام - فمجلاها ومحل ظهورها ومحل الظهور لها يسمى مرتبة المثال.

وإما أن تكون الموجودات المركبة كثيفة بالنسبة إلى تلك اللطائف - أو على الحقيقة بحيث تقبل التجزئة والتبعيض والخرق والالتئام - فمجلاها ومحل صفة ظهور ما يظهر لها فيه يسمى مرتبة الحس وعالم الشهادة وعالم الأجسام. والإنسان الحقيقي الكامل جامع للجميع. وقد انحصرت أقسام المراتب الكلية بعون الله.[١]

---

١ - مقدمة نقد النصوص/ ٤٣.

Qayṣarī writes, "The relative Unseen is divided into the two categories because spirits have imaginal forms corresponding to the Absolute Visible world, and an Intellectual, immaterial form corresponding to the Absolute Unseen.

The world of Kingdom is a manifestation of the Dominion, which is the Absolute Imaginal World, which in turn is a manifestation of the world of the Invincibility, that is, the world of immaterial beings, and it is a manifestation of the Permanent Archetypes, which is a manifestation of the world of divine names and the plane of Unity, which is a manifestation of the plane of the Singularity."[2]

Praise be to God, Lord of the worlds.

2 *Muqaddimat al-Qayṣarī 'ala fuṣūṣ al-ḥikam*, ed. Ḥasanzāde Āmūlī, p. 111.

قال القيصري: وإنما انقسم الغيب المضاف إلى قسمين، لأن للأرواح صورا مثالية مناسبة لعالم الشهادة المطلقة،وصورا عقلية مجردة، مناسبة للغيب المطلق.

فعالم الملك مظهر عالم الملكوت، وهو العالم المثالي المطلق، وهو مظهر عالم الجبروت، أي عالم المجردات، وهو مظهر عالم الأعيان الثابتة، وهو مظهر الأسماء الإلهية والحضرة الواحدية، وهي مظهر الحضرة الأحدية[٢].

والحمد لله رب العالميـن.

٢ - مقدمة القيصري على فصوص الحكم/ تحقيق حسـن زاده آملي/ ص ١١١.

Chapter 8

The Form and Contents of the Intellect

The Intellect is the foundation and source of all existential matters and those concerning divine Law. Upon it rests the creation of man, his divine responsibility and attainment to the highest degree and loftiest station, which is the degree and the station of the Intellect. God created it and desired it after freeing it from the fetters of materiality, Imagination and its self so that it would gaze upon the light of its Lord, just as He had originally created and adorned it.

The Prophet said, "God created the Intellect from a hidden, treasured light in His ancient knowledge, of which neither a sent messenger nor a proximate angel had any awareness. He made knowledge its soul, understanding its spirit, abstinence its head, modesty its eyes, wisdom its tongue, compassion its concern, mercy its heart. Then He adorned it and strengthened it with ten things: certainty, faith, truthfulness, serenity, sincerity, companionship, generosity,

الباب الثامن

صورة العقل وحشوه

العقل أساس الأمر التكويني والتشريعي ومرجعه، وعليه يترتب خلق الإنسان وتكليفه وبلوغه أعلى المراتب وارفع الدرجات، التي هي درجة العقل ومرتبته، كما خلقه الله واريد منه بعد التحرر من قيود المادة والمثال ونفسه، فينظر بنور ربه كما خلقه أول مرة وحشاه.

قال النبي ﷺ:«إن الله خلق العقل من نور مخزون مكنون في سابق علمه، الذي لم يطَّلع عليه نبيٌ مرسل ولا ملكٌ مقرب، فجعل العلمَ نفسه، والفهم روحه، والزهد راسه، والحياء عينه، والحكمة لسانه، والرأفة همّه، والرحمة قلبه، ثم حشاه وقواه بعشرة أشياء: باليقين والإيمان، والصدق، والسكينة، والإخلاص، والرفق، والعطية، والقنوع، والتسليم، والشكر، ثم قال عز

contentment, submission and gratitude. Then He commanded it to go back so the Intellect went back. Then God commanded it to draw near, so it drew near. Then He said, 'Speak!' It said, 'Praise be to God who does not have an opposite, nor equal, nor similar, nor substitute, nor equivalent, before whom all things are humble and abased.

God, the Almighty said, 'By My Might and Majesty, I have not created anything better than you, nor more obedient to me, nor loftier, nor nobler nor more honorable than you. By you I impose, I bestow, I am acknowledged as One, worshipped, called upon, hoped for, yearned for, feared and warned against. Reward is through you and punishment is through you.'"[1]

This is the form of the Intellect and its substance. It is the first of God's creation, so He did not gaze upon any other. None gained awareness of its reality and it did not see any but God. That is how it was and will be.

It is for these and other attributes that the Intellect became the criterion, the principle of the law, the scale of justice, the way of truth, the straight path. Indeed, it is the perfect and complete manifestation of it. It is the medium of divine grace and bestowal to all that is below it. The inferior does not arrive except by Intellect's grace and by ascending towards it, subsisting after having been annihilated in it, assuming its image, having been painted by its brush, created by its hand, adorned by its qualities, realized by its reality, as it had been by God.[2]

He who occupies this station is in need of the Intellect and cannot depart from this state. Rather, a being that is not illuminated by its light is in darkness and without its spirit is dead. Nothing has significance other than the significance bestowed by it.

---

1 Cited previously.

2 The relationship between the attributes and the Intellect is analogous to the relationship between God and the Intellect.

وجل ادبر فادبر، ثم قال له: اقبل فاقبل، ثم قال له: تكلم.

فقال: الحمد لله الذي ليس له ضد ولا ند ولا شبيه ولا كفؤ ولا عديل ولا مثل، الذي كل شيء لعظمته خاضع ذليل.

فقال الرب تبارك وتعالى: وعزتي وجلالي ما خلقت خلقا أحسن منك، ولا أطوع لي منك، ولا ارفع منك، ولا اشرف منك، ولا اعز منك، بك أؤخذ، وبك اعطي، وبك أوحد، وبك اعبد، وبك ادعى، وبك ارتجى، وبك ابتغى، وبك أخاف، وبك احذر، وبك الثواب، وبك العقاب»[١].

تلك صورة العقل وحشوها، وهو أول ما خلق الله فلم ينظر إلى غيره، ولم يطلع أحدا على حقيقته، ولم ينظر هو إلى غير الله، وعلى ذلك كان، وهو على ما كان.

لهذه الأوصاف وغيرها جرت له المقادير وسنت الأحكام، وصار ميزان العدل، والطريق الحق، والصراط المستقيم. بل هو المظهر الكامل التام لها، وواسطة الفيض والعطاء لما دونه. ولا يبلغ الأدون إلا بالتلقي عنه، والترقي إليه، والبقاء بعد الفناء فيه، فيكون على صورته، ويرسم بقلمه، ويخلق بيديه، ويتخلق بأخلاقه، ويتحقق بحقيقته، كما هو لله تعالى.[٢]

فمن كانت هذه منزلته لا يستغنى عنه، ولا يترك شانه. بل الخلق دون نوره ظلام، ومن غير روحه موت، ولا معنى لهم من غير معناه.

١ - سبق تخريجه.

٢ - أي كما أن نسبة العقل لله كذلك للأدون من الصفات المذكورة.

As such, it is necessary for the Intellect's light to dawn upon the human being and all that it entails and encompasses. Its spirit must infuse the human kingdom because all beings are created by its reality under the aegis of its light, spirit and meaning. God has not made it and its substance like an opaque wall which has neither movement nor reflective properties and is dark and lifeless.

One must perceive its light, spirit and meaning in every thought, idea, and sensation in the form that it occurs so that one may attain God and witness reality. This cannot be achieved by the speculative intellect since it is devoid of light, spirit and meaning in the actual divine form and the true, original plane of being.

If you have come to know this then know that Intellect is other than knowledge. So long as the Intellect does not govern through the reality upon which it was created, becoming actualized in itself and for others, knowledge alone cannot perceive the realities of perfection and reach the aspirations of the chivalrous.

Imam ʿAlī says, "He whose knowledge surpasses his Intellect is ruined."[3]

He also said, "Intellect will never drive one mad but knowledge without intellect will drive one mad."[4]

He said, "All knowledge that does not lead to the Intellect is misguidance."[5]

Finally, we ask God for success, support, mercy and grace. All praise be to God, the Lord of the Worlds.

---

3 *Ghurar al-ḥikam*, hadith no. 8601.

4 *Sharḥ Nahj al-balāgha*, v. 20, 323, 702.

5 *Ghurar al-ḥikam*, hadith no. 8601.

وعلى ذلك لابد من بزوغ نوره على الإنسان وما يلزمه وما يحيط به، وسريان روحه في كيانه، إذ الخلق دون نوره وروحه ومعناه من عين حقيقته التي منها خلق ، وما جعل الله له وحشاه كصورة جدارية ظلمانية لا حركة لها أو صورة مرآتية ظلمانية لا حياة فيها.

وعليه لابد من إدراك نوره وروحه ومعناه في كل معقول ومتصور و محسوس على الصورة التي هو عليها لبلوغ الحق وشهود الحقيقة. وهذا مما لا يتحصل للعقل الكسبي لافتقاره للنور والروح والمعنى بالصورة الإلهية الحقة، والنشأة الحقيقية الأولى.

وإذا علمت هذا فاعلم أن العقل غير العلم، فليس بالعلم وحده تدرك حقائق الكمال وتنال مقاصد الرجال ما لم يحكم العقل بحقيقته التي خلق عليها، ويتحقق بها عن نفسه وغيره.

قال أمير المؤمنين ﷺ: من زاد علمه على عقله كان وبالا عليه[٣].

وقال ﷺ: العقل لم يجن على صاحبه قط، والعلم من غير عقل يجني على صاحبه[٤].

و قال ﷺ: كل علم لا يؤيده عقل مضلة.[٥]

وأخيرا نسأل الله التوفيق والسداد، والرحمة والفضل،

والحمد لله رب العالمين.

---

٣ - غرر الحكم/ ح٨٦٠١.

٤ - شرح نهج البلاغة/ ٢٠/ ٣٢٣/ ٧٠٢.

٥ - غرر الحكم/ ٦٨٦٩.

Chapter 9

The Form and Contents of the Soul

The soul is an isthmus between the immaterial and material,[1]

---

1 Shaykh al-Āmulī says, "Since the rational soul is the comprehensive isthmus between the similar and dissimilar, the dividing line straddling the material and immaterial, it has two sides, each resembling that which corresponds to its world. Due to this correspondence, it is capable of knowing the existential reality of every divine name and an Intellectual world equivalent to the world itself, as God says, "We taught Adam all of the Names" and as Ṣadr al-Dīn al-Qūnawī states in *Mafātiḥ al-ghayb*, "It does not seek other than a correspondence which comprehends both sides. It partakes in each by removing distinctions, but not in an absolute sense, rather one that corresponds to each in its own right and in the aspect of correspondence. Each correspondence is fixed between the seeker and the sought, a subtle isthmus between them, extending its governance and form, sometimes on one side and at times on both sides. *Misbāḥ al-uns*, p. 95.

الباب التاسع

صورة النفس وحشوها

النفس برزخ بين المجرد و المادي[1]، تحُكَم بمن توجهت إليه، وقد تنشأُ

---

١ - قال الشيخ الاملي: ولما كانت النفس الناطقة برزخا جامعا بين المقارن والمفارق، وحداً فاصلاً متوسطاً بين المادي والمجرد، كانت لها جهتان تشبه بكل واحد منهما ما يناسب عالمها، وبتلك المناسبة قابلة لأن تصير عالمة بحقائق الأسماء الوجودية كلها، وعالما عقليا مضاهيا للعالم العيني، قوله علت كلمته ﴿ وَعَلَّمَ آدَمَ الْأَسْمَاءَ كُلَّهَا ﴾ وكما في مفاتيح الغيب للصدر الدين القونوي: لا يطلب شيء غيره دون مناسبة وهي أمر جامع بينهما، يشتركان فيه اشتراكا يوجب رفع الامتياز لا مطلقا بل من جهة ما يضاهي به كل منهما ذلك الأمر الجامع ومن حيث يشتركان فيه، ولكل مناسبة ثابتة بين طالب ومطلوب رقيقة بينهما هي مجرى حكمها وصورته، وتحدث تارة مع احد الطرفين وأخرى مع كليهما. / مصباح الأنس/ ص٩٥/ ط١.

and governed by the object of its orientation. It may arise as a new creation after acquiring knowledge, deeds, sincerity, intellect, mercy and grace. It cannot reach even a single perfection without the Intellect and the effulgence of its light upon it, emanating from the light of the hidden, treasured, ancient knowledge of God. [The soul] thereby knocks on the door of safety, disembarks and takes residence in the abode of nobility and the place of permanence, renouncing the urge to commit evil, —"I do not absolve my soul, for the soul incites to evil, except in that which my Lord has shown mercy. My Lord is All-forgiving, All-merciful" (12:53), — illuminates the types of darkness which have covered it, its illicit exhortations and weak prohibitions, makes its inner heart empty of all but the command of the Intellect. It forbids its trivialities which have blinded its vision and covered its sight whence it fumbled in the dark, unable to differentiate between correct and incorrect, truth and falsehood, permissible and forbidden, but now sees its ultimate goal and highest aim. [This occurs] by encountering and obeying the speech of the two prophets[2] and the two vicegerents of the inward and outward realms, each of which cannot do without the other. Deduction and imitation in the outward is of

---

It is said that Prophet Solomon relates some elegant words of Empedocles, the divine sage who lived in the Levant at the time of David, and obtained wisdom from Luqmān, the Wise. Concerning the middle, the human soul, Empedocles says, as cited by Shahrazūrī in *Nuzhat al-arwāḥ* "Whoever seeks knowledge from above—the first substance—finds it difficult to grasp, and whoever seeks knowledge from below, finds it difficult to comprehend sublime knowledge due to the problem of conveying the utterly insubstantial from the dense. Thus, he who seeks it from the middle, and knows it to its fullest, attains knowledge of both aspects and his seeking becomes effortless." After relating this Shahrazūrī says, "These wondrous words cannot be appreciated except by one who fathoms the middle, namely, the human soul" Shahrazūrī, *Nuzhat al-arwāḥ*, v. 1 p. 53, see also *Sharḥ al-manẓūma*, v. 2, pp. 40-41.

2 The Prophet and the Intellect.

خلقا جديدا من بعد علم وعمل وإخلاص وعقل ورحمة وفضل، وليس ثَمَّ كمال تبلغه إلا بحكم العقل وبزوغ نوره عليها المتجلي من عين النور المخزون المكنون في سابق علم الله، لتطرقَ باب السلامة وتنزل وتقيم في دار الكرامة ومحل الإقامة، تاركة ورائها الأمر بالسوء،﴿ مَا أُبَرِّئُ نَفْسِي إِنَّ النَّفْسَ لَأَمَّارَةٌ بِالسُّوءِ إِلَّا مَا رَحِمَ رَبِّي إِنَّ رَبِّي غَفُورٌ رَّحِيمٌ ﴾ [يوسف:٥٣]، كاشفة عن الظلمات التي غشيتها، وصيّرت فؤادها فارغا إلا من أمرها المُردي، ونهيها الواهي، فأعمت بصيرتها وأغشت بصرها، حتى عاشت لا تفرق بين صحيح وخطأ، وحق وباطل، وحلال وحرام. بل تراه الغاية القصوى والمقصد ألاسني. ولكن بالتلقي من لساني النبيين[٢] وخليفتي الدارين الظاهر والباطن والطاعة لهما - الذين لا غنى لاحدهما عن الآخر، ولا يستقيم الاجتهاد و

ومن لطائف كلمات الحكيم الرباني انباذقلس (قدس) وكان في زمن داود عليه السلام - وقد أخذ الحكمة عن لقمان الحكيم بالشام، وقيل عن سليمان النبي عليه السلام - ما قاله في تعريف هذا المتوسط - اعني به النفس الإنسانية، وقد نقله الشهرزوري في نزهة الأرواح:

«إن من رام أن يعرف الأشياء من علو - اعني من الجوهر الأول - عسر عليه إدراكها، ومن طلبها من اسفل عسر عليه إدراك العلم الأعلى لانتقاله من جوهر كثيف إلى جوهر في غاية اللطف، ومن طلبها من المتوسط وعرف المتوسط كنه المعرفة أدرك به علم الطرفين وسهل عليه الطلب».

قال الشهرزوري بعد نقل كلامه هذا: وهذا كلام عجيب لا يعرف قدره إلا من عرف المتوسط اعني النفس الإنسانية./ نزهة الأرواح للشهرزوري/ ج١ص٥٣، لاحظ شرح المنظومة ج٢ص٤٠-٤١.

٢ - النبي و العقل

no avail without assistance from the Intellect's lights and its original reality,[3] for all else[4] is walking in darkness, whether in being, in Law, or something else.[5] Finding itself engrossed in calamities, in a state of negativity and clothed in destructive forces, it begins to renounce [its deeds] and it censures itself, "I swear by the reproaching soul" (75:2). It continues to reject its state, censure its qualities, shun them and change from state to state in order to abstain from the cradle of destruction to receive breezes free of desire, "By the soul and order given to it. He inspired [the knowledge of] its wickedness and its rectitude" (91:7-8). It begins its ascent through receiving, drinking from the water of the Law to nourish its being, until it returns tranquil, pleased and pleasing [its Lord], "O tranquil soul, return to your Lord pleased and pleasing [Him]. Enter among my servants, enter My paradise" (89:27-30).[6]

---

3 The reality of the luminous Intellect, namely, that from which it was created, not the acquired intellect.

4 Deduction and blind conformity devoid of divine light.

5 What is inferior to deduction and blind conformity such as supposition and guesswork.

6 Imam 'Alī said, "The most beloved of God's servants is he whom God has assisted against his self, so inwardly he is clad in grief and outwardly he is clothed in fear. The lamp of guidance is burning in his heart and he has removed the garments of desire. He has abandoned all concerns except for one, and having isolated himself for it, has emerged from blindness and left the company of those who follow their passions. He has become the key to the doors of guidance, and the lock for the doors of destruction. Seeing it, he has tread the path, realized its signs and crossed its ocean. He has held fast to the strongest rope and the firmest mountain. His conviction is as bright as the sun." *Nahj al-balāgha*, sermon 87.

He also said, "He revived his Intellect and killed his desires until his body became tenuous and his corporeality became subtle. A brilliant light flashed before him and lighted the way for him, taking him on the path. Successive doors led him to the door of safety and the abode of permanence. His feet

التقليد مع الظاهر دون التسديد بأنوار العقل وحقيقته الأولى[٣]. فانه[٤] مشي في ظلماء، تكليفا وتكوينا سواء، فضلا عن غيره[٥] - تجد نفسها وتعرف حالها منغمسة بالمرديات، متلبسة بالمهلكات، فيغلب رفضها ويحكم لومها،﴿ وَلَا أُقْسِمُ بِالنَّفْسِ اللَّوَّامَةِ ﴾ [القيامة/ ٢]. ولا يزال الرفضُ حالها، واللوم وصفها يجنبها ويقلبها لتتجافى عن مضاجع الردى، وتتعرض للنفحات دون الهوى،﴿ وَنَفْسٍ وَمَا سَوَّاهَا ۞ فَأَلْهَمَهَا فُجُورَهَا وَتَقْوَاهَا ﴾ [الشمس:٧-٨]. فتنزل منزل الترقي بالتلقي. مستسقية بماء الشرع لنبتة وجودها. حتى ترجع مطمئنة راضية مرضية.﴿ يَا أَيَّتُهَا النَّفْسُ الْمُطْمَئِنَّةُ ۞ارْجِعِي إِلَى رَبِّكِ رَاضِيَةً مَّرْضِيَّةً ۞ فَادْخُلِي فِي عِبَادِي۞ وَادْخُلِي جَنَّتِي ﴾ [الفجر:٢٧-٣٠].[٦]

---

٣ - أي حقيقة العقل النورية لمن خلق منها دون العقل الكسبي.

٤ - أي الاجتهاد و التقليد من غير النور الإلهي.

٥ - مما هو دون الاجتهاد و التقليد كالظنون و التخمينات و غيرها.

٦ - قال أمير المؤمنين عليه السلام: «إن من أحب عباد الله إليه عبد أعانه الله على نفسه، فاستشعر الحزن وتجلبب الخوف، فظهر مصباح الهدى في قلبه قد خلع سرابيل الشهوات، وتخلى من الهموم إلا هما واحدا انفرد به، فخرج من صفة العمى ومشاركة أهل الهوى، وصار من مفاتيح أبواب الهدى ومغاليق أبواب الردى قد أبصر طريق وسلك سبيله وعرف مناره وقطع غماره، واستمسك من العرى بأوثقها، ومن الجبال بأمتنها، فهو من اليقين على مثل ضوء الشمس./ نهج البلاغة / ١/ ١٥١-١٥٢.

وفي كلام له عليه السلام: قد أحيا عقله، وأمات نفسه حتى دق جليله ولطف غليظه، وبرق له لامع كثير البرق، فأبان له الطريق، وسلك به السبيل، وتدافعته الأبواب إلى باب السلامة، ودار الإقامة، وثبتت رجلاه بطمأنينة بدنه في قرار الأمن والراحة بما استعمل قلبه وارضي ربه. نهج البلاغة/ / ٢٠٤.

The soul is not guided on the straight path nor the steadfast way without light, which is identical to the Intellect and its reality, its spirit and breath, "Is he who was dead and We revived, having given him a light by which he walks amongst people, like one who is in inexorable darkness? Thus, the deeds of the unbelievers are made to seem alluring to them" (6:122). The soul ascends on the ladder of perfection, attached to the Intellect which illuminates it, adorned by its virtues, actualized by its reality, created anew by its hidden, treasure light and inscribed by its pen. It makes knowledge its soul, understanding its spirit, abstinence its head, modesty its eye, wisdom its tongue, compassion its concern, mercy its heart, just as God had made the Intellect. It fills and strengthens it by ten things as God filled and strengthened the Intellect: Certainty, faith, truthfulness, tranquillity, sincerity, gentleness, generosity, contentment, submission and thankfulness.

The Intellect says to [the soul] what God said to it, since [the soul] is its manifestation and theophany. [The soul's] nature is from [the Intellect's] nature and its creation is from *its* creation.

---

became firm by the tranquility of his body in a place of safety and comfort, insofar as he used his heart and pleased his Lord." *Nahj al-balāgha*, sermon 219.

He also said, "The knowledge of realities rushes upon them so they feel the joy that arises from conviction. They take easily what the opulent regard as difficult. They endear towards that which the ignorant feel averse. They live in this world with their bodies but their spirits are suspended from high above. They are the vicegerents of God on His earth and the callers to His religion." (*Nahj al-balāgha*, hadith no. 147).

Fayḍ Kashanī writes in *al-Wāfī*: What is meant in, "They take easily what the opulent regard as difficult" is that they reject bodily desires and cut of worldly attachments which are a result of silence, keeping vigils, hunger, mindfulness and abstention from every meaningless thing. This is easy for one who renounces the realm of deception and ascends to the world of light and divine proximity, one who is estranged from all but God and makes Him his solitary concern.

فليس للنفس الهَدْي إلى الصراط المستقيم و الطريق القويم إلا بالنور، الذي هو عين العقل وحقيقته، وروحه ونفخه،﴿ أَوَمَن كَانَ مَيْتًا فَأَحْيَيْنَاهُ وَجَعَلْنَا لَهُ نُورًا يَمْشِي بِهِ فِي النَّاسِ كَمَن مَّثَلُهُ فِي الظُّلُمَاتِ لَيْسَ بِخَارِجٍ مِّنْهَا كَذَٰلِكَ زُيِّنَ لِلْكَافِرِينَ مَا كَانُوا يَعْمَلُونَ ﴾ [الأنعام:١٢٢]، يبزغ عليها لينيرها، فتعرج متدرجة في سلم الكمال، متعلقة به، متخلقة بأخلاقه، متحققة بحقيقته، مخلوقة من نوره المخزون المكنون خلقا جديدا، مصورة بقلمه على صورته، ليجعل العلم نفسها، والفهم روحها، والزهد راسها، والحياء عينها، والحكمة لسانها، والرأفة همها، والرحمة قلبها، كما جعل الله تعالى له. ويحشيها ويقويها بعشرة أشياء، كما حشاه وقواه:

باليقين، والإيمان، والصدق، والسكينة، والإخلاص، والرفق، والعطية، والقنوع، والتسليم، والشكر.

ويقول لها كما قال الله تعالى له، فإنها مظهره ومجلاه، خُلقها من خُلقه، وخَلقها من خَلقه:

وقال عليه السلام: هجم بهم العلم على حقائق الأمور، وباشروا رَوح اليقين، واستلانوا ما استوعره المترفون، وانسوا بما استوحش منه الجاهلون، وصحبوا الدنيا بأبدان أرواحها معلقة بالمحل الأعلى. أولئك خلفاء الله في ارضه والدعاة إلى دينه آه آه شوقا إلى رؤيتهم./ نهج البلاغة/ ٤ / ٣٨.

قال الفيض الكاشاني في الوافي: أراد عليه السلام بما استوعره المترفون: يعني المتنعمين رفض الشهوات البدنية، وقطع التعلقات الدنيوية، وملازمة الصمت والسهر والجوع والمراقبة والاحتراز عما لا يعني ونحو ذلك، وإنما يتيسر ذلك بالتجافي عن دار الغرور والترقي إلى عالم النور والأنس بالله والوحشة عما سواه وصيرورة الهموم جميعا هما واحدا الخ.

Go forth so it goes forth, draw near so it draws near, since there is but one light, it answers itself in its own question in its own language, for the soul is annihilated in itself and subsists in the Intellect. Thus, it solely responds to it and addresses in the best way saying, "Praise be to the one who does not have an opposite, nor equal, nor similar, nor equal, nor substitute, nor equivalent, and before whom all things are humble and abased."

Then [the Intellect] says what God said to it, "By My Might and Majesty, I have not created anything better than you, nor more obedient to me, nor loftier, nor nobler nor more honorable than you. By you I am taken, given, my acknowledged as One, worshipped, called upon, hoped for, yearned for, feared, cautioned against. Reward is through you and punishment is through you."

He who is governed by the Intellect alone, spreading its light and being encompassed by its light, his soul revels in another plane and a new creation. It embarks from its light and is formed from its form, dwelling in its presence, swimming in the sea of its lights, immersed in the ocean of its brilliance, surrounded by its majestic light, to which no ascending thing can rise,[7] nor envier can envy.[8]

The Prophet said, "The basis of a house is its foundation and the basis of religion is the gnosis of God and certainty, and the majestic Intellect." I asked, "What is the majestic Intellect?" He said, "Desisting from sin and eagerness in obeying God."[9]

All praise be to God, Lord of the worlds.

---

7 The soul's faculties and powers prevent it from ascension and annihilation.

8 Satanic

9 *Risālat al-Qushayriyya*, p. 438.

ادبري فتدبر، اقبلي فتقبل. إذ ليس إلا نور واحد يجيب نفسه من عين سؤاله، ويكون من عين قوله، لفنائها عن نفسها، وبقائها فيه فلا تجيب إلا جوابه، ولا تحسن إلا خطابه: «الحمد لله الذي ليس له ضد ولا ند ولا شبيه ولا كفؤ ولا عديل ولا مثل، الذي كل شيء لعظمته خاضع ذليل».

فيقول لها مقالة الرب تبارك وتعالى: «وعزتي وجلالي، ما خلقت خلقا أحسن منك، ولا أطوع لي منك، ولا أرفع منك، ولا أشرف منك، ولا أعز منك، بك أؤخذ، وبك اعطي، وبك أوحد، وبك أعبد، وبك أدعى، وبك أرتجى، وبك أبتغى، وبك أخاف، وبك أحذر وبك الثواب، وبك العقاب».

فمن حكم العقل نفسه، واستوسعها نورا، وأحاط بها نورا، كان لها معه نشأة أخرى وخلقا جديدا، تبتدع من نوره، وتصور على صورته، وتنزل حضرته، سابحة في بحر أنواره، مستغرقة في يم ضيائه، مسورة بسور نوره القامع، لا يطلع عليها طالع[٧]، ولا يطمع فيها طامع[٨].

قال النبي ﷺ: «إن من دعامة البيت أساسه، ودعامة الدين المعرفة بالله، واليقين، والعقل القامع. فقلت: بأبي و أمي: وما العقل القامع؟ قال: الكف عن المعاصي، والحرص على طاعة الله»[٩].

والحمد لله رب العالمين.

---

٧ – النفس من أعضاء و قوى تمنعها من الرقي و الفناء.

٨ – شيطاني.

٩ – الرسالة القشيرية/ ص ٤٣٨.

Chapter 10

The Form and Contents of the Body

The body is the vessel of the soul and becomes what the soul has become, being affected by it and affecting it. If the soul is illuminated, the body is affected by its light, and if it becomes dark, it is affected by its darkness. When the soul is illuminated by the light of the Intellect, its light spreads into the depths of the human earth so that the body, according to its capacity and receptivity, receives what the soul has received from the Intellect. It realizes the Intellect's light and is painted by its brush, or realizes the soul's light and is painted by *its* brush and becomes a new luminous creation, one that corresponds to the soul and Intellect. Thus, the human being becomes a unified, monotheist by the lights of God, possessing a pure body, chaste soul, sound intellect, and wholesome heart. "Is he who was dead and We revived, having given him a light by which he walks amongst people, like one who is in inexorable darkness? Thus, the deeds of the unbelievers are made to seem alluring to them" (6:122).

الباب العاشر

صورة البدن وحشوه

البدن قالب النفس يكون على ما عليه النفس، يتأثر بها ويؤثر بها، فإن تنورت أصابه من نورها، وان اظلمت أصابه من ظلمتها. فلما استضاءت النفس بنور العقل امتد نوره إلى تخوم الأرض البشرية، ليكون للبدن من العقل - على حسب استعداده وقابليته - ما كان للنفس من العقل، فيتحقق بنوره وينصبغ بصبغته، أو يتحقق بنورها وينصبغ بصبغتها، فينشا خلقا جديدا نورانيا يتناسب و خلقت النفس والعقل، ويصير الإنسان واحدا موحدا بأنوار الله، ذو بدن طاهرا، ونفس زكية، وعقل صحيحا، وقلب سليما، ﴿ أَوَمَن كَانَ مَيْتًا فَأَحْيَيْنَاهُ وَجَعَلْنَا لَهُ نُورًا يَمْشِي بِهِ فِي النَّاسِ كَمَن مَّثَلُهُ فِي الظُّلُمَاتِ لَيْسَ بِخَارِجٍ مِّنْهَا كَذَٰلِكَ زُيِّنَ لِلْكَافِرِينَ مَا كَانُوا يَعْمَلُونَ ﴾ [الأنعام:١٢٢].

The Prophet prayed, "O Allah, place light in my heart, light in my tongue, light in my hearing, light in my sight, light above me, light below me, light on my right, light on my left, light in front of me, light behind me; place light in my soul, make light abundant for me, make light abundant for me; make me light, make me light!

God, grant me light—light in my sinews, light in my flesh, light in my blood, light in my hair and light in my skin! God, grant me light — light in my grave, light in my bones, increase me in light, increase me in light, increase me in light and bestow upon me a light upon light!"[1]

In the Bible, Jesus used to say to the people, "I am the light of the world. Whoever follows me will never tread in darkness, but will have the light of life" [John 8:12].

Since the body is the manifestation of the soul and its vessel, the soul's reality will emerge in the body according to its nature and receptivity. Whatever the Intellect has placed in the soul, it will overflow to the body, so that the body becomes knowledge itself, in the same way the Intellect made the soul knowledge. God made knowledge its the Intellect, understanding its spirit, abstinence its head, modesty is eye, wisdom its tongue, compassion its concern, mercy its heart, then filled it and strengthened it with ten things as the soul was filled and strengthened, in the same way the Intellect was filled and strengthened. The theophany of divine lights extend to the creation of man, from the heaven of the Intellect to the depths of the human earth, accordingly. Thus, the reason for citing the prayer above, namely, were there no possibility for its realization, it would not have been asked. What manifests from the soul is the manifestation it receives from another, it fills below what it is filled with from above, such as certainty, faith, truthfulness, tranquility, sincerity, companionship, giving, contentment, submission, gratitude. It does not withhold manifesting these realities to the body as a corporeal manifestation and material locus in the earthly human frame.

---

1 See hadith no. 763 in *Muslim* and *Musannaf Ibn 'Abd al-Razzāq*, no. 3862.

ولمثل هذا سال النبي ﷺ ربه: «اللهم اجعل في قلبي نورا، وفي لساني نورا، وفي سمعي نورا، وفي بصري نورا، ومن فوقي نورا، ومن تحتي نورا، وعن يميني نورا، وعن شمالي نورا، ومن أمامي نورا، ومن خلفي نورا، واجعل في نفسي نورا، واعظم لي نورا، وعظم لي نورا، واجعل لي نورا، واجعلني نورا.

اللهم اعطني نورا، واجعل في عصبي نورا، وفي لحمي نورا، وفي دمي نورا، وفي شعري نورا، وفي بشري نورا.

اللهم اجعل لي نورا، نورا في قبري، ونورا في عظامي، وزدني نورا، وزدني نورا، وزدني نورا، وهب لي نورا على نور»[1].

و كان عيسى عليه السلام يقول كما في الإنجيل: «أَنَا نُورُ الْعَالَمِ. مَنْ يَتْبَعْنِي فَلاَ يَتَخَبَّطُ فِي الظَّلاَمِ بَلْ يَكُونُ لَهُ نُورُ الْحَيَاةِ» [إنجيل يوحنا/ أنا نور العالم].

ولما كان البدن مظهر النفس وقالبها فحيث تكون حقيقتها يكون له بما يتناسب وخلقته وقابليته. وما جعل لها من العقل يسري منها للبدن، فتجعل العلم نفسه،كما جعل العقل لها ذلك، وكما جعل الله العلم للعقل ، والفهم روحه، والزهد راسه، والحياء عينه، والحكمة لسانه، والرأفة همه، والرحمة قلبه. ثم تحشيه وتقويه بعشرة أشياء كما حشيت هي وتقوت، وكما حشي العقل وتقوى، فان مجالي الأنوار الإلهية تمتد في خلقة الإنسان من سماء العقل إلى تخوم الأرض البشرية كل بحسبه. ولذلك جاء الدعاء المذكور سابقا، ولولا إمكان تحققه لاستحال الطلب، وهكذا النفس يتجلى منها ما تجلى عليها، وتحشي ما دونها ما حشاه فوقها، باليقين، والإيمان، والصدق، والسكينة، والإخلاص، والرفق، والعطية، والقنوع، والتسليم، والشكر، فلا يمتنع تحقق هذه المعاني في البدن مظهرا، أي أن لها مظاهر جسمانية، ومواضع مادية في الهيكل الأرضي الإنساني.

---

١ - لاحظ رواية مسلم/ ٧٦٣، و مصنف إبن عبد الرزاق/ ٣٨٦٢.

Thereafter, by the governance of the emanations of the soul's lights upon the body and its dominance, the body becomes submissive and obedient to its command. It says to the body, as it was said to it beforehand, "Go forth!" so it goes forth, and "Draw near!", so it draws near. "Speak!" but it only speaks by way of realization, in its new, luminous plane of existence: "God makes it speak as He makes all things speak."

Praise be to God who does not have an opposite, nor equal, nor similar, nor equivalent, nor substitute, nor like, before whom all things are humble and abased. "They will say to their skins, 'Why have you testified against us?' They will say, 'God, who has made everything speak, made us speak. He created you the first time and to Him you will return" (41:21).

The body in this luminous state is not surpassed by anything in its world, and likewise there is no better creation than the soul in its world, nor anything better than the Intellect in its world, "He who perfected the creation of all things" (32:7). There is nothing more obedient than the body to the soul than the body after its [new] creation and guidance, "He said, 'Our Lord is He Who gave everything its nature, then guided it aright'" (20:50).

Likewise, there is nothing loftier, nobler and mightier than [the body], through which [blessings] are given and taken, God is acknowledged as one, worshipped, called upon, hoped for, yearned for, feared and warned against. Through it one is rewarded and punished, since it is the manifestation of the workings of the soul and Intellect in the material world. On that basis, the body, like the previous two aspects engages in creating, engendering, adorning and commanding to go forth and draw near, step by step and in stages. Were there another world below the material it would have had the same process and another rebirth and new creation, as the Prophet says quoting Jesus,

ومن ثم بحكم إشراف أنوار النفس على البدن، وغلبت نورها عليه يكون طوعا لها ممتثلا لأمرها، فتقول له ما قيل لها ادبر فيدبر، اقبل فيقبل، تكلم و لا يتكلم إلا من حيث تحققه، ونشأه النوراني الجديد، أنطقه الله الذي أنطق كل شيء.

الحمد لله الذي ليس له ضد ولا ند، ولا شبيه ولا كفؤ ولا عديل ولا مثل، الذي كل شيء لعظمته خاضع ذليل ﴿ وَقَالُوا لِجُلُودِهِمْ لِمَ شَهِدتُّمْ عَلَيْنَا قَالُوا أَنطَقَنَا اللهُ الَّذِي أَنطَقَ كُلَّ شَيْءٍ وَهُوَ خَلَقَكُمْ أَوَّلَ مَرَّةٍ وَإِلَيْهِ تُرْجَعُونَ ﴾ [فصلت/ ٢١].

فالبدن بهذه الخلقة النورية لا أحسن منه في عالمه، كذلك لا أحسن من النفس في عالمها، وفي عالم العقل لا أحسن منه ﴿ الَّذِي أَحْسَنَ كُلَّ شَيْءٍ خَلَقَهُ ﴾ [السجدة/ ٧]، ولا أطوع من البدن للنفس بعد خلقه وهديه، ﴿ قَالَ رَبُّنَا الَّذِي أَعْطَى كُلَّ شَيْءٍ خَلْقَهُ ثُمَّ هَدَى ﴾ [طه/ ٥٠]، كذلك لا أرفع منه ولا أشرف ولا أعز، وبه يؤخذ، وبه يعطى وبه يوحد، وبه يعبد، وبه يدعى، وبه يرتجى، وبه يبتغى، وبه يخاف، وبه يحذر، وبه الثواب وبه العقاب. إذ هو مظهر تصرف النفس والعقل في العالم المادي. وعلى ذلك يكون للبدن ما كان لسابقيه من الخلق والجعل والتحشية والقول، والإقبال والإدبار وغيرها، حذو النعل بالنعل و القذة بالقذة، ولو كان ثم عالم دون المادي لكان منه وله كما كان لغيره، وكان له ولادة أخرى وخلقة جديدة، كما قال النبي ﷺ، عن عيسى عليه السلام: «لن يلج ملكوت السماء من لم يولد مرتين»[٢].

---

٢ - تفسير النيسابوري/ ج٢/ ص٣٥٣.

"He who has not been born twice will never ascend to the heavens."[2]

The Bible says, "Now there was a Pharisee, a man named Nicodemus who was a member of the Jewish ruling council. He came to Jesus at night and said, "Rabbi, we know that you are a teacher who has come from God. For no one could perform the signs you are doing if God were not with him." Jesus replied, "Very truly I tell you, no one can see the kingdom of God unless they are born again." "How can someone be born when they are old?" Nicodemus asked. "Surely they cannot enter a second time into their mother's womb to be born!" Jesus answered, "Very truly I tell you, no one can enter the kingdom of God unless they are born of water and the Spirit. Flesh gives birth to flesh, but the Spirit gives birth to spirit. You should not be surprised at my saying, 'You must be born again.' The wind blows wherever it pleases. You hear its sound, but you cannot tell where it comes from or where it is going. So it is with everyone born of the Spirit." "How can this be?" Nicodemus asked. "You are Israel's teacher," said Jesus, "and do you not understand these things? Very truly I tell you, we speak of what we know, and we testify to what we have seen, but still you people do not accept our testimony. I have spoken to you of earthly things and you do not believe; how then will you believe if I speak of heavenly things? No one has ever gone into heaven except the one who came from heaven—the Son of man who is in heaven [John 3:1-13].

All praise be to God, Lord of the worlds.

---

2 *Tafsīr Nisabūrī*, v. 2, p. 353.

و في الإنجيل: غَيْرَ أَنَّ إِنْسَاناً مِنَ الْفَرِّيسِيِّينَ، اسْمُهُ نِيقُودِيمُوسُ، وَهُوَ عُضْوٌ فِي الْمَجْلِسِ الْيَهُودِيِّ، جَاءَ إِلَى يَسُوعَ لَيْلاً وَقَالَ لَهُ: «يَامُعَلِّمُ، نَعْلَمُ أَنَّكَ جِئْتَ مِنَ اللهِ مُعَلِّماً، لأَنَّهُ لاَ يَقْدِرُ أَحَدٌ أَنْ يَعْمَلَ مَا تَعْمَلُ مِنْ آيَاتٍ إِلاَّ إِذَا كَانَ اللهُ مَعَهُ». فَأَجَابَهُ يَسُوعُ: «الْحَقَّ الْحَقَّ أَقُولُ لَكَ: لاَ أَحَدَ يُمْكِنُهُ أَنْ يَرَى مَلَكُوتَ اللهِ إِلاَّ إِذَا وُلِدَ مِنْ جَدِيدٍ». فَسَأَلَهُ نِيقُودِيمُوسُ: «كَيْفَ يُمْكِنُ الإِنْسَانَ أَنْ يُولَدَ وَهُوَ كَبِيرُ السِّنِّ؟ أَلَعَلَّهُ يَسْتَطِيعُ أَنْ يَدْخُلَ بَطْنَ أُمِّهِ ثَانِيَةً ثُمَّ يُولَدَ؟» أَجَابَهُ يَسُوعُ: «الْحَقَّ الْحَقَّ أَقُولُ لَكَ: لاَ يُمْكِنُ أَنْ يَدْخُلَ أَحَدٌ مَلَكُوتَ اللهِ إِلاَّ إِذَا وُلِدَ مِنَ الْمَاءِ وَالرُّوحِ. فَالْمَوْلُودُ مِنَ الْجَسَدِ هُوَ جَسَدٌ، وَالْمَوْلُودُ مِنَ الرُّوحِ هُوَ رُوحٌ. فَلاَ تَتَعَجَّبْ إِذَا قُلْتُ لَكَ إِنَّكُمْ بِحَاجَةٍ إِلَى الْوِلاَدَةِ مِنْ جَدِيدٍ. الرِّيحُ تَهُبُّ حَيْثُ تَشَاءُ وَتَسْمَعُ صَفِيرَهَا، وَلكِنَّكَ لاَ تَعْلَمُ مِنْ أَيْنَ تَأْتِي وَلاَ إِلَى أَيْنَ تَذْهَبُ. هكَذَا كُلُّ مَنْ وُلِدَ مِنَ الرُّوحِ». فَعَادَ نِيقُودِيمُوسُ يَسْأَلُ: «كَيْفَ يُمْكِنُ أَنْ يَتِمَّ هَذَا؟» أَجَابَهُ يَسُوعُ: «أَنْتَ مُعَلِّمُ إِسْرَائِيلَ وَلاَ تَعْلَمُ هَذَا! الْحَقَّ الْحَقَّ أَقُولُ لَكَ: إِنَّنَا نَتَكَلَّمُ بِمَا نَعْلَمُ وَنَشْهَدُ بِمَا رَأَيْنَا، وَمَعَ ذلِكَ لاَ تَقْبَلُونَ شَهَادَتَنَا. إِنْ كُنْتُ حَدَّثْتُكُمْ بِأُمُورِ الأَرْضِ وَلَمْ تُؤْمِنُوا، فَكَيْفَ تُؤْمِنُونَ إِنْ حَدَّثْتُكُمْ بِأُمُورِ السَّمَاءِ؟ وَمَا صَعِدَ أَحَدٌ إِلَى السَّمَاءِ إِلاَّ الَّذِي نَزَلَ مِنَ السَّمَاءِ، وَهُوَ ابْنُ الإِنْسَانِ الَّذِي هُوَ فِي السَّمَاءِ. [إنجيل يوحنا/ الولادة الجديده من الروح]

والحمد لله رب العالمين.

Chapter 11

Finding and Losing

One seeks knowledge and performs deeds to ascend the stairway to perfection. The journey ends, but not wayfaring, since journeying ends with God, the final end, "To your Lord is your destination" (53:42). Wayfaring, however, is endless since theophanies are endless in any world and station, in whatever mode of seeking and ascension.

If the soul [seeks], it [seeks] itself and that is a loss, since every seeker of the self loses it. He who seeks his self loses it, and he who loses his self finds it, but in reality and knowledge,[1] whether it is in the Intellect, imagination or senses, for all are a single reality. Were it not for the manifestations of reality in the soul transforming it into a new creation, it would never find itself, like one seeking water in a mirage.

---

1 Fayḍ Kāshānī says in *Kalimāt al-maknūna*, "Anything that does not contain Him is non-existent, anything which contains Him is also non-existent because it is annihilated in Him.

الباب الحادي عشر

الوجد والفقد

يَطلبُ الإنسان العلم والعمل به ليرتقي في سُلَّم الكمال فينتهي سيراً لا سلوكاً، إذ السير ينتهى عند الرب وتمام المقام، ﴿ وَأَنَّ إِلَىٰ رَبِّكَ ٱلْمُنتَهَىٰ ﴾ [النجم/ ٤٢]، ولا ينتهي السلوك لأن المجالي لا تنتهي في أي دار ومقام، وكيف ما كان الطلب والارتقاء.

فإن كان من حيث النفس فهو لها وذلك فقد. إذ كل طالب نفسه فاقدها. فمن طلب نفسه فقدها، ومن فقد نفسه وجدها، ولكن بالحقيقة وعلمها[١]، عقليا كان أو مثاليا أو حسيا، فالجميع حقيقة واحدة. ولولا تجلي الحقيقة على النفس، وصيرورتها بها خلقا جديدا لما وجد نفسه أبداً، كمن يطلب الماء في السراب.

١ - قال الفيض الكاشاني في الكلمات المكنونة: أي شيء لم يكن هو فيه، فذلك الشيء غير موجود، وأي شيء كان فيه، فهو أيضاً غير موجود لأنه فان فيه.

The Bible says, "Jesus replied, 'The hour has come for the Son of man to be glorified. Truly, truly, I say to you, a grain of wheat remains alone unless it falls to the earth and dies. But if it dies, it produces many seeds. Whoever holds on to his life loses it, and whoever renounces his life in this world will keep it for eternal life. Whoever desires to serve me, he must follow me; and wherever I am, there my servant will also be. Whoever serves me, my Father will honor him'" (John 12:23-26).

One may lose his self but not his desires, like the smell that remains even after the particles of filth are removed, or in a positive sense, to love another more than oneself since a person is willing to sacrifice himself for his beloved. That is why you will find that trials are quicker to reach the believer. Something is taken in order to be given, even his self, so that you should know that the hand of God is one. The *hadith qudsī* states, "He who seeks Me, finds Me; he who finds Me, comes to know Me; he who comes to know Me, loves Me; he who loves Me, he is enthralled by Me; he who is enthralled by Me, I am enthralled by him; he whom I am enthralled by, I kill him; he whom I kill, I owe him blood-money; he to whom I owe blood-money, I am his blood-money."[2]

Let it be known that the only quest is the quest for Reality; it has a beginning but not an end because your soul becomes it. The first is attachment, then assuming [the divine characteristics],[3] then finally

2 *Mustadrak al-wasā'il*, v. 18, p. 419.

3 Tūsī writes, "If the gnostic detaches from himself and attaches to God he sees every power immersed in His power and attached to everything under His power. He sees all knowledge immersed in His knowledge, before which no object escapes, every intention immersed in His will, against which no contingent thing frustrates. In fact, everything and every perfection emanates from Him and effuses from Him. God becomes his vision by which he sees, his hearing by which he hears, the power by which he moves, the knowledge by which he knows, the being through which he exists. Thus, he becomes a gnostic truly assuming the divine characteristics. (*al-Kāfī*, p. 353; *Sharḥ al-asmā' al-ḥusna*, p. 112

و في الإنجيل: «فَقَالَ يَسُوعُ لَهُمَا: «قَدِ اقْتَرَبَتْ سَاعَةُ تَمْجِيدِ ابْنِ الإِنْسَانِ. الْحَقَّ الْحَقَّ أَقُولُ لَكُمْ: إِنَّ حَبَّةَ الْحِنْطَةِ تَبْقَى وَحِيدَةً إِنْ لَمْ تَقَعْ فِي الأَرْضِ وَتَمُتْ. أَمَّا إِذَا مَاتَتْ، فَإِنَّهَا تُنْتِجُ حَبّاً كَثِيراً. مَنْ يَتَمَسَّكْ بِحَيَاتِهِ، يَخْسَرْهَا. وَمَنْ نَبَذَهَا فِي هَذَا الْعَالَمِ يُوَفِّرُهَا لِلْحَيَاةِ الأَبَدِيَّةِ. مَنْ أَرَادَ أَنْ يَخْدِمَنِي فَلْيَتْبَعْنِي. وَحَيْثُ أَكُونُ أَنَا يَكُونُ خَادِمِي أَيْضاً. وَكُلُّ مَنْ يَخْدِمُنِي يُكْرِمُهُ أَبِي» [إنجيل يوحنا / الموت باب الحياة].

وقد يفقد الإنسان نفسه ولا يفقد شهواته، كرائحة النتانة بعد أزالت جرمها في السلب، ومحبة الأعزة دون نفسه في الإيجاب، فانه قد يضحي بنفسه لا جل من يحب.

ولأجل ذلك تجدُ المؤمن أسرع إلى البلاء، يؤخذ منه ليعطى، ولو نفسه، لتعلم أن يد الله واحدة. وفي الحديث القدسي: «من طلبني وجدني، ومن وجدني عرفني، ومن عرفني أحبني، ومن أحبني عشقني، ومن عشقني عشقته، ومن عشقته قتلته، ومن قتلته فعلي ديته، ومن علي ديته فأنا ديته»[٢].

ولتعلم: انه لا طلب إلا للحقيقة وبها ابتداءا، ويمتنع انتهاءا، لتحقق نفسك بها. فالأول تعلق وتخلق[٣]، والآخر تحقق[٤] ينتهي عنده الطلب كما ينتهي

---

٢ - مستدرك الوسائل/ ١٨/ ٤١٩.

٣ - قال الطوسي: العارف إذا انقطع عن نفسه واتصل بالحق رأى كل قدرة مستغرقة في قدرته المتعلقة بجميع المقدورات، وكل علم مستغرقا في علمه الذي لا يعزب عنه شيء من الموجودات، وكل إرادة مستغرقة في إرادته التي لا يتأبى عنه شيء من الممكنات. بل كل وجود وكل كمال وجود فهو صادر عنه فائض من لدنه، فصار الحق حينئذ بصره الذي به يبصر، وسمعه الذي به يسمع، وقدرته التي بها يفعل، وعلمه الذي به يعلم ووجوده الذي به يوجد، فصار العارف حينئذ متخلقا بأخلاق الله بالحقيقة./ الكافي ٢/ ٣٥٣، وشرح الأسماء الحسنى ٢ / ١١٢.

realization,[4] which is the end of his quest and journeying. Reality is God's secret so whoever tries to find it by other than Him, does not find it and one who worships God [through another] worships the other, no matter how far he reaches in his quest and his worship.

How strange it is to face God through one's own self. How can one orient towards God by other than God and claim to be facing Him with sincerity?

God is not sought except through Himself, and there is nothing other than God. "God was and there was nothing else with Him,"[5] and He is now as He always was. He was a hidden treasure and loved to be known.[6] Thus, none can know Him except through Him; He is one.

---

4 Imam al-Ṣādiq says, "The body of the gnostic is with creation but his heart is with God. Were he to become heedless of God even for the blink of an eye, he would perish out of yearning. The gnostic is the trustee and caller to God. He is the treasure of His secrets, the source of His lights, the guide to His mercy towards His creation, the bearer of His knowledge, the measure of His grace and justice. He is free from creation and worldly aims. He has no confidant save God. He only speaks, indicates and breathes through God, from God, by God and with God. He is reposed in the garden of His sanctity, nourished by the abundance of His grace, with gnosis as the foundation and faith as its branch. (*Misbāḥ al-sharīʿa*, p. 191, *Biḥār al-anwār*, v. 3, p. 14.)

Imam ʿAlī said, "Verily God Almighty has a wine for His friends (*awliyāʾ*), so that when they drink it, they become intoxicated; when they become intoxicated, they delight; when they delight, they melt away; when they melt away, they become pure; when they become pure, they seek; when they seek, they find; when they find, they attain; when they attain they unite, so when they unite, there remains no difference between them and their Beloved." (*al-Dharīʿa*, v. 19, p. 184, *Tuḥfat al-Sannīya*, p. 84).

Imam al-Ṣādiq says, "The spirit of the believer is more connected to the spirit of God than the Sun's rays are connected to the Sun." (*al-Kāfī*, v. 2, p. 116; *Biḥār al-anwār*, v. 81, p. 268).

5 *Biḥar al-anwār*, v. 53, p. 234. Junayd added, "He is now as He was."

6 As stated in the *hadith qudṣī*, "I was a hidden treasure and I loved to be

السير. والحقيقة سر الحق تعالى، فكل من يطلبه مع وجود غيره لا يجده، ومن يعبدُه عَبَدَ غيره، ولو بلغ ما بلغ بطلبه وعبادته.

والعجب لمن يتوجه إلى الله بنفسه، فكيف يتوجه إلى الله بغير الله، ويدعى توجه وإخلاص ؟

بلى لا يطلب الله إلا بالله. فليس إلا الله وحده، «كان الله ولم يكن معه شيء» وهو الآن كما كان[5]، وكان كنزا مخفيا فأحبّ أن يعرف[6]، ولا يُعرف إلا

---

٤ - عن الصادق عليه السلام: العارف شخصه مع الخلق، وقلبه مع الله لو سهى قلبه عن الله طرفة عين لمات شوقا إليه، والعارف أمين ودائع الله وكنز أسراره ومعدن أنواره ودليل رحمته على خلقه ومطية علومه وميزان فضله وعدله، قد غنى عن الخلق والمراد والدنيا، ولا مؤنس له سوى الله ولا نطق ولا إشارة ولا نفس إلا بالله ولله ومن الله ومع الله، فهو في رياض قدسه متردد، ومن لطائف فضله إليه متزود، والمعرفة اصل فرعه الإيمان./ مصباح الشريعة/ ١٩١، وبحار الأنوار/ ٣/ ١٤.

عن أمير المؤمنين عليه السلام: إن لله تعالى شرابا لأوليائه إذا شربوا سكروا، وإذا سكروا طربوا، وإذا طربوا طابوا، وإذا طابوا ذابوا، وإذا ذابوا خلصوا، وإذا خلصوا طلبوا، وإذا طلبوا وجدوا، وإذا وجدوا وصلوا، وإذا وصلوا اتصلوا، وإذا اتصلوا لا فرق بينهم وبين حبيبهم./ الذريعة/ ١٩/ ١٨٤، والتحفة السنية / ٨٤.

وعن الصادق عليه السلام: إن روح المؤمن لأشدّ اتصالا بروح الله من اتصال شعاع الشمس بها./ الكافي ٢/ ١١٦، والبحار / ٧١/ ٢٦٨.

٥ - بحار الأنوار/ ٥٤/ ٢٣٤. وأضاف الجنيد، وهو الآن كما كان.

٦ - حديث قدسي: كنتُ كنزاً مخفياً، فأحْببتُ أن أُعرَف فخلقتُ الخلقَ لكي أُعرف. وفي عبارة أخرى: فخلقت الخلق وتعرفت إليهم فعرفوني.

If something remains in you and you still have something, remember, you have not reached perfection, you have not perceived the farthest limit of seeking, you will not have concluded at your Lord and not attained unity as you ought to have! You will not have realized the reality which you are without yourself, which is true unity, since there is no otherness in divine unity.

Abū ʿAbdallah says, "He who claims to know God through a veil, a form or a similitude is a polytheist, because a veil, form or similitude is other than Him, for He is One, Singular. How can He be Singular if one claims to know Him through something else. Only one who has come to know God through Him knows Him. He who has not come to know Him through Him does not know Him, but only knows other than Him. The creatures do not perceive anything except through God and gnosis of God is not attained except through God.[7]

Imam ʿAlī says, "Know God through God, the messenger through the message and the people of authority through [the commands of] enjoining good, justice and goodwill.[8]

What he means when he says know God through God is that God created people, lights, substances and individuals. Individuals are bodies, substances are spirits, which are magnificent and great that do not resemble bodies or spirits. None has authority or cause for the creation of the sensible, perceiving spirit. He is solitary in creating spirits and bodies.

---

known so I created the creation so that I may become known." In other words, I created the creation and I made myself known to them so they came to know Me.

Absolute Being descends from the empyrean of absoluteness and the condition of [divine] Identity. It manifests in the mirror of the individuations and individual theophanies. This is an allusion to the nature of engendering.

7 *al-Tawḥīd*, p. 143, no. 7.

8 *al-Kāfī: None knows but through Him*, p. 51.

به، هو وحده، فإن بقي فيك ولك شيء يذكر ما بلغت الكمال، ولا أدركت منتهى الطلب، فلم تنتهي إلى الرب ولم تتم التوحيد كما ينبغي لك، وليس تحقيقا للحقيقة التي هي أنت بلا أنت. وهو التوحيد الحقيقي. إذ لا غيرية مع التوحيد.

عن أبي عبد الله عليه السلام: من زعم أنه يعرف الله بحجاب أو بصورة أو بمثال فهو مشرك، لأن الحجاب والمثال والصورة غيره، وإنما هو واحد موحد، فكيف يوحد من زعم انه عرفه بغيره؟ إنما عرف الله من عرفه بالله، فمن لم يعرفه به فليس يعرفه إنما يعرف غيره، لا يدرك مخلوق شيئا إلا بالله، و لا تدرك معرفة الله إلا بالله[٧].

وعنه عليه السلام قال: قال أمير المؤمنين عليه السلام: اعرفوا الله بالله، والرسول بالرسالة، وأولي الأمر بالأمر بالمعروف والعدل والإحسان.[٨]

ومعنى قوله عليه لسلام: اعرفوا الله بالله يعني أن الله خلق الأشخاص والأنوار والجواهر والأعيان، فالأعيان: الأبدان. والجواهر: الأرواح. وهو جل وعز لا يشبه جسما ولا روحا، وليس لاحد في خلق الروح الحساس الدرّاك أمر ولا سبب، هو المتفرد بخلق الأرواح والأجسام، فإذا انتفى عنه الشبهين: شبه الأبدان وشبه الأرواح فقد عرف الله بالله، وإذا شبهه بالروح أو البدن أو النور فلم يعرف الله بالله[٩].

فإن الوجود المطلق تنزل من سماء الإطلاق وقيد الهوية، وتجلي في مرائي التعينات ومجالي التشخصات. إشارة إلى لمية الإيجاد.

٧ - التوحيد/ ١٤٣/ ٧.

٨ - أصول الكافي/ الشيخ الكليني/ كتاب التوحيد/ باب انه لا يعرف إلا به/ ص٥١.

٩ - المصدر السابق.

Thus, if you forego comparing Him to spirits or bodies you will have come to know God through God. But if you compare Him to a spirit, body, or light then you have not come to know Him through Him.[9]

Imam 'Alī was asked, "How have you come to know your Lord?" He replied, "The way He has made Himself known to me." "How has He made Himself known to you?" He said, "He is unlike any form, nor sensed through the senses, nor compared to the people. He is near in His distance, distant in His proximity, above all things and nothing can be said to be above Him. He is before all things and nothing can be said to be before Him. He is in all things but not in the way that something is inside of another. He is outside of all things but not in the way something is outside of another. Glory be to the One who is thus and none is like so. He is the Origin of everything."[10]

Manṣūr ibn Ḥāzim relates from Abu 'Abdallah, "I saw a people and said to them, 'God is more majestic, greater and nobler than that He can be known through His creation. In fact, the creatures are known through Him. May God have mercy on you."[11]

Imam Bāqir says, "One is called knowledgable and powerful because God has endowed knowledge to the knower and power to the powerful. However much you describe Him through the subtlety of meaning in your imaginations, it is still a creation, engendered like yourselves, which returns back to you. But God is the bestower of life and determiner of death. Perhaps a small ant supposes that God has two antennas[12] because it is a perfection for it, and that one who does not have them is deficient.[13]

---

9 Cited above.

10 Cited above.

11 Cited above.

12 Sensory appendages on the front of the head.

13 *al-Rawāshiḥ al-samāwiyya*, p. 133, *Sharḥ al-asmā' al-ḥusna*, v. 1, p. 41.

وسئل أمير المؤمنين عليه السلام: بم عرفت ربك ؟ قال: بما عرفني نفسه، قيل: وكيف عرفك نفسه ؟ قال: لا يشبهه صورة، ولا يحس بالحواس، ولا يقاس بالناس، قريب في بعده، بعيد في قربه، فوق كل شيء، ولا يقال شيء فوقه، إمام كل شيء، ولا يقال له إمام، داخل في الأشياء لا كشيء داخل في شيء، وخارج من الأشياء لا كشيء خارج من شيء، سبحان من هو هكذا، ولا هكذا غيره، ولكل شيء مبتدأ[١٠].

عن منصور بن حازم قال: قلت لابي عبد الله عليه السلام: إني ناظرت قوما، فقلت لهم: إن الله جل جلاله أجل وأعز وأكرم من أن يعرف بخلقه. بل العباد يعرفون بالله، فقال: رحمك الله[١١].

وقال الباقر عليه السلام: هل يسمى عالما قادرا إلا لأنه وهب العلم للعلماء، والقدرة للقادرين، وكلما ميزتموه بأوهامكم في أدق معانيه، فهو مخلوق مصنوع مثلكم مردود إليكم، والباري تعالى واهب الحياة ومقدر الموت، ولعل النمل الصغار تتوهم أن لله زبانيتين[١٢] لأنهما كمالها، وتتصور أن عدمهما نقصان لمن لا يكونان له.[١٣]

---

١٠ - المصدر السابق.

١١ - المصدر السابق.

١٢ - شعرتان في مقدمة الرأس، بهما تحس عن بعد.

١٣ - الرواشح السماوية ١٣٣، شرح الأسماء الحسنى ١/ ٤١.

وفي الدعاء: كيف يستدل عليك بما هو في وجوده مفتقر إليك، أيكون لغيرك من الظهور ما ليس لك حتى يكون هو المظهر لك، متى غبت حتى تحتاج إلى دليل يدل عليك، ومتى بعدت حتى تكون الإثار هي التي توصل إليك، عميت عين لا تراك ولا تزال عليها رقيبا، وخسرت صفقة عبد لم تجعل له من حبك نصيبا. بحار الأنوار ٦٤/ ١٣٢.

In conclusion, the human being cannot reach his ultimate end and perfection, nor is he capable of it, nor does he perceive reality unless the light of God is realized inwardly and outwardly, externally and in the unseen. Thus, through the Intellect endorsed by light he becomes a new creation. He knows God through God, without which it is impossible to attain perfection and completion.

Imām al-Ṣādiq says, "The pillar of man is his Intellect from which astuteness, understanding, memory and knowledge arise. Through his Intellect he becomes complete. It is his guide, his evidence and the key to his affairs. If his intellect is augmented by [divine] light, he has knowledge, memory, remembrance, astuteness and understanding, and knows how, why and where. He recognizes one who advises him and one who wishes to defraud him. If he knows all that, he will come to

---

In the supplication: How can that which is in need of You for its very existence prove Your existence? Does something have a manifestation that You lack which would make You manifest? When have You been hidden so that You would need a trace to indicate towards You? Blind is the eye that does not see You and that You are ever watchful over it. The servant for whom You have not dedicated a share of Your love has failed. (*Biḥar al-anwār*, v. 64, p. 142).

Fayḍ Kāshānī writes, "Just as everything has a quiddity, which is the face of its essence, everything has a reality that encompasses it, upholds its essence, manifests its effects and attributes, the force that destroys and harms it, and the power that benefits and brings it felicity. It is the aspect which faces God, referred to by the verses, "He Encompasses all things" (41:54), "He is a Witness to all things" (41:53), "He is with you wherever you are" (57:4), "We are nearer to him than his jugular vein" (50:4), "We are nearer to him than you are, but you do not see" (56:85), and "Everything will perish save His countenance" (28:88).

This reality is what will remain after all things are annihilated. Thus, if we look at things in this way and know God in this manner, we will know God through God, in fact, we will also know things through God. (Kashānī, *Qurrat al-ʿUyūn*, p. 19).

وحاصل ما تقدم: إن الإنسان لا يبلغ منتهاه وكماله وما يسر له ولا يدرك الحقيقة إلا أن يتحقق بنور الله ظاهرا وباطنا، غيبا وشهادة، ويكون خلقا جديدا بالعقل المؤيد بالنور، فيعرف الله بالله، ومحال غير هذا كمالا و تماما.

قال أبو عبد الله ﷺ: دعامة الإنسان العقل، والعقل منه الفطنة، والفهم، والحفظ، والعلم، وبالعقل يكمل، وهو دليله ومبصره ومفتاح أمره. فإذا كان تأييد عقله من النور كان عالما، حافظا، ذاكرا، فطنا، فهما، فعلم بذلك كيف، ولم، وحيث، وعرف من نصحه، ومن غشه، فإذا عرف ذلك عرف مجراه، وموصوله، ومفصوله، واخلص الوحدانية لله والإقرار بالطاعة، فإذا فعل ذلك كان مستدركا لما فات، وواردا على ما هو آت، يعرف ما هو فيه، ولأي

قال الفيض الكاشاني: كما أن لكل شيء ماهية هو بها، وهي وجهه الذي إلى ذاته، كذلك لكل شيء حقيقة محيطة به بها قوام ذاته وبها ظهور آثاره وصفاته، وبها حوله عما يرديه ويضره، وقوته على ما ينفعه ويسره، وهي وجهه الذي إلى الله سبحانه واليه أشير بقوله عز وجل: ﴿ إِنَّهُ بِكُلِّ شَيْءٍ مُّحِيطٌ ﴾ [فصلت:٥٤]، و ﴿ أَنَّهُ عَلَىٰ كُلِّ شَيْءٍ شَهِيدٌ ﴾ [فصلت:٥٣]، وقوله سبحانه: ﴿وَهُوَ مَعَكُمْ أَيْنَ مَا كُنتُمْ ﴾ [الحديد :٤]، وبقوله تعالى: ﴿ وَنَحْنُ أَقْرَبُ إِلَيْهِ مِنْ حَبْلِ الْوَرِيدِ ﴾، [ق:١٦]، وبقوله عز وجل: ﴿ وَنَحْنُ أَقْرَبُ إِلَيْهِ مِنكُمْ وَلَكِن لَّا تُبْصِرُونَ ﴾ [الواقعة:٨٥]، وبقوله عز اسمه: ﴿ كُلُّ شَيْءٍ هَالِكٌ إِلَّا وَجْهَهُ ﴾ [القصص:٨٨].

فان تلك الحقيقة هي التي تبقى بعد فناء الأشياء، فإذا نظرنا إلى الأشياء بهذا الوجه وعرفنا الله عز وجل بهذا النظر فقد عرفنا الله بالله، بل عرفنا الأشياء أيضاً بالله. / قرة العيون/ ص١٩.

know his path, his means of arrival and the things which derail him. He then becomes sincere in the profession of God's unity and the confirmation of obedience towards Him. When he has done that he will redress his losses and usher what is to come. He will know what he is in, for what purpose he is here, how he can fulfill it and where he is heading. All that is from the assistance of the Intellect."[14]

Praise be to God, Lord of the worlds.

---

14 *al-Kāfī: The Book of Knowledge and Ignorance*, p. 19, hadith no. 23.

Know also that complete faith, adherence in the authority of God, the Prophet and the holders of authority depends on luminosity. Imam 'Alī says, "He whose outward exceeds his inward with respect to our spiritual authority the scale of his deeds is meagre. O Salman, the believer's faith is not complete until he knows me through luminosity and if he knows me in this way, he is a believer whose heart God has tested for faith and whose breast He has expanded for Islam. He has gnosis in his religion and has insight. He who falls short of that remains in doubt and uncertainty. O Salman and O Jundub, gnosis of me through luminosity is gnosis of God, and gnosis of God is gnosis of me; this is pure religion. (*'Uyūn al-hikam wa'l mawā'iẓ*, p. 167; *Mashāriq anwār al-yaqīn*, p. 257).

شيء هو ها هنا، ومن أين يأتيه والى ما هو صائر، وذلك كله من تأييد العقل[١٤].

والحمد لله رب العالميـن.

---

١٤ - أصول الكافي/ الشيـخ الكليني/ كتاب العقل و الجهل/ ص١٨/ ٢٣/ ح٢٣.

واعلـم أيضـاً أن تمـام الإيمان والولاية لله والرسـول وأولي الأمـر معقود عـلى النورانية، قال الإمـام عـلي عليه السلام: مـن كان ظاهـره في ولايتـي اكثر مـن باطنـه خفـت موازينه، يا سـلمان لا يكمـل المؤمـن إيمانه حتـى يعرفني بالنورانيـة، وإذا عرفني بذلك فهو مؤمـن امتحن الله قلبه للإيـمان وشرح صـدره للإسـلام، وصـار عارفا بدينـه مسـتبصرا، ومن قصر عـن ذلك فهو شـاك مرتاب، يا سـلمان ويا جنـدب، أن معرفتـي بالنورانية معرفة الله ومعرفـة الله معرفتي، وهو الدين الخالص.../ عيون الحكم والمواعظ / ١٦٧، مشـارق أنوار اليقين/ ٢٥٧-٢٥٨.

Chapter 12

The Intellect's Composition and Perfection

It was mentioned that the first thing God created was the Intellect. However, its composition within each person differs, as Isḥāq bin 'Umar relates from Abū 'Abdallah, "I said to Abu 'Abdallah, 'I approach a certain type of person and say only a portion of what I have to say but he comprehends all of it. I approach another and say all that I have to say and he retains it and repeats it to me just as I had said it. Then I speak to yet another who asks me to repeat what I have just said.' He said, 'O Isḥāq do you know why that is?' I said, 'No.' He said, 'As for the one to whom you spoke only a part and he understands the whole, his seed was kneaded with his Intellect. He who absorbs everything and repeats your words verbatim, his Intellect was formed in his mother's womb. He who asks you to repeat what you said, his Intellect developed when he matured; thus, he asks you to repeat.'"[1]

---

1 *al-Kāfī: The Book of Intellect and Ignorance*, hadith no. 27.

الباب الثاني عشر

تركيب العقل وكماله

تقدم الكلام في أن الله تعالى أول ما خلق العقل، ومع ذلك يختلف تركيبه في الأفراد الإنسانية لقول أبي عبد الله عليه السلام، عن إسحاق بن عمار، قال: قلت لأبي عبد الله عليه السلام: الرجل آتيه وأكلمه ببعض كلامي فيعرفه كله، ومنهم من آتيه فاكلمه بالكلام فيستوفي كلامي كله، ثم يرده على كما كلمته، ومنهم من آتيه فاكلمه فيقول أعد علي، فقال: «يا إسحاق: وما تدري لم هذا؟ قلت: لا. قال: الذي تكلمه ببعض كلامك فيعرفه كله، فذاك من عجنت نطفته بعقله، وأما الذي تكلمه فيستوفي كلامك ثم يجيبك على كلامك فذاك الذي ركب عقله فيه في بطن أمه، وأما الذي تكلمه بالكلام فيقول أعد علي، فذاك الذي ركب عقله فيه بعد ما كبر، فهو يقول لك أعد علي»[1].

١ - أصول الكافي/ الشيخ الكليني/ كتاب العقل و الجهل/ ص ١٩/ ح ٢٧.

The Intellect does not develop and reach the highest degree amongst the Prophets and [their] inheritors until its soldiers gather within it and expel the soldiers of its rival.

Samāʿa ibn Mihrān said, "I was with Abū ʿAbdallah when a group of his followers were also with him. The topic of Intellect and ignorance arose so Abū ʿAbdallah said, 'Know the Intellect and its soldiers—you will be guided. Know Ignorance and its soldiers—you will be guided.' The listener said, 'May I sacrifice myself for you! We do not know except what you have taught us.' Then Abū ʿAbdallah said, 'God created the Intellect—the first creature among the spiritual beings (*rūḥāniyyūn*)—from His light on the right side of His Throne. He said to it, "Retreat!" so it retreated. Then He said, "Approach!" so it approached. Then He said, "I have created a great creature and ennobled it above all My creation."

Then He created Ignorance from a briny, dark ocean and said, "Retreat!" so it retreated. Then He said, "Approach!" but it did not approach. So God said, "Have you become arrogant?" So He cursed it.

Then God appointed for the Intellect seventy-five soldiers. When Ignorance saw how God had ennobled the Intellect and what it had been given, it conceived a hidden enmity towards it. Ignorance said, "O Lord, this is a creature like me. You have created it, ennobled it and given it strength, while I am its opposite and I have no strength against it. Grant me soldiers the likes of which You have given it."

So God said, "Yes, but if you disobey Me from now onwards, I will banish you and your army from My mercy." Ignorance said, "I accept," So God gave it seventy-five soldiers.

He made good the vizier of the Intellect and evil its contrary, which is the vizier of Ignorance, then faith and its contrary disbelief, attestation and its contrary denial, hope and its contrary despair, justice and its contrary inequity, contentment and its contrary resentment, gratitude and its contrary ungratefulness, eagerness and its contrary

ولا يكمل العقل ويبلغ الدرجة العليا مع الأنبياء والأوصياء حتى يجتمع إليه جنده، و ينقى من جنود ضده.

عن سماعة بن مهران قال: كنت عند أبي عبد الله عليه السلام، وعنده جماعة من مواليه، فجرى ذكر العقل والجهل، فقال أبو عبد الله عليه السلام: «اعرفوا العقل وجنده والجهل وجنده تهتدوا، قال سماعة: فقلت جعلت فداك لا نعرف إلا ما عرفتنا.

فقال أبو عبد الله عليه السلام: إن الله عز وجل خلق العقل وهو أول خلق من الروحانيين عن يمين العرش من نوره، فقال له: ادبر فادبر، ثم قال له اقبل فاقبل، فقال له الله تبارك وتعالى خلقتك خلقا عظيما، وكرمتك على جميع خلقي.

قال: ثم خلق الجهل من البحر الأجاج ظلمانيا فقال له: ادبر فادبر، ثم قال له: اقبل فلم يقبل، فقال له: استكبرت فلعنه، ثم جعل للعقل خمسة وسبعين جندا، فلما رأي الجهل ما أكرم الله به العقل، وما أعطاه أضمر له العداوة، فقال الجهل:

يا رب هذا خلق مثلي خلقته وكرمته وقويته، وأنا ضده ولا قوة لي به، فاعطني من الجند مثل ما أعطيته فقال: نعم، فان عصيت بعد ذلك أخرجتك وجندك من رحمتي.

قال: قد رضيت، فأعطاه خمسة وسبعين جندا.

فكان مما اعطي العقل من الخمسة والسبعين الجند: الخير وهو وزير العقل، وجعل ضده الشر وهو وزير الجهل، والإيمان وضده الكفر، والتصديق وضده الجحود، والرجاء وضده القنوط، والعدل وضده الجور، والرضا وضده السخط، والشكر وضده الكفران، والطمع وضده اليأس، والتوكل وضده

resignation, reliance and its contrary greed, clemency and its contrary cruelty, mercy and its contrary anger, knowledge and its contrary ignorance, understanding and its contrary stupidity, modesty and its contrary shamelessness, renunciation and its contrary craving, gentleness and its contrary harshness, reverence and its contrary impudence, humility and its contrary pride, deliberation and its contrary haste, discernment and its contrary foolishness, silence and its contrary idle talk, submission and its contrary arrogance, surrender and its contrary doubt, patience and its contrary uneasiness, pardon and its contrary vengeance, wealth and its contrary poverty, remembrance and its contrary deliberation, memory and its contrary forgetfulness, vengeance reality, sympathy and its contrary severing ties, contentment and its contrary greed, altruism and its contrary deprivation, friendship and its contrary enmity, loyalty and its contrary treachery, obedience and its contrary disobedience, humility and its contrary haughtiness, safety and its contrary tribulation, love and its contrary hatred, truthfulness and its contrary lying, truth and its contrary falsehood, trustworthiness and its contrary betrayal, sincerity and its contrary corruption, acuity and its contrary dullness, comprehension and its contrary foolishness, recognition and its contrary rejection, masking and its contrary exposing, security and its contrary guile, confidentiality and its contrary disclosure, prayer and its contrary neglect, fasting and its contrary breaking fast, jihad and its contrary cowering, Hajj and its contrary breaking the covenant, guarding one's tongue and its contrary slandering, filial piety and its contrary disobedience, reality and its contrary ostentation, virtue and its contrary vice, covering and its contrary displaying, guarding and its contrary advertising, fairness and its contrary partiality, preparedness and its contrary inequity, cleanliness and its contrary filth, shame and its contrary indecency, moderation and its contrary excess, rest and its contrary fatigue, ease and its contrary difficulty, blessing and its

الحرص، والرأفة وضدها القسوة، والرحمة وضدها الغضب، والعلم وضده الجهل، والفهم وضده الحمق، والعفة وضدها التهتك، والزهد وضده الرغبة، والرفق وضده الخرق، والرهبة وضده الجرأة، والتواضع وضده الكبر، والتؤدة وضده التسرع، والحلم وضده السفه، والصمت وضده الهذر، والاستسلام وضده الاستكبار، والتسليم وضده الشك، والصبر وضده الجزع، والصفح وضده الانتقام، والغنى وضده الفقر، والتذكر وضده السهو، والحفظ وضده النسيان، والتعطف وضده القطيعة، والقنوع وضده الحرص، والمؤاساة وضدها المنع، والمودة وضدها العداوة، والوفاء وضده الغدر، والطاعة وضدها المعصية، والخضوع وضده التطاول، والسلامة وضدها البلاء، والحب وضده البغض، والصدق وضده الكذب، والحق وضده الباطل، والأمانة وضدها الخيانة، والإخلاص وضده الشوب، والشهامة وضدها البلادة، والفهم وضده الغباوة، والمعرفة وضدها الإنكار، والمداراة وضدها المكاشفة، وسلامة الغيب وضدها المماكرة، والكتمان وضده الإفشاء، والصلاة وضدها الإضاعة، والصوم وضده الإفطار، والجهاد وضده النكول، والحج وضده نبذ الميثاق، وصون الحديث وضده النميمة، وبر الوالدين وضده العقوق، والحقيقة وضدها الرياء، والمعروف وضده المنكر، والستر وضده التبرج، والتقية وضدها الإذاعة، والإنصاف وضده الحمية، والتهيئة وضدها البغي، والنظافة وضدها القذر، والحياء وضدها الجلع، والقصد وضده العدوان، والراحة وضدها التعب، والسهولة وضده الصعوبة، والبركة وضدها المحق، والعافية وضدها البلاء، والقوام وضده المكاثرة، والحكمة وضدها الهواء، والوقار وضده الخفة، والسعادة وضدها الشقاوة، والتوبة وضدها الإصرار،

contrary obliteration [of reward], health and its contrary trial, measure and its contrary excess, wisdom and its contrary caprice, dignity and its contrary frivolity, happiness and its contrary misery, repentance and its contrary persistence [in sin], seeking forgiveness and its contrary self-deception, mindfulness and its contrary carelessness, supplication and its contrary disdainfulness, liveliness and its contrary indolence, joy and its contrary sorrow, familiarity and its contrary separateness, generosity and its contrary stinginess.

All of these qualities of the Intellect's soldiers converge only in a prophet, an inheritor [of a prophet], or a believer whose heart God has tested for faith. As for the rest of our devotees, they possess some of these soldiers insofar as they perfect themselves and expunge the soldiers of Ignorance. Then they will be at the highest station with the prophets and their successors, which is attained by knowing the Intellect and its soldiers and eschewing Ignorance and its soldiers. May God grant us and you success to serve Him and earn His good pleasure."[2]

Know that the Intellect is bestowal — he who burdens it increases in ignorance. Conduct is exertion — he who strives for it acquires it. So put things in their proper place in discipline.

Imām al-Riḍā said, "O Hāshim, Intellect is a gift from God and refined conduct (*adab*) is acquired through effort. One who strives to refine his conduct is able to do so, but he who strives to acquire Intellect increases only in ignorance."[3]

Abu 'Abdallah relates that Imam 'Alī used to say, "The depths of wisdom are mined through the Intellect, the depths of Intellect are mined through wisdom. Good management fosters discipline."[4]

He said, "Contemplation is the revival of the heart of the insightful, like one who walks in darkness with a light, gracefully avoiding pitfalls and minimizing delay." Praise be to God, the Lord of the Worlds.

---

3 *al-Kāfī*, v. 1, hadith no. 18.

4 Ibid., v. 1, hadith no. 34.

والاستغفار وضده الاغترار، والمحافظة وضدها التهاون، والدعاء وضده الاستنكاف، والنشاط وضده الكسل، والفرح وضده الحزن، والألفة وضدها الفرقة، والسخاء وضده البخل.

فلا تجتمع هذه الخصال كلها من أجناد العقل إلا في نبي أو وصي نبي أو مؤمن قد امتحن الله قلبه للإيمان، وأما سائر ذلك من موالينا فان احدهم لا يخلو من أن يكون فيه بعض هذه الجنود حتى يستكمل وينقى من جنود الجهل، فعند ذلك يكون في الدرجة العليا مع الأنبياء والأوصياء، وإنما يدرك ذلك بمعرفة العقل وجنوده، وبمجانبة الجهل وجنوده، وفقنا الله وإياكم لطاعته ومرضاته.[٢]

ومع العقل وآدابه اعلم: أن الأول حباء من تكلّفه ازداد جهلا، والثاني كُلفة من تكلفه قدر عليه، فلا بد أن توضع الأمور في مواضعها عند التربية.

قال الرضا عليه السلام: يا أبا هاشم العقل حِباء من الله والأدب كلفة فمن تكلف الأدب قدر عليه، ومن تكلف العقل لم يزدد بذلك إلا جهلا».[٣] عن أبي عبد الله عليه السلام، قال: كان أمير المؤمنين يقول: «بالعقل استخرج غور الحكمة، وبالحكمة استخرج غور العقل، وبحسن السياسة يكون الأدب الصالح».

قال: وكان يقول: «التفكر حياة قلب البصير، كما يمشي الماشي في الظلمات بالنور بحسن التخلص وقلة التربص».[٤] والحمد لله رب العالمين.

---

٣ - الكافي/ الشيخ الكليني / ١/ ٢٤/ ١٨].

٤ - المصدر السابق/ ١/ ٢٨/ ٣٤].

2 *al-Kāfī: The Book of Intellect and Ignorance*, p. 16, hadith no. 14. Māzandarānī says concerning this hadith: *God created the Intellect—the first creature among the spiritual beings*: The Intellect is the first of the spiritual beings. 'Intellect' refers to the human immaterial substance which is the first of the engendered things and prior to every other contingent being in primordiality and origination. This is affirmed by the Prophet's statement, "The first thing God created was the Intellect." Whether this refers to a creature, quality or state, it is nonetheless, the first creature with respect to the spiritual beings, but it may not be that it is the first creature among the other contingent beings unless one posits that the creation of spiritual beings precedes the creation of all other contingent entities. Supporting this idea is beyond the scope of this discussion. However, the evidence that the Intellect is absolutely the first creature in reality to the exclusion of every other contingent being is rejected on account of the following:

There is no evidence that the Intellect is the absolute first being unless one entertains certain remote possibilities. Secondly, there is no evidence that God brought forth other beings through the Intellect, which is clear.

Rūḥ (spirit) is made masculine, feminine and its plural is '*arwāḥ*'. It is mentioned frequently in the Qur'ān and the hadith with various meanings: Gabriel, as in God saying, the Trusted Spirit and the Holy Spirit. It also means the angels, the power by which the body is sustained and is living, and the human faculty of rationality through which man is expresses 'I'.

Philosophers, theologians and others have differed as to its reality, making various claims, holding many an unfounded idea and lacking any real insight. None knows its reality except God and those He has taught among His servants, saying, "They ask you about the spirit. Say: The spirit is from my Lord's command. You have only been given a little knowledge of it" (17:85). Most of the theologians, scholars and mystics hold this view.

Rūḥānī (spiritual) is a singular adjective and *rūḥānīyīn* is plural with a *dhamma* on the *rā'* on both and the *alef* and *nūn* to indicate the adjectival form. Abū 'Ubayda says that any place that is pleasant and spacious is *rawḥānī*, with the *fatḥa*. *Rūḥānīyūn* refers to the immaterial world, the Unseen, the world of Dominion (*malakūt*) and the world of Command (*'amr*), just as

٢ - أصول الكافي/ الشيخ الكليني/ كتاب العقل و الجهل/ ص/ ١٦/ ح ١٤.

قال المازندراني في الحديث المذكور: إن الله خلق العقل وهو أول خلق من الروحانيين، ما حاصله: الجار والمجرور إن كان خبر بعد خبر، أي هو أول خلق وهو من الروحانيين، فأفاد الكلام أن العقل يعني الجوهر المجرد الإنساني أول المبدعات ومقدم على غيره من الممكنات كلها في الفطرة والإيجاد ويؤيده قوله صلى الله عليه وآله وسلم: أول ما خلق الله العقل. وإن كان بيانا لخلق أو صفة أو حالا عنه أفاد انه أول خلق بالنسبة إلى الروحانيين، واما انه أول خلق بالنسبة إلى غيره من الممكنات كلها فلا إلا إذا ثبت تقدم الروحانيين على سائر الممكنات في الإيجاد وثبوت ذلك خارج عن مفاد هذا الكلام، فما قيل: من أن فيه دلالة على أن العقل هو المبدع الأول بالحقيقة وعلى الإطلاق دون غيره من الممكنات لأنها بتوسطه فمدفوع:

إما أولا فلانه لا دلالة فيه على تقدم العقل على غيره على الإطلاق إلا في بعض الاحتمال الذي هو أبعد الاحتمالات فلا يتم بذلك ما ادعاه. وإما ثانيا فلانه لا دلالة فيه على أن غير العقل من الممكنات صدر منه تعالى بتوسط العقل وهو ظاهر.

والروح يذكر ويؤنث ويجمع على الأرواح، وقد تكرر ذكره في القرآن والحديث على معان منها جبرئيل عليه السلام في قوله تعالى: روح الأمين و روح القدس ومنها سائر الملائكة، ومنها القوة التي تقوم بهذا الجسد وتكون به الحياة، ومنها القوة الناطقة الإنسانية التي يعبر عنها بالإنسان بقوله: أنا.

واختلف المتكلمون والحكماء وغيرهما في حقيقته، وقالوا فيه أقوالا كثيرة، وظنوا فيه ظنونا متقاربة صدرت عنهم من غير بصيرة فانه لا يعلم حقيقته إلا الله سبحانه ومن علمه من عباده كما قال جل شانه: ﴿وَيَسْأَلُونَكَ عَنِ الرُّوحِ ۖ قُلِ الرُّوحُ مِنْ أَمْرِ رَبِّي وَمَا أُوتِيتُم

this world is called the sensory, material, visible, Kingdom (*mulk*) and the world of creation (*khalq*). It may be said that the *rūḥānīyūn* are immaterial luminous substances that are independent of bodies and physicality. If it is in need of bodies for its activity and movement, it is called soul, otherwise it is called an Intellect, and so on for every light is a single reality which does not differ in quiddity and accidents, but differ only in intensity, perfection, deficiency of original light and being. God knows best.

From the right of the Throne: This relates to either creation or the state of the spiritual beings. The right is the stronger and nobler side than the left. Lexically, a throne is the seat of a king. Their being from the right of the Throne is symbolic of their nobility, loftiness and sublime station in comparison with the other creatures. Thus, they repose at the right-hand side of the King, which means three things in religious tradition: The first, the kingdom; the second, the body which encompasses every other body; the third, the nine celestial spheres, and all-encompassing knowledge. Each one of these is a symbolized by the king's throne, which may be what is intended here. As for the first, it indicates the entirety of existence which contains both right and left, yet the right is stronger and nobler side and thus takes precedence in the order of creation. Anything that is closer to Him in creation is 'right' in comparison to what follows, for it is stronger and nobler.

As for the second, if the all-encompassing body is called the Throne, it has both a right and a left side like the seat of a king, yet those at the right are the possessors of nobility and rank just like those standing to the right of the king's seat.

The third is similar to what was mentioned in the second, or even the first, namely, that knowledge associated with the right is 'right' compared to the knowledge that follows it; its knowledge is simple and multiplicity arises due to multiplicity of the objects of knowledge.

It is possible to say that the Throne also refers to the two worlds:
The first consists of the entire world of bodies, called the Physical Throne. The second consists of the immaterial world, called the Intellectual Throne and the Spiritual Throne. The meaning of Throne here likely refers to the

مِنَ الْعِلْمِ إِلَّا قَلِيلاً ﴾ [الإسراء/ ٨٥] . وهو مذهب اكثر المتكلمين وأرباب المعاني وأهل الباطن.

وتقول في نسبة الواحد: الروحاني، وفي نسبة الجمع: الروحانيين بضم الراء فيهما، والألف والنون من زيادات النسب، وزعم أبو عبيدة أن العرب تقول لكل شيء فيه روح ومكان روحاني بالفتح، أي طيب، ثم الروحانيون يطلق عليهم عالم المجردات وعالم الغيب وعالم الملكوت وعالم الأمر كما يطلق على هذا العالم المحسوس عالم الماديات وعالم الشهود وعالم الملك وعالم الخلق. وقد يقال إن الروحانيين جواهر مجردة نورانية غير مفتقرة في وجودها إلى جسم وجسمانيات، فان كان في فعلها وتصرفها مفتقرة إليها فهي نفس، وإلا فهي عقل أو غيره، وان الأنوار كلها حقيقة واحدة لا تفاوت بينها في المهية وعوارضها، بل في الشدة والضعف والكمال والنقص في اصل النورية والوجود والله اعلم بحقيقة الحال.

«عن يمين العرش»، متعلق بخلق أو حال عن الروحانيين، واليمين الجانب الأقوى والأشرف خلاف الشمال، والعرش في اللغة: سرير الملك، وكونهم عن يمين العرش كناية عن كرامتهم وعلو منزلتهم ورفعة شانهم من بين المخلوقات، لأن من عظمت منزلته تبوا عن يمين الملك، وفي عرف المتشرعة يطلق على ثلاثة أمور: احدها: الملك.

وثانيها: الجسم المحيط بسائر الأجسام، وهو الفلك التاسع.

وثالثها: العلم المحيط بجميع الأشياء، وكل ذلك على سبيل التشبيه بسرير الملك، ويمكن إرادة كل واحد منها هنا، أما الأول فلان الملك وهو عبارة عن جميع الكائنات له يمين وشمال ويمينه أي جانب أقواه وأشرفه هو يلي المبدا الأول في ترتيب الإيجاد وتقدمه، فكل ما هو اقرب منه جل شانه في الإيجاد فهو ايمن بالقياس إلى ما بعده لكونه أقوى واشرف.

وأما الثاني: فلان ذلك الجسم المحيط إذا سمي عرش كان له يمين وشمال كما كان لسرير الملك، ثم الكاين على يمينه من أهل الكرامة والمنزلة كالكاين عن يمين

Spiritual Throne and its right, the nobler side which is closer to God in the order of creation. It may be said that what is meant by the Throne is the human heart because it is the Throne of the All-merciful. The right is the side which inclines towards God and the left is the side distant from Him. This is because it is capable of two types of spiritual movement, the path of Truth and the path of falsehood.

It is also said that the Throne means the human immaterial substance also called the Intellect and the Intellectual Throne vis-à-vis the nine celestial spheres known as the Physical Throne. Each side faces another. What is intended by 'right' is all sides, and has been named 'right' to ennoble and magnify it.

It is said that the Throne is an intermediate substance between the immutable Intellectual world and the mutable and renewable world, whether they be mutable souls or bodies. God engendered the Permanent Archetypes through His Essence, without intermediary and engendered the mutable things through the Throne. The Permanent Archetypes are the right in the order of creation because of their proximity to Him.

From His light. This relates to the creation of the intellect, namely, its being created from His Essence without intermediary or material consideration. Or it indicates the state of the Intellect that relates to its nobility and honor, as in the case of Jesus, the spirit of God, or the state of spiritual beings given that they are all luminous beings and the Intellect is the first and the best of them. Accordingly, there is evidence that the Intellect is a divine light from which God distinguishes truth from falsehood, right from wrong, just as light illuminates what is veiled by darkness, and that its light emanates from the light of His Essence, without the intermediary of any other luminous thing. The turbidity of dark matter does not make it turbid. Thus, if it is freed from fetters and severed from attachments it connects with God completely. That is why it is said that distance does not exist in the spiritual world.

It is possible that what is meant by light is justice, since it is not uncommon to carry this meaning in the exegesis of Qāḍī and others in reference to the verse, "The earth was illuminated by the Light of its Lord." It means that

سرير الملك.

وأما الثالث: فلمثل ما ذكرناه في الثاني، أو في الأول باعتبار المعلومات لأن العلم المتعلق باليمين يمين بالنسبة إلى العلم المتعلق بما بعده، وان كان علمه بالأشياء بسيطا والتكثر إنما هو في المعلومات.

ولا يبعد أن يقال: يجوز أيضاً إطلاق العرش على عالمين:

احدهما: عالم الجسمانيات كلها، ويسمى بالعرش الجسماني.

وثانيهما: عالم المجردات كلها ويسمى بالعرش العقلاني والعرش الروحاني. ويجوز أن يراد بالعرش هنا العرش الروحاني وبيمينه اشرف جانبيه وهو ما يقرب من الحق في سلسلة الإيجاد وإن يقال يجوز أيضاً أن يراد بالعرش القلب الإنساني لأنه عرش الرحمن، ويمينه الجانب المائل إلى الحق، وشماله الجانب البعيد عنه، لأنه قابل لسلوك الطريقين: طريق الحق وطريق الباطل.

هذا وقيل: المراد بالعرش هنا الجوهر المجرد الإنساني المسمى بالعقل وبالعرش العقلاني وهو بإزاء الفلك التاسع المسمى بالعرش الجسماني وكل منهما في جانب مقابل لجانب آخر، والمراد بيمينه مطلق جانبه وسمي يمينا للتشريف والتعظيم.

وقيل: العرش جوهر متوسط بين العالم العاقل الثابت وبين العالم المتغير المتجدد نفوسا كانت المتغيرات أو أجساما، والله سبحانه أوجد الثابتات بنفس ذاته بلا واسطة، وأوجد المتغيرات بواسطة العرش والثابت هو اليمين في سلسلة الإيجاد لأنه اقرب منه تعالى.

«من نوره» متعلق بخلق العقل أي خلقه من ذاته بلا واسطة شيء ولا اعتبار مادة أو حال عن العقل والإضافة للتشريف والتكريم كما في عيسى روح الله، أو حال عن الروحانيين بناء على أن الروحانيين كلهم نورانيون والعقل أولهم وأفضلهم، وعلى التقادير فيه إشارة إلى أن العقل نور رباني لأنه يظهر به الحق عن الباطل والصواب عن الخطأ كما يظهر بالنور الأشياء المحتجبة بالظلام وأن نوريته مستفادة من نور ذاته

God created the Intellect as a being originating in His justice, since the very purpose of creating the human being is justified by the Intellect. His justice necessitates creating a being of this type so that the purpose is not lost. He said, "retreat" away from the forbidden, or descend to the lower world and physical stations which are at the farthest distance from the divine worlds. So it 'retreated' to obey His command and surrender to His authority without ever losing its luminosity and immateriality. Its retreat was simply the emanation of its light in the material world.

Then He said, "approach" towards obedience and whatever entails entering the compass of His generosity and proximity. Or, approach [Me] from the hidden elements of corporeality, the stations among the types of human darkness and the manifestations of ignorance from the natural world, to the luminous world of immaterial beings, the stations of witnessing of the divine. "Approach," obedient to His command, surrendering to His authority, renouncing His disobedience, ascending gradually to become an active Intellect and attain the degree of certainty itself. Thus, it returns from whence it began and ends at the beginning.

This type of hadith and its commentary can be found at the beginning of the Book of Intellect, however there is a discrepancy in the wording between these two. The command to approach in the former precedes the command to retreat whereas, here, it is reversed. Unless the divine directive is a series of statements then it is clear otherwise it would be objectionable, unless it is said that there was the command to approach then retreat then approach. Thus, in the hadith above, the command to approach after retreating is omitted and in this version the command to approach before retreating is omitted. In either case, one can derive benefit and ponder.

God addressed it, magnifying and honoring it and emphasized that it should be grateful for this obvious blessing.

I have made you a great creation. True greatness is only for God. All others are great relative to their proximity to God and obedience to His command. These two aspects were realized in the Intellect, thus, *I have honored you*, that is, I have ennobled you and preferred you over the rest of creation, as He says "The most honorable among you are the most God-conscious." "Above the rest

سبحانه بلا توسط شيء نوراني غيره ولا تكدره كدرة المواد الظلمانية، ولذلك إذا عرى عن العوائق وانقطع عن العلائق اتصل بالخالق اتصالا تاما، ومن ثم قيل: لا مسافة في العالم الروحاني.

ويحتمل أن يراد بالنور العدل وإطلاق النور على العدل سايغ شايع كما صرح به القاضي وغيره في تفسيره قوله تعالى «وأشرقت الأرض بنور ربها» والمعنى أن الله سبحانه خلق العقل خلقا ناشيا من عدله إذ لولا العقل لبطل الغرض من إيجاد الإنسان فعدله اقتضى خلق هذا النوع من المخلوق لئلا يفوت الغرض « فقال له: ادبر» عن المنهيات أو انزل إلى عالم السفلي والمنازل الجسمية التي هي في غاية البعد عن العوالم الربوبية «فادبر»، وأطاع أمره عز شانه، وانقاد لحكمه من غير أن يفارق نوريته وتجرده. وإنما كان إدباره بمجرد إشراقات نوره في العالم الجسماني.

«ثم قال له: اقبل» إلى الطاعات وما يوجب النزول في ساحة كرامته تعالى من القربات أو أقبل من مكامن المواد الجسمية ومنازل الظلمات البشرية ومظاهر الجهالات الطبيعية إلى عالم المجردات النورية ومنازل الشواهد الربوبية «فاقبل» مطيعا لأمره منقادا لحكمه تاركا لمعصيته متدرجا في الصعود من طور إلى طور حتى صار عقلا فعالا وترقى حتى مرتبة عين اليقين، وهناك رجع إلى ما نزل منه وانتهى إلى ما بدا منه.

وقد مر مثل هذا الحديث وشرحه في صدر كتاب العقل إلا أن بينهما مغايرة في الجملة لأن الأمر بالإقبال في السابق مقدم على الأمر بالإدبار، وهنا بالعكس فان كانت القضية في الخطاب متعددة فالأمر واضح وإلا ففيه أشكال، اللهم إلا أن يقال: كان في الواقع أمر الإقبال ثم أمر بالإدبار ثم أمر بالإقبال ففي الحديث السابق لم يذكر الأمر بالإقبال بعد الأمر بالإدبار وفي هذا الحديث لم يذكر الأمر بالإقبال قبل الأمر بالإدبار، ومن مجموعهما يستفاد ما كان في الواقع فليتأمل.

«فقال الله تعالى»، تعظيما وتكريما له وحثا له على أداء شكر هذه النعمة الجليلة.

«خلقتك خلقا عظيما»، العظيم الحقيقي ليس إلا الله سبحانه، وأما غيره فعظمته

of creation," Greatness, nobility and preference without the precondition of receptivity and capacity indicates that the Intellect is superior to even the proximate angels.

Then He created Ignorance. Ignorance here does not mean compound ignorance, which is a form in the mind that does not correspond to reality, nor simple ignorance, which is not knowing something that should be known, upon which obedience and disobedience is dependent, as is culpability. He says, "So, if you disobey me from now onwards, I will expel you and your army from my Mercy." Ignorance in the previous two meanings is included among the soldiers of Ignorance and differs from it, since in a second sense, it is non-existent. What is non-existent is uncreated, whether in the sense of pure negation or the lack of an attribute. What is meant by Ignorance here is the origin of evil and wickedness and what is meant by Intellect is the origin of goodness and virtue.

Perhaps these two origins refer to qualities of the soul, the faculty of ignorance and the faculty of intellect. What is meant by this is the soul's essence, namely, the immaterial substance governing the body needed for its activity and movement, which is autonomous from the body in existence and activity. If something has this [immateriality] and shines its light on another, it becomes intelligent through it. Even if it does not transfer it to another, the Intellect still remains intelligent and receptive, in and of itself. The soul is called ignorance metaphorically because it is the locus of simple and compound ignorance. However, it can be said that the soul is the origin of all ignorance, evil and the source of corrupt and false imaginal forms, the root of desire and anger, animality and all the other bodily powers. If these corruptions acquire agency and become established in the soul, it becomes pure ignorance, utterly satanic and distant from God. The more they become established and rooted, the more the soul becomes ignorant, satanic and veiled from God, until it reaches sheer ignorance and complete misguidance, becoming the archetype of the rebellious and the chief of the arrogant.

From the dark, briny sea. Ujāj means salty and bitter and 'dark' refers to the state of ignorance or the briny sea and indicates divine wrath because it is bitter and whose flavor and smell is hated by the taste of the drinkers

باعتبار قربه منه وإطاعته لأمره، وقد تحقق هذان الوجهان في العقل «وكرمتك» أي شرفتك وفضلتك ومنه «إن أكرمكم عند الله اتقاكم»، «على جميع خلقي» فيه أن العظمة والشرافة والفضيلة من باب التفضيل منه تعالى من غير اشتراط القابلية والاستعداد وان العقل اشرف من الملائكة المقربين.

«قال ثم خلق الجهل» ليس المراد بالجهل هنا الجهل المركب اعني الصور العلمية الغير المطابقة للواقع، ولا الجهل البسيط اعني عدم العلم عما من شانه العلم لأن إطاعته وعصيانه غير متصورة فلا يلائم قوله: «فإذا عصيت بعد ذلك أخرجتك وجندك من رحمتي»، ولان الجهل بهذين المعنيين من جنود الجهل المذكور هنا وجند الشي غيره، ولان الجهل بالمعنى الثاني أمر عدمي والإعدام غير مخلوقة سواء كانت سلوبا محضة أو ملكات. بل المراد به مبدا الشرور والمقابح، كما أن المراد بالعقل مبدا الخيرات والمحاسن.

ويمكن أن يراد بهذين المبدأين صفة النفس المسماة بالقوة الجاهلة وصفتها المسماة بالقوة العاقلة، وإن يراد بهما ذات النفس أي الجوهر المجرد المدبر للبدن المحتاج في فعله وتصرفه إليه و ذات الجوهر المستغني عن البدن في وجوده وفعله الذي إذا حصل لغيره وأشرق نوره فيه كان ذلك الغير عاقلا به إذا لم يحصل له وقام بذاته كان عاقلا ومعقولا، وتسمية النفس بالجهل من باب المجاز لأنها محل للجهل المركب والبسيط، بل يمكن أن يقال: إنها من باب الحقيقة، لأن النفس وإن كانت مبدأ للجهالات ومنشأ للشرور كلها ومصدرا للصور الوهمية الكاذبة الباطلة ومقتضيات القوى الشهوية والغضبية والبهيمية وسائر القوى البدنية، لكن إذا تمكنت فيها هذه الأباطيل ورسخت فيها صارت جهلا محضا وشيطانا صرفا بعيدا عن الحق جل شانه، وكلما ازداد التمكن والرسوخ ازدادت جهالتها وشيطنتها واحتجابها عن الحق حتى بلغت النهاية في الجهالة والغاية في الضلالة وصارت قدوة المتمردين وإمام المتكبرين.

«من البحر الأجاج ظلمانيا»، ماء أجاج أي مالح مر و«ظلمانيا»، حال عن الجهل أو البحر الأجاج والمراد به الغضب الإلهي، لأنه مر كريه الطعم و الرائحة على مذاق

and sense of smell of the gnostics. Or, it means the totality of the soul's faculties, some which are good and some ugly, and the soul's fermentation therein. This aggregate is equivalent to bitter, turbid water that is admixed with the dust of base habits the bitterness of vile attributes, the saltiness of ugly outcomes and the coarseness of dishonorable behavior. It is called a sea because of the accumulation of these attributes and their multiplicity. It is described as dark because of its veiling of the lights of the Intellects, becoming a barrier between it and its insight. Or, it means primordial bodily matter which is pure receptivity and the cause of soul's attachment to it and its individuation. It is called a dark sea because of the accumulation of the waters of evil and contrary and opposing attributes, like the relationship between the sea and the waves.

He said, "Retreat!" He commanded it to go down from the world of Dominion and light to the world of darkness and evils, orienting itself to those desires with which it has sympathy, with an eye for its wants and pleasures. So it descended due to a certain necessity which was a trial for the servants. It was in order to govern the land and develop the earth, lest the human being remain like the angels, stripped of the adornment of procreating and multiplying, farming and developing the earth. This would have undermined the very purpose of creating this species, earthly vicegerency, and consequently, invalidate reward and punishment. The divine attributes, their realities and effects would not be revealed, such as justice, retribution, omnipotence, dominance, forgiveness and pardoning, etc.

Then He said, "Approach, but it did not approach." After the command to retreat, He commanded it to approach Him and return to sublime stations and lofty honors that He possesses, which are not easily attainable unless one moves from the base to the sublime, from a low state to a high state, from the ephemeral plane to the eternal plane. Thus, it moves state to state and from perfection to perfection, until it reaches the pinnacle of witnessing God, the endpoint of perceiving God's lights and enjoying the high heaven whose fruits are near at hand. But it refuses to travel the path of righteousness, grasp the lasso of obedience, adhere to the fulfillment of the promise and harken to sound advice to uproot wicked deeds. This is all due to the

الشاربين ومشام العارفين، أو المراد به مجموع الصفات النفسانية التي بعضها حسن وبعضها قبيح لتخمير النفس بها، وهذا المجموع من حيث هو بمنزلة ماء كدر مر ممتزج بغبار الملكات الدنية ومرارة الصفات الشنيعة وملوحة قبايح الآثار وخشونة فضايح الأطوار، وعبر عنه بالبحر للدلالة على تراكم تلك الصفات وكثرتها، ووصفه بالظلمة لسترها أنوار العقول حايلا بينها وبين بصيرتها، أو المراد به المواد البدنية الهيولانية التي هي محض الاستعداد وعلة قابلية لتعلق النفس بها وتشخصها وعبر عنها بالبحر الظلماني لتراكم مياه الشرور والصفات المتغايرة المتضادة فيها ونسبتها إليها كنسبة البحر إلى الأمواج.

«فقال له ادبر فادبر»، أمره بالهبوط من الملكوت والنور إلى عالم الظلمات والشرور والتوجه إلى ما يلايمه من المشتهيات والنظر إلى ما فيه هواه من المستلذات فهبط لما في ذلك من مصلحة، وهي ابتلاء العباد ونظام البلاد وعمارة الأرض إذ لولا ذلك لكان الناس بمنزلة الملائكة عارين عن حلية التناكح والتناسل والزراعة وتعمير الأرض وبطل الغرض المطلوب من هذا النوع من الخلق وبطل خلافة الأرض، ولزم من ذلك بطلان الثواب والعقاب وعدم انكشاف صفات الباري وانجلاء حقائقها وآثارها مثل العدالة والانتقام والجبارية والقهارية والعفو والغفران وغيرها

«ثم قال له: اقبل فلم يقبل» أمره بعد الإدبار بالإقبال إليه تعالى والرجوع إلى ما لديه من المقامات العلية والكرامات الرفيعة التي لا يتيسر الوصول إليها إلا بالانتقال من طور أخس إلى طور اشرف، ومن حالة أدني إلى حالة أعلى، ومن نشأة فانية إلى نشأة باقية، وهكذا من حال إلى حال ومن كمال إلى كمال حتى يبلغ إلى غاية مشاهدة جلال الله ونهاية ملاحظة أنوار الله ويرتع في جنة عالية قطوفها دانية، فأبى السلوك في سبيل الرشاد والتقيد بربقة الانقياد والمسك بلوازم الوعظ والنصيحة والانقلاع عن الأفعال القبيحة، كل ذلك لشدة احتجابه بحجاب الظلمات وانغماسه في بحر ذمائم الصفات لتوهمه أن تلك الذمائم الخاسرة والصفات الظاهرة والمشتهيات الحاضرة كمال له فاغتر

intensity of the veils of darkness and immersion in the sea of blameworthy attributes, supposing that these blameworthy defects, outward qualities and ever-present desires are its perfection. Thus, it becomes seduced by them and waxes proudly, embodying these qualities and becomes arrogant.

So, He says, "Have you become arrogant? So He cursed it." The interrogative is intended for reproach and blame and curse implies expulsion and distance from goodness. That is, you have arrogantly abandoned My command, which is advantageous to both realms, whereas I commanded obedience for the sake of humility and neediness. You have exchanged the better, that which leads to happiness and serenity for the worse, out of ignorance. That you have been imprisoned by ignorance and evil it is no wonder that you are far from mercy, banished from the station of greatness and nobility.

Then He gave the Intellect seventy-five soldiers. Lexically, *jund* refers to a group prepared for war. The plural is *ajnād* and *junūd*. In *al-Siḥāḥ* it refers to helpers and supporters. Each one of the aforementioned [qualities] is an army due to the multiplicity of individuals and divisions. Since the path of God is treacherous, there are divisions for each step taken and for each division there are foes, adversaries and mortal enemies leading the wayfarer towards perdition and misguidance. The woes of ignorance necessitated that in order to tread the path the Intellect should have supporters and helpers to ward the enemies and overcome the hostile foes. So, God in His grace, mercy and perfect compassion gave armies to bolster it in the places of conflict and in the battlefields, to ensure peace in the stations of proximity and nobility. These seventy-five armies, as they have been mentioned here, are actually seventy-eight in number. There is no discrepancy here since what is meant here is not a numerical limit but the concept of enumeration and of no real significance, as we have explained in the principles of jurisprudence.

Shaykh Bahā' writes, "Perhaps the three extras are one of the two lines on hope and greed, understanding, and peace and safety. The copyists included them unaware that they are repeated. We will explain further at its appropriate place, God willing.

When Ignorance saw how God ennobled the Intellect, through purifying it with the light of the Essence and strengthening it with many armies and

بها أو افتخر وأخذها بضاعة له واستكبر.

«فقال له: استكبرت فلعنه»، الاستفهام للتوبيخ والتعيير واللعن والطرد والابعاد من الخير يعني تركت أمري بما يصلح في النشأتين استكبارا وجعلت الامتثال به مذلة وافتقارا، واستبدلت الذي هو أدنى بالذي هو خير لجهلك بما يوجب قرارة العين والسرور، واحتباسك بقدر الجهالة والشرور، فلا جرم أنت بعيد عن الرحمة والسلامة، مطرود عن مقام العزة والكرامة.

«ثم جعل للعقل خمسة وسبعين جندا»، في المعرب الجند جمع معدّ للحرب وجمعه اجناد، وفي الصحاح الجند الأعوان والأنصار، وفي عد كل واحد من الأمور المذكورة جندا باعتبار تكثر أفراده وشعبه، ولما كان الطريق إلى الله مخوفا، وفي كل قدم منه شعبه وعلى كل شعبة منه عدو مقاتل وخصم مجالد يقود سالكه إلى مهاوي الضلالة ومساوي الجهالة احتاج سلطان العقل في قطع هذا الطريق إلى أعوان وأنصار يستعين بهم في دفع الأعداء والمحاربة مع الخصماء، فأعطاه الله سبحانه بفضل رحمته وكمال رافته جنودا تعينه في مواضع الجدال ومواطن القتال وتوصله على السلامة إلى منازل القرب والكرامة.

وهذه الجنود خمسة وسبعون على ما في العنوان والمذكور في التفصيل ثمانية وسبعون ولا منافاة بينهما إذ ليس في العنوان ما يفيد الحصر إلا مفهوم العدد وهو ليس بمعتبر كما بيناه في أصول الفقه.

وقال الشيخ بهاء الملة والدين رحمه الله على ما نقل عنه: لعل الثلاثة الزائدة إحدى فقرتي الرجاء والطمع، وإحدى فقرتي الفهم و إحدى فقري السلامة والعافية، فجمع الناسخون بين البدلين غافلين عن البدلية، وسنشير إلى توضيح ذلك في موضعه إن شاء الله تعالى.

«فلما رأى الجهل ما اكرم الله به العقل»، من تصفيته بنورانية الذات وتقويته بكثرة الجنود وشرائف الصفات التي بنضارتها تشرق قلوب العارفين، وبإنارتها تضي صدور السالكين، وبإضائتها يسيرون إلى أعلى المقامات وينالون اشرف المكانات «أضمر له

noble qualities, whose effulgence illuminates the hearts of the gnostics, brilliance irradiates the breasts of the wayfarers, radiance drives it to the highest of stations and attain the noblest of honors, *it harbored enmity*. The Intellect and Ignorance are contrary in essence because the Intellect is a luminous substance and Ignorance is turbid and dark; this in itself is the cause of enmity. That is why there is enmity between the intelligent and the ignorant, the believer and the unbeliever until the Day of Judgement. Thus, God says, "There has arisen, between you and us enmity and hostility until the Day of Judgement. However, since both light and darkness were equal in domination and repulsion, it was as if Ignorance did not harbor hostility in this aspect, but in the aspect of God's ennobling the Intellect, strengthening it with armies, bounties and perfections with which it would certainly dominate it. Thus, out of envy it harbored enmity but did not manifest it for it was not strong enough to have an effect. It asked for an army equal in strength and number. *Ignorance said, "My Lord this is a creation like me."* It is like me in that it is also created, or its essence is like mine so it does not exceed me in essential virtue. This statement originates from self-deception, in the same way that the ignorant considers himself equal to the intelligent. He is either unaware of the grave difference between light and darkness or knows but makes a claim due to pride, lest its self is diminished before the Intellect. Otherwise, wherein is the comparison between the two essences, one which has been created by the water of mercy and divine light and one which has been created by the fire of wrath and the dark, briny sea. Satan became arrogant because he could not distinguish between the two and refused to prostrate before Adam claiming, "You created me from fire and created him from clay." Because of his myopia he only saw the clay of Adam and neglected his luminosity. Had he known that he would have realized the falsity of his argument.

You created it, ennobled it and strengthened it. That is, You created it from Your light and ennobled it over all Your creation and strengthened it by armies enabling it to move to the world of proximity and progress to the world of sanctity. *I am its opposite but have no power against it*, in being its contrary and adversary, and moving towards my ultimate end and final

العداوة» بين العقل والجهل تضاد بحسب الذات، لأن العقل جوهر نوراني والجهل كدر ظلماني، وهذا يصح أن يكون منشا لعداوته، ولذلك كانت العداوة بين العاقل والجاهل والمؤمن والكافر قائمة إلى قيام الساعة كما قال سبحانه «وبدا بيننا وبينكم العداوة والبغضاء إلى يوم القيامة»، ولكن لما كان النور والظلمة متساويين في الغلبة والتدافع كانه لم يحصل للجهل من هذه الجهة عداوة، وإنما حصلت العداوة على من جهة إكرام العقل بالجنود وتقويته بالفضائل والكمالات الموجبة لغلبته على الجهل، فلذلك اضمر الجهل عداوة له حسدا ولم يظهرها لعدم القدرة على إمضاء آثارها، بل طلب لنفسه مثل جنوده في القوة والعدد كما أشار إليه بقوله «فقال الجهل يا رب هذا خلق مثلي»، أي مثلي في كونه مخلوقا، أو مثلي بحسب الذات ولا مزية له علي في المحاسن الذاتية، وهذا القول منه على الأخير تمويه واغترار بنفسه، كما هو شأن الجاهل حيث يعد نفسه مماثلا للعاقل، وهو إما غافل عن التفاوت الفاحش بين النور والظلمة أو عالم به، لكنه قال ذلك ادعاءا واستنكافا لانحطاط ذاته عن ذات العقل وإلا فأين المماثلة بحسب الذات بين المخلوق من ماء الرحمة والنور الرباني وبين المخلوق من نار الغضب والبحر اللجاج الظلماني ولعدم الفرق بينهما استكبر الشيطان لعنه الله وأبى أن يسجد لآدم عليه السلام وتمسك بقوله «خلقتني من نار وخلقته من طين» وهو لقصر نظره لا حظ طينية آدم وغفل عن نورانيته ولو علم ذلك لعلم بطلان قياسه.

«خلقته وكرمته وقويته»، يعني خلقته من نورك وكرمته على جميع خلقك وقويته بجنود يتقوى بها في الحركة إلى عالم الأنس والانتقال إلى عالم القدس «وأنا ضده ولا قوة لي به»، في المضادة والمقابلة والانتقال إلى ماهو غاية مرامي ونهاية مقامي في اللذات التي عاينتها والحركة إلى أقصى مدارجها «فاعطني من الجند مثل ما أعطيته» في العدد والقوة، طلب ذلك ليحصل له قوة بسبب جنوده على معارضة العقل وجنوده فيتيسر له الوصول إلى غاية منيته ونهاية بغيته «فقال نعم»، أعطيك مثل جنود العقل اختبارا وامتحانا لك وتكميلا للحجة عليك باعطاء سؤلك وانتظارا لرجعتك إلى درجة رفيعة

station which are the desires under my gaze and reaching their climax. *So grant me armies the likes of which You have given it*, in number and in strength. It sought that to obtain power through its armies to challenge the Intellect and its armies. So God facilitated reaching the culmination of its desired aim and said, "*Yes,*" I have granted you similar to the armies of the Intellect, as a trial and test for you and to fulfill the proof against you, by granting you your request and waiting for you to return to a lofty degree and noble station. One who obeys out of compulsion or inability is not like one who obeys while having the power to disobey. The latter are greater in degree and higher in station. For this reason, the worship, humility, and penitence of the youth is more valuable than that of old men.

If you disobey me from now onwards, that is, after that act of disobedience when you did not approach, or after I have granted you armies and helpers to confront the Intellect and its helpers, *I will remove you and your armies from my Mercy*, which is reserved for the obedient. So, you will become wretched, enter the camp of the wicked, and be worthy of entering the lowest level of hellfire. The soul's disobedience with its armies is a greater cause for expulsion from [divine] mercy that its disobedience without armies, because in the latter case, it is weak and without helpers so its acts are deficient. Its wretchedness is not severe and deserving of expulsion from [divine] mercy. In contrast, if it is strong with helpers and powers, its trajectory towards wretchedness and movement towards misguidance is more intense. Its acquiring blameworthy qualities, vices and immersion in the darkness of transgression and ruin is more grave, so the distance from divine mercy and God's gentleness is greater and stronger. It is more worthy to enter into the pits of hellfire and more deserving of a painful punishment.

It said, "I accept." It was pleased that God accepted its request or the fact of being excluded from [divine] mercy to the extent of its sin. Even if the soul mildly inclines towards corruption with these ill qualities and armies, it is not stripped of freewill and is not compelled to wickedness. It is indeed possible for it to attain health and safety from satanic insinuations through medicine and prescribed remedies that repel diseases of the soul. Even after the soul has been strengthened with armies and qualities which

ومنزلـة شريفـة، فـان المطيـع مـع العجـز وفقـد الآلات ليـس مثـل المطيع مـع القـدرة على المخالفـة، بـل أولئـك أعظـم درجـة وارفـع منزلـة، ولذلك كانـت عبـادة الشبان وإنباتهم وإخباتهـم أحسـن وأشرف من عبـادة الشـيوخ وانباتهـم واخباتهم.

«فـان عصيـت بعـد ذلـك»، أي بعد ذلـك العصيـان بـترك الإقبـال أو بعـد أن أعطيتك جنـودا وأنصـارا مقابلـة جنـود العقـل وأنصـاره «أخرجتـك وجندك مـن رحمتـي»، المعدة للمطيعين فتشـقى بذلك وتدخل في زمرة الأشرار وتسـتحق الدخول في الدرك الأسـفل من النـار، والوجـه لكـون معصية النفس مـع الجنود موجبـا للخروج من الرحمـة دون معصيتها لامعهـا أن النفـس إذا كانت ضعيفة فاقـدة للأنصار كانت أفعالها ناقصة، فلم تكن شـقاوتها شـديدة موجبـة للخروج مـن الرحمة بخلاف مـا إذا كانت قويـة واجـدة لأنصارها وآلاتها، فـان سـلوكها في طريـق الشـقاوة وسـيرها في منهـج الضلالـة أفحـم، واكتسـابها للأخلاق الذميمـة والرذائـل وانهماكهـا في ظلـمات الغـي والغوائل اعظم فيكـون تباعدهـا عن الرحمة الإلهيـة والألطـاف الربانية اكثر وأقـوى ودخولهـا في دركات الجحيم واسـتحقاقها للعذاب الأليـم اقرب وأولى.

«قـال: رضيـت»، رضي عن الحق بإجابة سـؤاله أو رضي بالخروج عـن الرحمة على تقدير معصيتـه، والنفس وان كانت مائلة إلى الفسـاد عليلة بأمراض تلـك الصفات والأجناد لكن ذلـك لا يسـلب عنهـا الاختيـار ولا يوجـب صـدور القبائـح عنها عـلى سـبيل الاضطرار، بـل يمكن لهـا تحصيل الصحـة والسـلامة عن الوسـاوس الشـيطانية بالأدويـة والعلاجات المقـررة لدفـع الأمـراض النفسـانية، وبالجملة النفـس بعد تقويتهـا بالجنـود والصفات التي هـي بمنزلـة العلـل والأمراض لهـا اختيـار في أعمالها وقدرة عـلى أفعالها وليـس صدور تلك الأعـمال والأفعـال عنهـا عـلى سـبيل اللجـاء والاضطـرار، فلهـا أن تـترك مقتضيـات تلك الصفـات وترتقـي إلى أعـلى مـدارج الكـمالات الأبديـة حتى تسـتحق أن يقـال لها «يـا أيتها النفـس المطمئنـة ارجعـي إلى ربـك راضية مرضيـة» ولها أن تمـضي تلك المقتضيـات وتسرح في مراعـي هـذه الصفـات حتـى ترتد إلى اسـفل سـافلين وتبتعد عـن رحمـة رب العالمين.

are, in relation to it, illness and disease, it has freewill and agency over its actions. These acts and deeds do not arise out of compulsion and coercion. Thus, it must eschew the consequences of these qualities and ascend to the highest stages of everlasting perfection, so that it deserves to be addressed, "O tranquil soul, return to your Lord, content and accepted." It must remove these effects and desist from succumbing to these attributes so that it turns back from the lowest of the low, which is far from the mercy of the Lord of the worlds.

So He gave it seventy-five armies, equivalent to what He had given Intellect; given that they are contraries so too are their armies. Thus, there is a balance in creation and the [outward] realization of opposition and contrariness which will remain until the last day. That is due to an obvious benefit that the people of Intellect recognize and hidden one known only by the Knower of the Unseen.

It should be known that the types of virtues according to the philosophers are four: wisdom, bravery, temperance, and justice. That is because the human being has three separate faculties which give rise to various effects in combination with the will. If one of them predominates, the others are subjugated or deficient.

The first is the rational faculty which is called the angelic soul. It is the basis of thinking about concepts and perceiving realities.

The second is the faculty of anger which is called predatory soul. It is the source of anger, threat, domination and ascendancy over others.

The third is the faculty of desire which is also called the bestial soul. It is the source of desire, hunger, passion for food, drink and sex. If the rational faculty moves with equanimity and acquires certain knowledge, it attains the virtues of knowledge and wisdom. If the faculty of anger becomes balanced and obeys the rational faculty in all that it considers its share without contravening any of its commands, it attains the virtues of forbearance and bravery. If the faculty of desire becomes balanced and obeys the rational faculty in all that it considers its share, without contravening any of its commands, it attains the virtues of temperance and generosity. If these three virtues are admixed and combined there arises another thing

«فأعطاه خمسة وسبعين جندا» في مقابلة ما أعطى العقل وكما انهما متقابلان كذلك جنودهما متقابلان فحصل التكافؤ في الإيجاد وتحقق التعاند والتضاد وبقيت العداوة بينهما إلى يوم التناد، وذلك لمصلحة ظاهرة يعلمها أولي الألباب وخفية لا يعلمها إلا علام الغيوب.

وينبغي أن يعلم أن أجناد الفضائل باتفاق الحكماء أربعة:

الأول الحكمة، والثاني الشجاعة، والثالث العفة، والرابع العدالة، وذلك لأن للإنسان قوى ثلاثة متباينة هي مبادي لآثار مختلفة مع مشاركة الإرادة وإذا غلبت احدها على البواقي صارت البواقي مغلوبة أو مفقودة.

وتلك القوى أولها قوة ناطقة وتسمى نفسا ملكية وهي مبدا الفكر في المعقولات والنظر في حقائق الأمور.

وثانيها القوة الغضبية وتسمى نفسا سبعية، وهي مبدا الغضب والإقدام على الأهوال والتسلط والترفع على الغير.

وثالثها القوة الشهوية، وتسمى نفسا بهيمية وهي مبدا الشهوة وطلب الغذاء وشوق الالتذاذ بالماكل والمشارب والمناكح، وإذا تحركت القوة الناطقة بالاعتدال في ذاتها واكتسب المعارف اليقينية حصلت فضيلة العلم والحكمة، وإذا تحركت القوة الغضبية بالاعتدال وانقادت للقوة العاقلة فيما تعده حظا ونصيبا لها ولم تتجاوز عن حكمها حصلت فضيلة الحلم والشجاعة، وإذا تحركت القوة الشهوية بالاعتدال وانقادت للقوة العاقلة واقتصرت على ما تعده العاقلة نصيبا لها ولم تخالفها في حكمها حصلت فضيلة العفة والسخاء، وإذا تركبت هذه الفضائل الثلاثة وتمازجت حصلت حالة متشابهة هي فضيلة العدالة.

ثم انه يندرج تحت هذه الأجناس الأربعة أنواع غير محصورة من الفضائل.

أما الحكمة فالمشهور من أنواعها سبعة: الذكاء، وسرعة الفهم، وصفاء الذهن، وسهولة التعلم، وحسن التعقل، والتحفظ والتذكر.

وأما الشجاعة فالمشهور من أنواعها احد عشر: كبر النفس، والنجدة، والهمة،

which is the virtue of justice.

Thereafter, innumerable virtues are subsumed under these four types. There are seven well-known virtues subsumed under wisdom: astuteness, quick-wittedness, perspicacity, cleverness, reasoning, precaution and memory.

There are eleven notable virtues subsumed under bravery: confidence, courage, determination, resolve, forbearance, gravity, noble-mindedness, endurance, humility, protectiveness and gentleness.

There are twelve notable virtues subsumed under temperance: modesty, companionship, beauty, serenity, conciliation, equanimity, patience, contentment, dignified bearing, piety, consistency, freedom and generosity.

There are eight virtues subsumed under generosity: generosity, sacrifice, forgiveness, chivalry, nobility, empathy, magnanimity and pardon.

There are twelve virtues subsumed under justice: friendship, affection, loyalty, sympathy, kinship, recompense, partnership, fulfilling trusts, love, submission, reliance and worship.

Likewise, one must know that the vices are also four and for every virtue there is a corresponding vice: Ignorance is contrary to wisdom; cowardice is contrary to bravery; covetousness is contrary to temperance.; injustice is contrary to justice.

This is the case at first glance, however, upon closer inspection there are actually eight, because each virtue has a defined limit which if exceeded in the direction of excess or deficiency results in a vice. Virtue is equivalent to the center and vice is the extreme. Thus, the eight vices are the following:

Cunning and stupidity are the extremes of wisdom, cunning an excess and stupidity a deficiency. Brashness and cowardice are the extremes of bravery; covetousness and indolence are the extremes of temperance; oppression and submissiveness are the extremes of justice. Just as every type of virtue has two types of vice, every subtype of virtue has two vices, one which is an excess and the other a deficiency. Some subtypes have names and others do not. As you have come to know that there are seven types of wisdom, there are fourteen types of vice related to them:

Maliciousness and stupidity are the extremes of astuteness, the former an excess and the latter a deficiency; shrewdness and dim-wittedness are the

والثبات، والحلم، والسكون، والشهامة، والتحمل، والتواضع، والحمية، والرقة.

وأما العفة فالمشهور من أنواعها اثني عشر: الحياء، والرفق، وحسن، الهدى، والمسالمة، والدعة، والصبر، والقناعة، والوقار، والورع، والانتظام، والحرية، والسخاء. ثم السخاء نوع يندرج تحته أصناف كثيرة من الفضائل والمشهور منها ثمانية: الكرم، والإيثار، والعفو، والمروة، والنبل، والمواساة، والسماحة، والمسامحة.

وأما العدالة فالمشهور من أنواعها اثني عشر: الصداقة، والألفة، والوفاء، والشفقة، و صلة الرحم، والمكافأة، وحسن الشركة، وحسن القضاء، والتودد، والتسليم، والتوكل، والعبادة.

وكذا ينبغي أن يعلم أن أجناس الرذائل أيضاً أربعة بإزاء كل جنس من الفضيلة جنس من الرذيلة.

الأول: الجهل وهو ضد الحكمة ، الثاني: الجبن وهو ضد الشجاعة ، الثالث: الشره وهو ضد العفة ، الرابع: الجور وهو ضد العدالة.

هذا بحسب بادي النظر. وأما بعد التأمل فأجناس الرذائل ثمانية، لأن كل فضيلة لها حد معين إذا جاوزته في طرف الإفراط أو في التفريط تنتهي إلى رذيلة، فالفضيلة بمثابة الوسط والرذيلة بمثابة الأطراف فيكون أجناس الرذائل ثمانية:

السفه والبله - وهما في طرف الحكمة، السفه في طرف الإفراط والبله في طرف التفريط، والتهور والجبن، وهما في طرفي الشجاعة والشره وخمود الشهوة وهما في طرفي العفة، والظلم والانظلام - وهما في طرفي العدالة - وكما أن لكل جنس من الفضائل جنسين من الرذائل كذلك لكل نوع من الفضائل نوعان من الرذائل:

احدهما في جانب الإفراط والآخر في جانب التفريط، ولبعض تلك الأنواع اسم خاص دون بعضها وقد عرفت أن أنواع الحكمة سبعة أنواع فأنواع ضدها أربعة عشر:

الخبث والبلادة - وهما في طرفي الذكاء الخبث في طرف الإفراط والبلادة في طرف التفريط - وسرعة التخيل والإبطاء - وهما في طرفي سرعة الفهم - وظلمة الذهن

extremes of quick-wittedness; mental cloudiness, which prevents one from conceptualizing, and dementia are the extremes of perspicacity, gullibility and prejudice are the extremes of cleverness; over-thinking and brooding over irrelevant concepts are the extremes of reasoning; restraint in the unnecessary and lack of restraint in the necessary are the extremes of precaution; remembering the superfluous and forgetting the incumbent are the extremes of memory. Apply this accordingly to the rest of the types.

Some types may have well-known names such as impudence and folly which are the extremes of temperance; extravagance and stinginess which are the extremes of generosity; arrogance and servility which are the extremes of humility; depravity and prudishness which are the extremes of worship.

If you have come to know this then we say that in this hadith the virtues and vices that have been mentioned by the Imam, some are types, some are subtypes and some are particulars, which is clear to the perceptive individual. *Sharḥ uṣūl al-kāfī*, v. 1, pp. 202-210.

المانعة من إدراك المطالب والتهابة المانع من الإقامة على المطلوب - وهما في طرفي صفاء الذهن - والمبادرة المانعة من استثبات الصور والتعصب المودي إلى التعذر - وهما في طرفي سهولة التعلم - وصرف الفكر في إدراك ما هو زائد على تعقل المطلوب وصرفه في إدراك ما هو ناقص عنه - وهما في طرفي حسن التعقل - وضبط ما لا فائدة فيه وترك ضبط ما هو مهم - وهما في طرفي التحفظ - وتذكر ما يوجب تضييع الأوقات والنسيان الموجب لإهمال مراعات الواجبات - وهما في طرفي التذكر - وقس عليه أنواع بواقي الأجناس.

وربما يكون لبعض الأنواع اسم مشهور كالوقاحة والخرق وهما في طرفي الحياء - والإسراف والبخل - وهما في طرفي السخاء - والتكبر والتذلل - وهما في طرفي التواضع - والفسق والتحرج - وهما في طرفي العبادة.

إذا عرفت هذا فنقول: ما ذكره عليه السلام في هذا الحديث من الفضائل والرذائل بعضه من الأجناس وبعضه من الأنواع وبعضه من الأصناف وبعضه من الجزئيات كما لا يخفى على المتأمل انتهى/ شرح أصول الكافي/ ١/ ٢٠٢-٢١٠.

Chapter 13

Intellectual Beauty and Majesty

Know that the beauty of a man is his light and there is nothing more luminous than the Intellect endorsed by light. Thus, beauty is measured in relation to light, its type and the world from which it originates. The light and beauty of the people of the Intellectual world is not like the light and beauty of the people of the Imaginal world, nor that of the people of the material world, even if the source of it is a single reality and a single light, which is the hidden, treasured light of God. Theophanies differ according their worlds and sources of effusion.

The Prophet said, "A servant who says, 'There is no god but God' a hundred times God resurrects him on the Day of Judgment like a full moon. On that day He will not raise anyone's deeds more than his except for one who says the same or more."[1]

---

1 Narrated by Tabrānī from Abū al-Dardā' from ibn 'Umar.

الباب الثالث عشر

الجمال والجلال العقلي

اعلم أن جمال المرء بنوره، ولا أنور من العقل المؤيد بالنور، فالجمال على قدر النور ونوعه من أي عالم كان، يتلون بلونه. فليس نور أهل العالم العقلي وجمالهم كنور أهل العالم المثالي و جمالهم، ولا كنور أهل العالم المادي وجمالهم، وان كان مرجع الجميع إلى حقيقة واحدة، ونور واحد وهو نور الله المخزون المكنون، ولكن المجالي مختلفة على حسب عوالمها ومنبع عيونها.

قال النبي ﷺ: «ليس من عبد يقول لا اله إلا الله مائة مرة إلا بعثه الله تعالى يوم القيامة ووجهه كالقمر ليلة البدر، ولا يرفع لاحد يومئذ عمل أفضل من عمله إلا من قال مثل قوله أو زاد»[١].

---

١ -رواه الطبراني عن أبى الدرداء و عن ابن عمر.

He also said, "Among my nation seventy thousand or seven hundred thousand people shall certainly enter paradise, each holding the other's hand and none will enter unless the other enters with him. Their faces will be like the full moon."[2]

Tomorrow, their forms will be like the full moon because it is the most evident and sublime manifestations [of beauty]. The same holds true for those in every world, from the farthest to the nearest, such as the people of the night prayer and those who retire in seclusion with their Lord. God clothes them with a light from His light and they become superlative in beauty, most refined of body, softest in skin, most handsome of figure, soundest of heart; though their eyes sleep their hearts are awake.

In the Bible the beauty of the Intellect is described in the following, "Do not think that I have come to abolish the Law or the Prophets; I have not come to abolish them but to fulfill them. For truly, I say to you, until heaven and earth pass away, not an iota, not a dot, will pass from the Law until all is accomplished. Therefore whoever relaxes one of the least of these commandments and teaches others to do the same will be called least in the kingdom of heaven, but whoever does them and teaches them will be called great in the kingdom of heaven. For I tell you, unless your righteousness exceeds that of the scribes and Pharisees, you will never enter the kingdom of heaven" (Matthew 5: 17-20).

"You have heard that it was said, 'An eye for an eye and a tooth for a tooth.' But I say to you, do not resist the one who is evil. But if anyone slaps you on the right cheek, turn to him the other also. And if anyone would sue you and take your tunic, let him have your cloak as well. And if anyone forces you to go one mile, go with him two miles. Give to the one who begs from you, and do not refuse the one who would borrow from you" (Matthew 5:38-42).

---

2 *Saḥīḥ Bukhārī*, hadith no. 6070.

وعنه ﷺ: «ليدخلن الجنة من أمتي سبعون ألفا أو سبعمائة ألف متماسكون أخذ بعضهم بيد بعض لا يدخل أولهم حتى يدخل آخرهم، وجوههم على صورة القمر ليلة البدر»[٢].

وإنما يكونون على صورة القمر ليلة البدر غدا، لأن ذلك أجلى مظاهر التحقق وأعلاه. والأمر كما هو في كل العوالم من أقصاها إلى أدناها، كأهل صلاة الليل الذين خلو بربهم فكساهم الله نورا من نوره، فصاروا أنظر الناس وجها، وأرق جسما، وألين جلدا، وأصح بدنا، وأسلم قلبا، ونامت عيونهم ولم تنم قلوبهم.

و في الإنجيل يظهر الجمال العقلي بهذا النص و أمثاله: «لاَ تَظُنُّوا أَنِّي جِئْتُ لأُلْغِيَ الشَّرِيعَةَ أَوِ الأَنْبِيَاءَ. مَا جِئْتُ لأُلْغِيَ، بَلْ لأُكَمِّلَ. فَالْحَقَّ أَقُولُ لَكُمْ: إِلَى أَنْ تَزُولَ الأَرْضُ وَالسَّمَاءُ، لَنْ يَزُولَ حَرْفٌ وَاحِدٌ أَوْ نُقْطَةٌ وَاحِدَةٌ مِنَ الشَّرِيعَةِ، حَتَّى يَتِمَّ كُلُّ شَيْءٍ. فَأَيُّ مَنْ خَالَفَ وَاحِدَةً مِنْ هَذِهِ الْوَصَايَا الصُّغْرَى، وَعَلَّمَ النَّاسَ أَنْ يَفْعَلُوا فِعْلَهُ، يُدْعَى الأَصْغَرَ فِي مَلَكُوتِ السَّمَاوَاتِ. وَأَمَّا مَنْ عَمِلَ بِهَا وَعَلَّمَهَا، فَيُدْعَى عَظِيماً فِي مَلَكُوتِ السَّمَاوَاتِ. فَإِنِّي أَقُولُ لَكُمْ: إِنْ لَمْ يَزِدْ بِرُّكُمْ عَلَى بِرِّ الْكَتَبَةِ وَالْفَرِّيسِيِّينَ، لَنْ تَدْخُلُوا مَلَكُوتَ السَّمَاوَاتِ أَبَداً» [إنجيل متى/ موقف المسيح من الشريعة].

و قال: «وَسَمِعْتُمْ أَنَّهُ قِيلَ: عَيْنٌ بِعَيْنٍ وَسِنٌّ بِسِنٍّ. أَمَّا أَنَا فَأَقُولُ لَكُمْ: لاَ تُقَاوِمُوا الشَّرَّ بِمِثْلِهِ، بَلْ مَنْ لَطَمَكَ عَلَى خَدِّكَ الأَيْمَنِ، فَأَدِرْ لَهُ الْخَدَّ الآخَرَ؛ وَمَنْ أَرَادَ مُحَاكَمَتَكَ لِيَأْخُذَ ثَوْبَكَ، فَاتْرُكْ لَهُ رِدَاءَكَ أَيْضاً؛ وَمَنْ سَخَّرَكَ أَنْ تَسِيرَ مِيلاً، فَسِرْ مَعَهُ مِيلَيْنِ. مَنْ طَلَبَ مِنْكَ شَيْئاً، فَأَعْطِهِ. وَمَنْ جَاءَ يَقْتَرِضُ مِنْكَ، فَلاَ تَرُدَّهُ خَائِباً!» [إنجيل متى/ الانتقام].

---

٢ - صحيح البخاري/ ح٦٠٧٠.

"You have heard that it was said, 'You shall love your neighbor and hate your enemy.' But I say to you, love your enemies and pray for those who persecute you, so that you may be sons of your Father who is in heaven. For He makes His sun rise on the evil and on the good, and sends rain on the just and on the unjust. For if you love those who love you, what reward do you have? Do not even the tax collectors do the same? And if you greet only your brothers, what more are you doing than others? Do not even the Gentiles do the same? You therefore must be perfect, as your heavenly Father is perfect" (Matthew 5:43-46).

The majesty of a man is his light and there is nothing more luminous than the Intellect assisted by the bridling light. The Prophet said, "The basis of a house is its foundation and the basis of religion is the gnosis of God and certainty, and the bridling intellect." I asked, "What is the bridling Intellect?" He said, "Desisting from sin and eagerness in obeying God, gratitude for all of His favors, bounties and wholesome trials."[3]

He who covers character flaws with his virtues and fights his desires with his Intellect, goodwill becomes secure and love becomes manifest.

Imām 'Alī said, "The Intellect is a sharp sword."[4]

He also said, "The Intellect is a covering mantle, grace is outward beauty, so cover your character flaws by your grace and fight your desires with your Intellect, you will secure goodwill and love will prosper.[5]

It says in the Bible, "Do not think that I have come to bring peace to the earth. I have not come to bring peace, but a sword. For I have come to set a man against his father, and a daughter against her mother, and a daughter-in-law against her mother-in-law. And a

---

3 *Risālat al-Qushayrī*, p. 438.

4 *Ghurur al-ḥikam wa durar al-kilam*, v. 1, p. 9.

5 *Mawsū'at al-Imām 'Alī ibn abī Ṭālib*, chapter on the various branches of knowledge.

و قال: «وَسَمِعْتُمْ أَنَّهُ قِيلَ: تُحِبُّ قَرِيبَكَ وَتُبْغِضُ عَدُوَّكَ. أَمَّا أَنَا فَأَقُولُ لَكُمْ: أَحِبُّوا أَعْدَاءَكُمْ، وَبَارِكُوا لاَعِنِيكُمْ، وَأَحْسِنُوا مُعَامَلَةَ الَّذِينَ يُبْغِضُونَكُمْ، وَصَلُّوا لأَجْلِ الَّذِينَ يُسِيئُونَ إِلَيْكُمْ وَيَضْطَهِدُونَكُمْ، فَتَكُونُوا أَبْنَاءَ أَبِيكُمُ الَّذِي فِي السَّمَاوَاتِ: فَإِنَّهُ يُشْرِقُ بِشَمْسِهِ عَلَى الأَشْرَارِ وَالصَّالِحِينَ، وَيُمْطِرُ عَلَى الأَبْرَارِ وَغَيْرِ الأَبْرَارِ. فَإِنْ أَحْبَبْتُمُ الَّذِينَ يُحِبُّونَكُمْ، فَأَيَّةُ مُكَافَأَةٍ لَكُمْ؟ أَمَا يَفْعَلُ ذَلِكَ حَتَّى جُبَاةُ الضَّرَائِبِ؟ وَإِنْ رَحَّبْتُمْ بِإِخْوَانِكُمْ فَقَطْ، فَأَيَّ شَيْءٍ فَائِقٍ لِلْعَادَةِ تَفْعَلُونَ؟ أَمَا يَفْعَلُ ذَلِكَ حَتَّى الْوَثَنِيُّونَ؟ فَكُونُوا أَنْتُمْ كَامِلِينَ، كَمَا أَنَّ أَبَاكُمُ السَّمَاوِيَّ هُوَ كَامِلٌ!»[إنجيل متى/ محبة الأعداء].

وجلال المرء بنوره، ولا أنور من العقل المؤيد بالنور القامع.

قال النبي ﷺ:«إن من دعامة البيت أساسه، ودعامة الدين المعرفة بالله، واليقين والعقل القامع. فقلت بأبي و أمي: وما العقل القامع؟

قال: الكف عن المعاصي، والحرص على طاعة الله، والشكر على جميع إحسانه وأنعامه وحسن بلائه»[٣]. ومن ستر خلل خلقه بفضله، وقاتل هواه بعقله، سلمت له المودة، وظهرت له المحبة. قال أمير المؤمنين عليه السلام: «العقل حسام قاطع»[٤].

و قال أيضاً: «العقل غطاء ستير، والفضل جمال ظاهر، فاستر خلل خلقك بفضلك، وقاتل هواك بعقلك، تسلم لك المودة، وتظهر لك المحبة»[٥].

و في الإنجيل يظهر الجلال العقلي بهذا النص وأمثاله: «لاَ تَظُنُّوا أَنِّي جِئْتُ لأُرْسِيَ سَلاماً عَلَى الأَرْضِ. مَا جِئْتُ لأُرْسِيَ سَلاَماً، بَلْ سَيْفاً. فَإِنِّي جِئْتُ لأَجْعَلَ الإِنْسَانَ عَلَى خِلاَفٍ مَعَ أَبِيهِ، وَالْبِنْتَ مَعَ أُمِّهَا، وَالْكَنَّةَ مَعَ

---

٣ – سبق تخريجه.

٤ – غرر الحكم و درر الكلم/ ج ١/ ص ٩.

٥ – موسوعة الإمام علي بن أبي طالب/ باب فروع مختلفة من العلوم.

person's enemies will be those of his own household. Whoever loves his father or mother more than me is not worthy of me, and whoever loves his son or daughter more than me is not worthy of me. And whoever does not take his cross and follow me is not worthy of me. Whoever finds his life will lose it, and whoever loses his life for my sake will find it. Whoever receives you receives me, and whoever receives me receives Him who sent me. The one who receives a prophet because he is a prophet will receive a prophet's reward, and the one who receives a righteous person because he is a righteous person will receive a righteous person's reward. And whoever gives one of these little ones even a cup of cold water because he is a disciple, truly, I say to you, he will by no means lose his reward" (Matthew 10: 34-42).

It also says in the Bible, "I came to cast fire on the earth, and would that it were already kindled! I have a baptism to be baptized with, and how great is my distress until it is accomplished! Do you think that I have come to give peace on earth? No, I tell you, but rather division. For from now on in one house there will be five divided, three against two and two against three. They will be divided, father against son and son against father, mother against daughter and daughter against mother, mother-in-law against her daughter-in-law and daughter-in-law against mother-in-law."

He also said to the crowds, "When you see a cloud rising in the west, you say at once, 'A shower is coming.' And so it happens. And when you see the south wind blowing, you say, 'There will be scorching heat,' and it happens. You hypocrites! You know how to interpret the appearance of earth and sky, but why do you not know how to interpret the present time?

"And why do you not judge for yourselves what is right? As you go with your accuser before the magistrate, make an effort to settle with him on the way, lest he drag you to the judge, and the judge hand you

حَمَاتِهَا. وَهَكَذَا يَصِيرُ أَعْدَاءَ الإِنْسَانِ أَهْلُ بَيْتِهِ. مَنْ أَحَبَّ أَبَاهُ أَوْ أُمَّهُ أَكْثَرَ مِنِّي، فَلاَ يَسْتَحِقُّنِي. وَمَنْ أَحَبَّ ابْنَهُ أَوِ ابْنَتَهُ أَكْثَرَ مِنِّي، فَلا يَسْتَحِقُّنِي. وَمَنْ لاَ يَحْمِلْ صَلِيبَهُ وَيَتْبَعْنِي، فَهُوَ لاَ يَسْتَحِقُّنِي. مَنْ يَتَمَسَّكْ بِحَيَاتِهِ، يَخْسَرْهَا؛ وَمَنْ يَخْسَرْ حَيَاتَهُ مِنْ أَجْلِي، فَإِنَّهُ يَرْبَحُهَا. مَنْ يَقْبَلْكُمْ، يَقْبَلْنِي؛ وَمَنْ يَقْبَلْنِي، يَقْبَلِ الَّذِي أَرْسَلَنِي. مَنْ يُرَحِّبْ بِنَبِيٍّ لِكَوْنِهِ نَبِيّاً، فَإِنَّهُ يَنَالُ مُكَافَأَةَ نَبِيٍّ؛ وَمَنْ يُرَحِّبْ بِرَجُلٍ بَارٍّ لِكَوْنِهِ بَارّاً، فَإِنَّهُ يَنَالُ مُكَافَأَةَ بَارٍّ. وَأَيُّ مَنْ سَقَى وَاحِداً مِنْ هَؤُلاَءِ الصِّغَارِ وَلَوْ كَأْسَ مَاءٍ بَارِدٍ، فَقَطْ لأَنَّهُ تِلْمِيذٌ لِي، فَالْحَقَّ أَقُولُ لَكُمْ: إِنَّ مُكَافَأَتَهُ لَنْ تَضِيعَ أَبَداً» [إنجيل متى/ يسوع والعالم].

و كذلك في الإنجيل: جِئْتُ لأُلْقِيَ عَلَى الأَرْضِ نَاراً، فَلَكَمْ أَوَدُّ أَنْ تَكُونَ قَدِ اشْتَعَلَتْ؟ وَلكِنَّ لِي مَعْمُودِيَّةً عَلَيَّ أَنْ أَتَعَمَّدَ بِهَا، وَكَمْ أَنَا مُتَضَايِقٌ حَتَّى تَتِمَّ! أَتَظُنُّونَ أَنِّي جِئْتُ لأُرسِيَ السَّلاَمَ عَلَى الأَرْضِ؟ أَقُولُ لَكُمْ: لاَ، بَلْ بِالأَحْرَى الانْقِسَامَ: فَإِنَّهُ مُنْذُ الآنَ يَكُونُ فِي الْبَيْتِ الْوَاحِدِ خَمْسَةٌ فَيَنْقَسِمُونَ: ثَلاَثَةٌ عَلَى اثْنَيْنِ، وَاثْنَانِ عَلَى ثَلاثَةٍ، فَالآبُ يَنْقَسِمُ عَلَى ابْنِهِ، وَالابْنُ عَلَى أَبِيهِ، وَالأُمُّ عَلَى بِنْتِهَا، وَالْبِنْتُ عَلَى أُمِّهَا، وَالْحَمَاةُ عَلَى كَنَّتِهَا، وَالْكَنَّةُ عَلَى حَمَاتِهَا!» وَقَالَ أَيْضاً لِلْجُمُوعِ: «عِنْدَمَا تَرَوْنَ سَحَابَةً تَطْلُعُ مِنَ الْغَرْبِ، تَقُولُونَ حَالاً: الْمَطَرُ آتٍ! وَهكَذَا يَكُونُ. وَعِنْدَمَا تَهُبُّ رِيحُ الْجَنُوبِ، تَقُولُونَ: سَيَكُونُ حَرٌّ! وَهَكَذَا يَكُونُ. يَا مُرَاؤُونَ! تَعْرِفُونَ أَنْ تُمَيِّزُوا مَنْظَرَ الأَرْضِ وَالسَّمَاءِ، فَكَيْفَ لاَ تُمَيِّزُونَ هَذَا الزَّمَانَ؟ وَلِمَاذَا لاَ تُمَيِّزُونَ مَا هُوَ حَقٌّ مِنْ تِلْقَاءِ أَنْفُسِكُمْ؟ فَفِيمَا أَنْتَ ذَاهِبٌ مَعَ خَصْمِكَ إِلَى الْمُحَاكَمَةِ، اجْتَهِدْ فِي الطَّرِيقِ لِتَتَصَالَحَ مَعَهُ، لِئَلاَّ يَجُرَّكَ إِلَى الْقَاضِي، فَيُسَلِّمَكَ الْقَاضِي إِلَى الشُّرطِيِّ، وَيُلْقِيَكَ الشُّرطِيُّ فِي السِّجْنِ. أَقُولُ لَكَ: إِنَّكَ لَنْ تَخْرُجَ مِنْ هُنَاكَ أَبَداً حَتَّى تَكُونَ قَدْ وَفَّيْتَ مَا عَلَيْكَ إِلَى

over to the officer, and the officer put you in prison. I tell you, you will never get out until you have paid the very last penny." (Luke 12:49-59).

If these prophetic ethical qualities that have been mentioned are considered to be the divine law (*sharī'a*), then the saint is the model of that law, with respect to both the intellect and the law. Therefore, what issues from him are beatific and majestic rulings of the intellect that are harmonious with His law and He who prescribed it.

If the human being manifests the beatific and majestic perfection of the rational Intellect, namely, acquire its qualities and act in accordance with the governance of the Intellect in the visible and hidden aspects of the human kingdom, friendship is secured and God and His creation love him. However, this primarily originates from his own soul, not from his Lord, and produces both positive and negative effects that may or may not be supported.

If the human being manifests the beatific and majestic perfection of the Intellect endorsed by light, friendship is secured and God and His creation love him. It gives rise to positive effects that are agreeable to all with whom he interacts and he is supported.

All praise be God, the Lord of the Worlds.

آخِرِ فَلْسٍ!» [إنجيل لوقا/ يسوع والعالم].

و إن كانت هذه الأخلاق النبوية المذكورة شرعية إلا أن الولي نسخة الشرع عقلا و شرعا فيصدر منه أحكام عقلية جمالية و جلالية مماثلة لشرعه و مَن عيّنه.

و الإنسان إن ظهر بكمال عقله الكسبي الجمالي و الجلالي، أي اتصف بصفات و أدى أفعال من حيث الحكم العقلي لغيب مملكته الإنسانية وشهادتها، سلمت له المودة وظهرت له المحبة من الله وخلقه، ولكن هذا يغلب أن يكون من حيث نفسه لا من حيث ربه، فتترتب عليه آثار مرجوة و غير مرجوة، وقد لا يعان عليهما.

و إن ظهر بكمال عقله المؤيد بالنور الجمالي و الجلالي، سلمت له المودة، وظهرت له المحبة من الله وخلقه، فتترتب عليه آثار مرجوة موفقة مع جميع ما يرتبط به، ويعان عليها. والحمد لله رب العالميـن.

Chapter 14

The White Pearl and the Red Ruby

Since the First Intellect is the highest of all contingent entities, the supreme, noblest and intensely simple in substance, free from every corruption, it is called the White Pearl. This is because the pearl is the highest and the noblest gem of the sea. It is a heavenly drop of water that falls into the salty sea, pure from any earthly contamination, as mentioned in the hadith. "The first thing that God created was the Intellect and the first thing that God created was the white pearl."[1]

Due to the admixture of the soul's luminosity with the darkness of bodily attachment, unlike the 'discrete' Intellect, is called the Red Ruby and the Green Emerald as these are the most resplendent of earthly gems.

---

[1] Kashānī, *Laṭa'if al-i'lām fī ishārāt ahl al-ilhām*, p. 474.

الباب الرابع عشر

الدرة البيضاء والياقوتة الحمراء

لما كان العقل الأول أعلى الموجودات الممكنة وافضلها وأشرفها واشدها بساطة ونزاهة عن الفساد سمي بالدرة البيضاء. إذ الدر أعلى الجواهر البحرية وافضلها وأشرفها، وهو ماء سماوي صافي في غاية الصفاء عما يشوبه من الكدورات الأرضية يدر من مدرار السماء فينزل إلى البحر المالح، كما جاء في الحديث: أول ما خلق الله العقل، وأول ما خلق الله درة بيضاء[1].

ولامتزاج نورية النفس بظلمة التعلق بالجسم بخلاف العقل المفارق، كنوا عنها بالياقوتة الحمراء والزمردة الخضراء، لأنها اجل الجواهر الترابية الأرضية.

---

١ - لطائف الاعلام في اشـارات أهل الاهام/ الشيخ عبد الرزاق القاساني/ ص٤٧٤.

According to this depiction of the Intellect and of the soul, and their being named pearl, ruby or emerald, the colors of the perfect humans and the people of God differ with respect to their individual stations. One whose station corresponds with the Intellectual world is called the White Pearl. His is the purest, highest and noblest of gems whose lights and colors are white. Those who are of the Imaginal and sensory worlds are called the Red Ruby and the Green Emerald. Each have their colors, a governing divine name and an invocation.

Kashānī writes in *Laṭā'if al-iʿlām*, "The White Pearl is the First Intellect. It is called so because it is the most intensely simple and pure among the entities. Thus, it is not colored as the hadith states, "The first thing that God created was the Intellect and the first thing that He created was the White Pearl. Since the First Intellect is the highest, supreme and noblest of all contingent entities, it is called the white pearl. This is because the pearl is the highest, supreme and noblest gem of the sea. The pearl is a heavenly drop of water that falls from the sky into the salty sea, absolutely pure from any earthly contamination. The oyster receives it and it is formed in the sea according to the specific receptivity of the oyster, transforming it accordingly. Likewise, the role of the Intellect is like that of the receptive oyster of contingency [receiving] the water of life that flows from the Sea of Necessity [carried] by the air of the breath of the All-merciful and arising from the empyrean of Lordship.

The First Intellect, existentially, is the pearl of the Sea of Necessity whose origin is the water of life from the breath of the All-merciful. It is also the pearl in the sea of contingency from the perspective that there is existential unity among realities in the manifestation of entities. It is white because white is the best color and the nearest in relation to light. That is why the soul is called the Emerald and the Red Ruby, since red, green and all colors besides white and black are an isthmus, just as the soul is an isthmus between the intellect and nature.[2]

2 Kashānī, *Laṭā'if al-iʿlām fī ishārāt ahl al-ilhām*, p. 474.

فعلى هذه الصورة المذكورة للعقل والنفس، وللمناسبة في تسميتهما بالدرة والياقوتة أو الزمردة يكون مقام الكمّل وغيرهم من أهل الله وتتعين ألوانهم من حيث منازلهم، فالذي كان من العالم العقلي يسمى بالدرة البيضاء، وله من الجواهر أصفاها و أعلاها وأشرفها، ومن الأنوار والألوان البياض، والذي كان من العالم المثالي والحسي، يسمى بالياقوتة الحمراء والزمردة الخضراء، وله من الجواهر ألوانها. وكل له اسم وذكر يحكمه.

قال القاشاني في لطائف الأعلام: الدرة البيضاء هو العقل الأول، سمي بذلك لكونه اشد الممكنات بساطة ونزاهة، فلا يكون متلون، وفي الحديث: أول ما خلق الله العقل. وأول ما خلق الله درة بيضاء. فلما كان العقل أعلى الموجودات الممكنة و افضلها وأشرفها سمي بالدرة، إذ الدرر أعلى الجواهر البحرية وأشرفها وافضلها، والدر ماء سماوي خالص في غاية الصفاء، عما يشوب غيره من الكدورات الأرضية يدر من مدرار السماء، فينزل إلى البحر المالح فيتلقاه الصدف فيتكون وينعقد في البحر بخصوص قابلية في الصدف، ويتكيف فيه بكيفية في تعينه بحسبه، وكذلك العقل وجوده دار إلى صدف قابلية الإمكان من ماء الحياة الفائضة من بحر الوجوب الجاري في هواء النفس الرحماني من فوقية سماء الربوبية.

فالعقل الأول من حيث وجوده درة بحر الوجوب واصلها من ماء الحياة النفس الرحماني، وهو أيضاً درة بحر الإمكان باعتبار أحدية جمع حقائق مظهريات الممكنات، وبياضها لأن البياض أفضل الألوان، وأتمها مناسبة بالنور، ولهذا سميت النفس بالزمردة، وبالياقوتة الحمراء، لأن الحمرة والخضرة وغيرهما من الألوان مما هو غير البياض، والسواد لها البرزخية بينهما، فكذا النفس لها البرزخية بين العقل والطبيعة[٢].

---

٢ - لطائف الأعلام في إشـارات أهل الإلهام/ الشيخ عبد الرزاق القاساني/ ص٤٧٤.

The Bible says, "The kingdom of heaven is like treasure hidden in a field, which a man found and covered up. Then in his joy he goes and sells all that he has and buys that field. Again, the kingdom of heaven is like a merchant in search of fine pearls, who, on finding one pearl of great value, went and sold all that he had and bought it" (Matthew 13:44-45). All praise be to God, the Lord of the Worlds.

و في الإنجيل: «يُشَبَّهُ مَلَكُوتُ السَّمَاوَاتِ بِكَنْزٍ مَطْمُورٍ فِي حَقْلٍ، وَجَدَهُ رَجُلٌ، فَعَادَ وَطَمَرَهُ. وَمِنْ فَرَحِهِ، ذَهَبَ وَبَاعَ كُلَّ مَا كَانَ يَمْلِكُ وَاشْتَرَى ذلكَ الْحَقْلَ. وَيُشَبَّهُ مَلَكُوتُ السَّمَاوَاتِ أَيْضاً بِتَاجِرٍ كَانَ يَبْحَثُ عَنِ اللآلِيءِ الْجَمِيلَةِ. فَلَمَّا إِنْ وَجَدَ لُؤْلُؤَةً ثَمِينَةً جِدّاً، حَتَّى ذَهَبَ وَبَاعَ كُلَّ مَا يَمْلِكُ، وَاشْتَرَاهَا»[إنجيل متى/ مثل الكنز و مثل اللؤلؤة]. والحمد لله رب العالميـن.

Chapter 15

The Intellectual Paradise

Know that paradise and hellfire originate from the human soul, originating with every soul from inception to maturity and created by a person's deeds, qualities, perceptions and habits, accumulated from the beginning of life until its end. Both can be witnessed as a reality within us as we move between them but not in actual form. God says, "Certainly not! If you only knew with the knowledge of certainty. You would surely behold the Hellfire. Then you would surely behold it with the eye of certainty" (105:5-7).

It is related that the Prophet was sitting in the mosque when he heard a loud thud. The Prophet asked, "Do you know what that was?" They replied, "God and His Messenger know best." He then told us, "That was a stone which was thrown into the Hellfire seventy years ago, it was sinking further into the Fire and had just reached the bottom."

الباب الخامس عشر

الجنة العقلية

اعلم أن الجنة والنار تنشآن من النفس الإنسانية، وتحدثان لكل نفس بحدوثها وبلوغها، وتعمران بأعمالها وأخلاقها ومدركاتها وملكاتها الحاصلة لها من أول العمر إلى آخره. وهما مشهودتان لنا محلا لا صورة نتقلب في احدهما قال تعالى: ﴿ كَلَّا لَوْ تَعْلَمُونَ عِلْمَ الْيَقِينِ ۝ لَتَرَوُنَّ الْجَحِيمَ ۝ ثُمَّ لَتَرَوُنَّهَا عَيْنَ الْيَقِينِ ﴾ [التكاثر: ٥-٧]، ﴿ إِنَّ الَّذِينَ يَأْكُلُونَ أَمْوَالَ الْيَتَامَىٰ ظُلْمًا إِنَّمَا يَأْكُلُونَ فِي بُطُونِهِمْ نَارًا وَسَيَصْلَوْنَ سَعِيرًا ﴾ [النساء: ١٠].

وقد روي أن النبي ﷺ كان قاعدا في المسجد فسمعوا هدة عظيمة فارتاعوا، فقال النبي ﷺ: «أتعرفون ما هذه الهدة ؟ قالوا: الله و رسوله أعلم.

قال ﷺ: «حجر القي من أعلى جهنم منذ سبعين سنة الآن وصل إلى قعرها، فكان وصوله إلى قعرها وسقوطه فيها هذه الهدة.

No sooner than he finished speaking that a shriek was heard from the house of the hypocrite announcing his death; he was seventy years old. The Prophet exclaimed, "God is Greater!" Thereupon, the knowledgeable among the companions understood that the stone was that very hypocrite who was falling towards hellfire since his inception until he reached its bottom when he died at the age of seventy.

God says, "The hypocrites occupy the lowest depths of hell." (4:145).[1]

Imām Sajjād says, "Know that one who opposes a friend of God and adopts a religion other than God's religion and takes matters in his own hands without the consent of God's representative will be in the burning fire. The fire eats the body while the spirit has departed and they have been overcome by wretchedness. They are dead who will not find the hellfire, and were they alive they would have felt the anguish of the fire. So take lesson, O people of insight, and praise God in what he has guided you."[2]

If you have come to know this, then know that there is an intellectual, spiritual paradise that arises from the various types of true knowledge, gnostic [realities] endowed with certainty, and light of the Intellect, since gnosis is the seed of witnessing and the gnosis of God through God is the most distinct and noble types of gnosis.

Imām al-Ṣādiq says, "If people only knew the excellence in the gnosis of God they would never cast a glance on the adornments and worldly comforts of which the enemies [of God] take pleasure. The world would be less valuable than what their feet trample upon. They would repose in the gnosis of God, take pleasure in it as one who is presently enjoying the gardens of paradise with the saints of God."[3]

In contrast to the paradise of the Intellect is the fire which arises from the loss of gnosis and perfections of the Intellect, either through

---

1 See Kāshānī, *Qurrat al-'uyūn*, p. 216, and al-*'Uhūd al-Muḥammadiyya*, p. 783.

2 *al-Kāfī*, v. 8, p. 17.

3 *al-Kāfī*, v. 8, p. 247.

فلما فرغ من كلامه إلا والصراخ في دار منافق من المنافقين قد مات وكان عمره سبعين سنة. فقال صلى الله عليه وآله وسلم: الله أكبر.

فعلمت علماء الصحابة أن هذا الحجر هو ذلك المنافق وانه منذ خلقه يهوي في جهنم، وبلغ عمره سبعين سنة، فلما مات حصل في قعرها».

قال الله تعالى: ﴿إِنَّ الْمُنَافِقِينَ فِي الدَّرْكِ الْأَسْفَلِ مِنَ النَّارِ﴾ [النساء/ ١٤٥][1].

وقال الإمام السجاد عليه السلام: «اعلموا أن من خالف أولياء الله و دان بغير دين الله واستبد بأمره دون أمر ولي الله كان في نار تلتهب، تأكل أبدانا قد غابت عنها أرواحها وغلبت عليها شقوتها، فهم موتى لا يجدون حر النار، ولو كانوا أحياء لوجدوا مضض حر النار، فاعتبروا يا أولي الأبصار واحمدوا الله على ماهداكم»[2].

وإذا علمت هذا فاعلم أن من الجنان جنة عقلية روحانية تنشا من العلوم الحقيقية والمعارف اليقينية والأنوار العقلية. إذ المعرفة بذرة المشاهدة، ومعرفة الله بالله أجلى المعارف وأشرفها.

فعن الصادق عليه السلام: «لو يعلم الناس ما في فضل معرفة الله تعالى ما مدوا أعينهم إلى ما متع به الأعداء من زهرة الحياة الدنيا ونعيمها، وكانت دنياهم أقل عندهم مما يطؤنه بأرجلهم، ولنعموا بمعرفة الله وتلذذوا بها تلذذ من لم يزل في روضات الجنان مع أولياء الله»[3].

ويقابل الجنة العقلية النار التي تنشا من فقدان المعارف والكمالات العقلية نكرانا أو وحرمانا بعد الإدراك وغير ذلك، وعن الرسول صلى الله عليه وآله: «ما منكم إلا وله منزلان منزل في الجنة ومنزل في النار، فان مات ودخل النار

---

١ - لاحظ قرة العيون/ الفيض الكاشاني/ ص٢١٦، و العهود المحمدية/ ٧٨٣.

٢ - الكافي/ ٨/ ١٧.

٣ - الكافي/ ٨/ ٢٤٧.

denial or deprivation after having perceived them, and so forth. The Prophet says, "Each one of you has two places, a place in paradise and a place in the fire. He who dies and enters the fire someone from the people of paradise will inherit his place.[4]

Despite what has been mentioned that paradise corresponds to the worlds and the stations of its people, a theophany is not limited to a single world or station since the loci of theophany are limitless and effusion is endless. Man has been created for permanence, not for extinction.

Theophanies and specifics of the Intellectual world correspond to the degrees of its people, "We favored some messengers over others; God spoke to some, while others He raised in rank. We gave Jesus, the son of Mary, clear proofs and We strengthened him with the Holy Spirit. If God had so willed, their followers would not have fought each other after clear signs had come to them. But they differed, some believing and some disbelieving. If God had so willed, they would not have fought each other, but God does what He wills" (2:253).[5] Praise be to God, Lord of the Worlds.

---

4 *Biḥār al-anwār*, v. 8, p. 91.

5 Fayḍ Kāshānī writes, "There are two paradises, a spiritual paradise for the proximate ones that arises from certain kinds of true knowledge and true gnosis. Gnosis in the world is the seed for witnessing in the hereafter and complete rapture is contingent on witnessing, since existence is delightful and its perfection even more so. If gnostic truths that conform to the nature of the intellectual faculty, such as the knowledge of God, His angels, His books, His prophets and the Last Day are witnessed, then the soul experiences indescribable rapture.

The second is a physical paradise which is for the people of the right. It arises from virtuous character, truthful speech and righteous deeds, on account of which the human soul creates maidens, palaces, youths, pearls, rubies and coral in its world and plane. The soul is capable of that by God's permission. As long as it is in this plane these effects are not produced in it for it is too weak and preoccupied with sensory things. However, if it becomes strong, purified and its preoccupations cease, and all of its faculties

ورث أهل الجنة منزله»[٤].

و سوى ما ذكر من الجنان على حسب العوالم ومقامات أهلها، ولا ينحصر التجلي في العالم و المقام بواحد، إذ المجالي لا حصر لها و الفيض دائم، و الإنسان خلق للبقاء لا للفناء.

وههنا تتناسب التجليات و خصوصيات العالم العقلي التي تتفاضل بتفاضل درجات أهله ﴿ تِلْكَ الرُّسُلُ فَضَّلْنَا بَعْضَهُمْ عَلَىٰ بَعْضٍ مِّنْهُم مَّن كَلَّمَ اللهُ وَرَفَعَ بَعْضَهُمْ دَرَجَاتٍ وَآتَيْنَا عِيسَى ابْنَ مَرْيَمَ الْبَيِّنَاتِ وَأَيَّدْنَاهُ بِرُوحِ الْقُدُسِ وَلَوْ شَاءَ اللهُ مَا اقْتَتَلَ الَّذِينَ مِن بَعْدِهِم مِّن بَعْدِ مَا جَاءَتْهُمُ الْبَيِّنَاتُ وَلَكِنِ اخْتَلَفُوا فَمِنْهُم مَّنْ آمَنَ وَمِنْهُم مَّن كَفَرَ وَلَوْ شَاءَ اللهُ مَا اقْتَتَلُوا وَلَكِنَّ اللهَ يَفْعَلُ مَا يُرِيدُ ﴾ [سورة البقرة/ ٢٥٣][٥]. والحمد لله رب العالمين.

---

٤ - بحار الأنوار/ ٨/ ٩١.

٥ - قال الفيض الكاشاني ما حاصله: الجنة جنتان: جنة روحانية للمقربين، تنشا من العلوم الحقة و المعارف اليقينية، فان المعرفة في الدنيا بذرة المشاهدة في الآخرة، واللذة الكاملة موقوفة على المشاهدة، فان الوجود لذيذ وكماله ألذّ، فالمعارف التي هي مقتضى طباع القوة العاقلة من العلم بالله وملائكته وكتبه ورسله واليوم الآخر إذا صارت مشاهدة للنفس كانت لها لذة لا يدرك الوصف كنهها.

وجنة جسمانية: لهم أيضاً ولأصحاب اليمين، تنشا من الأخلاق الفاضلة والأقوال الصادقة والأعمال الصالحة بإبداع النفس الإنسانية المتصفة بها الصور الملذة من الحور والقصور والغلمان واللؤلؤ والياقوت والمرجان في عالمها وصقعها. فان للنفس اقتدارا على ذلك بإذن الله تعالى، ولكنها ما دامت في هذه النشأة لا يترتب عليها آثارها لضعفها واشتغالها بالمحسوسات، فإذا قويت وصفت وزالت الشواغل، وانحصرت القوى كلها في قوة واحدة ذات تخيل حتى صارت عينا باصرة للنفس وقدرة فعالة لها وانقلب العلم

become one faculty possessing an imagination, a seeing eye for the soul and an active power that transforms knowledge into witnessing. Thereafter, whatever occurs in the mind that the soul inclines towards becomes a state sanctioned by God, whereby it sees it with the eyes and senses it stronger than ever before. He only has to say 'Be!' to something and it is, as it states in the Ḥadith *Qudṣī*, "O mankind, I have created you for permanence. I am the Living and do not die. Obey me in what I have commanded you and desist from what I have forbidden you, and I will make you like Me, alive and never dying. I am the One who says to a thing 'Be!' and it is. Obey me in what I have commanded you, I will make you like Me, if you say to a thing 'Be!' it will be." (*Mustadrak al-wasā'il*, v. 11, p. 25).

"I have prepared for My righteous servants what no eye has seen no ear has heard or entered in the heart of any man." (*Biḥār al-anwār*, v. 8, p. 92).

In the Qur'ān, "No soul knows what joy is kept hidden in store for them as a reward for their actions" (32:17).

The hellfire is also of two types: A spiritual fire which ascends over the hearts of the hypocrites, the arrogant and the untruthful. It arises by means of the world of Intellect due to the loss of gnosis and Intellectual perfections, either through denying, rejecting, or being deprived of them after having perceived them and having yearned for them. It results from experiencing their contrary, which is compound ignorance and the loss of pure potentiality and the acquisition of Satanic actuality, deviation, being entrenched in false doctrines of personal conjecture. These are indeed painful.

There is no pain due to natural deficiencies but it is like death and chronic disease of the organs without the feeling of pain. Both are not capable of being amended in the hereafter, although stupidity is less capable of being cured than cleverness. In any case, torment for these types is severe as well.

They feel the fire along with those who committed cardinal sins, in accordance with their deeds. It is the continuation of the worldly plane because of the loss of pleasures after becoming habituated and attached to them, lingering in them. It also due to committing evil deeds, speaking lies and possessing vices, since the soul creates correspondingly painful forms

مشاهدة، فلا يخطر بالبال شيء تميل إليه النفس إلا ويوجد بالحال بإذن الله تعالى بحيث يراه رؤية عيان ويحس به إحساسا قويا لا أقوى منه، فلا يقول لشي كن إلا ويكون، وفي الحديث القدسي: «يابن آدم خلقتك للبقاء وأنا حي لا أموت اطعني فيما أمرتك به وانته عما نهيتك عنه أجعلك مثلي حيا لا تموت، وأنا الذي أقول لشيء كن فيكون اطعني فيما أمرتك به أجعلك مثلي إذا قلت لشيء كن فيكون»./ مستدرك الوسائل / ١١/ ٢٥٨.

وفيه أعددت لعبادي الصالحين ما لا عين رأت ولا أُذن سمعت ولا خطر على قلب بشر./ البحار/ ٨/ ٩٢.

وفي القرآن: ﴿ فَلَا تَعْلَمُ نَفْسٌ مَا أُخْفِيَ لَهُمْ مِنْ قُرَّةِ أَعْيُنٍ جَزَاءً بِمَا كَانُوا يَعْمَلُونَ ﴾ [سورة السجدة:١٧].

والنار ناران: نار روحانية: تطلع على الأفئدة للمنافقين والمتكبرين والمكذبين، تنشأ بوسيلة عالم العقل بسبب فقدان المعارف والكمالات العقلية، إما بإنكارها وجحودها أو بالحرمان عنها بعد إدراكها والشوق إليها بحسب حصول أضدادها بالجهل المركب وفقدان القوة الهيولانية وحصول فعلية الشيطنة والاعوجاج ورسوخ العقائد الباطلة في الوهم، وهي مؤلمة جدا.

وأما النقص بحسب الغريزة فلا الم بسببه بل هي بمنزلة الموت والزمانة في الأعضاء من غير شعور بألم وكلاهما مشتركان في عدم الانجبار في الأخرة إلا أن البلاهة أدنى إلى الخلاص من فطانة تبرء «خ/ بتراء» فالعذاب لهؤلاء عظيم ولأولئك اليم.

ونار محسوسة لهم ولأهل الكبائر على قدر أعمالهم تنشا بتبعية هذه النشأة الدنياوية بسبب فقدان متاعها بعد حصول الألف له والتعلق له والأخلاد إليه وارتكاب الأعمال السيئة والأقوال الكاذبة والأخلاق الردية، فان النفس بسبب ذلك تنشئ في عالمها صورا مؤذية مناسبة لها من الحيات والعقارب والسموم واليحموم وغيرها، فتتأذى بها ولا تقدر على عدم إنشائها.

كما أنها إذا أصابتها في الدنيا مصيبة فكلما يخطر ببالها اغتمت بها وتأذت ولا يمكنها

---

in its world such as snakes, scorpions, poisons, black smoke, and so on. It will be pained by them and will be unable to not create them.

As in this world, the soul is distressed whenever it thinks of a tribulation. It feels its pain and it can hardly bear to think of it. In this world, some distraction might make it forget for a while, but in the hereafter, it will not be able to turn its attention away from the pain due to some other preoccupation. This is because the purity and potency of that realm, the various faculties will transform into a single faculty possessing imagination and the soul will still desire what it cannot find, long for what harms it, seek what it detests, choose what pains it, and flee from what rectifies it, saying, "Ah, would that between me and you there were the distance of the two horizons—what an evil companion!" (43:38). This will be the case unless these forms are foreign to the very substance of the soul whereby they do not remain in it and discontinue after a period of time, according to the degree, intensity and depth of attachment or lack thereof, God willing. Thus, whoever has an iota of faith will exit the fire. "So whoever does an iota of good shall see it, and whoever does an iota of evil shall see it" (99:7-8). "God does not forgive that one ascribe a partner for Him, but He forgives everything else for those whom He wills" (4:48).

The Prophet said, "He who sent me in truth as a bearer of glad tidings, God shall never punish the monotheist in the fire. The people of divine unity will intercede and receive intercession. (*al-Amālī*, p. 372).

Imām al-Ṣādiq relates from his forefathers that the Prophet said, "Whomever God has promised a reward for a deed, He will certainly fulfill it, and whomever God has warned about a punishment for a deed, God has a choice in the matter. *Maḥasin al-Barqī*, p. 246, *al-I'tiqadāt*, p. 67. See also, *Qurrat al-'uyūn*, p. 252.

أن تخطرها، ولكنها في الدنيا تغفل عنها أحيانا بسبب الشواغل بخلاف الأخرة فإنها لا تغفل عنها لعدم الشاغل وصفاء المحل وقوته وصيرورة القوى كلها قوة واحدة ذات تخيل، فلا يزال يريد ما لا يجده ويشتهي ما يضره ويفعل ما يكره ويختار ما يعذبه ويهرب عما يصحبه قائلا: ﴿ يا لَيْتَ بَيْنِي وَبَيْنَكَ بُعْدَ الْمَشْرِقَيْنِ فَبِئْسَ الْقَرِينُ ﴾ [سورة الزخرف:٣٨]. إلا أن هذه الهيئات لما كانت غريبة عن جوهر النفس وكذا ما يلزمها فلا يبعد أن تزول في مدة من الدهر متفاوتة على حسب تفاوت العلائق في رسوخها وضعفها وكثرتها وقلتها إن شاء الله، فيخرج من النار من في قلبه ذرة من الإيمان ﴿ فَمَن يَعْمَلْ مِثْقَالَ ذَرَّةٍ خَيْرًا يَرَهُ ۝ وَمَن يَعْمَلْ مِثْقَالَ ذَرَّةٍ شَرًّا يَرَهُ ﴾ [سورة الزلزلة:٧-٨]،﴿ إِنَّ اللهَ لَا يَغْفِرُ أَن يُشْرَكَ بِهِ وَيَغْفِرُ مَا دُونَ ذَٰلِكَ لِمَن يَشَاءُ ﴾ [سورة النساء:٤٨]. قال النبي ﷺ: والذي بعثني بالحق بشيرا لا يعذب الله بالنار موحد أبداً، وان أهل التوحيد يشفعون فيشفعون./ الأمالي، الشيخ الصدوق/ ٣٧٢

وعن الصادق عليه السلام عن ابائه عليهم السلام قال: قال رسول الله ﷺ: من وعده الله على عمل ثوابا فهو منجز له، ومن أوعده على عمل عقابا فهو فيه بالخيار./ محاسن البرقي/ ٢٤٦، والاعتقادات / ٦٧. لاحظ قرة العيون / ص ٢٥٢.

Chapter 16

The Culmination of the Intellect and its Completion

There is a great amount of disagreement among scholars concerning the origin, division, rank and nobility of the Intellect, and the heart, spirit, soul, etc., the realities of which are compounded with one another. Some maintain that each is a separate entity but others have said that it is a single thing that possesses various aspects giving rise to the multiplicity of terms. With respect to its attachment to its essence and its Originator, its particular mode of individuation, the delimitation of what it perceives and the defining of its forms, it is called the Intellect. With respect to its lordship over the body, being the source of sensory life and the wellspring of the soul's faculties, it is called the spirit (*rūḥ*). With respect to its attachment to and management of the body, it is called the soul (*nafs*). With respect to the aspect which orients towards God, receiving from Him lights and the aspect which is oriented towards the animal soul, bestowing upon the

الباب السادس عشر

منتهى العقل وتمامه

اختلف اختلافا كثيرا بين أهل العلم تأصيلا و تفريعا في أولية وشرفية العقل والقلب والروح والنفس وغيرها في المسائل المتعلقة بها ذكر، وتداخلت هذه الحقائق مع بعضها. فذهب البعض إلى تغايرهم. وقال فريق هم شيء واحد إلا بالاعتبارات التي تقتضي التسمية. فباعتبار تعقله ذاته وموجده، وتقيده بتعين خاص، وتقييده ما يدركه ويضبطه بحصره إيّاها فيما تصوّره سمى عقلا، وباعتبار ربوبيته للبدن، وكونه مصدر الحياة الحسية، ومنبع فيضانها على جميع القوى النفسانية سمي روحا، وباعتبار تعلقه بالبدن وتدبيره إيّاه سمي نفسا، وباعتبار تقلبه بين الوجه الذي يلي الحق فيستفيض منه الأنوار، وبين الوجه الذي يلي النفس الحيوانية، فيفيض عليها ما استفاض من موجدها

soul according to its capacity what it has received from its Originator, it is called the heart (*qalb*). From the perspective of it being affected from its source it is called *fūʾād*, since *fāʾd* means affected and when it is the source of lights and arises from the body it is called the breast (*ṣadr*), and so on.[1]

In any case, with the assistance of [divine] light all of them culminate in a new creation, singular and unified in theophany and manifestation. Nonetheless, we will add what was mentioned earlier that relates to the perfection of the Intellect, its culmination and essence.

The first thing that God created was the Intellect. It was a perfect creation, and nothing better, nor more obedient, nor loftier, nor nobler nor more honorable, and contingent upon it was imposition, bestowal, divine unity, worship, supplication, hope, yearning, fear, caution, reward and punishment as God Almighty has said, "By My Might and Majesty, I have not created a creation better than you, nor more obedient to me, nor loftier, nor nobler nor more honorable than you. By you I impose, I bestow, My oneness realized, I am worshipped, called upon, hoped for, yearned for, feared and cautioned against. Through you there is reward and punishment." Intellect has a soul, which in its reality is knowledge, a spirit, which in its reality is understanding, a head, which is abstention, modesty, which is its eye, wisdom, which is its tongue, concern, which is compassion, a heart, which is mercy, and so on.

God gave all of this to it at the time of its creation for it has no soul besides its own soul, nor spirit besides its own spirit, nor heart besides its own heart. Thus, there is no second creation besides its own being.

If it manifests the Intellect, it contemplates its Lord, if it manifests the heart, it fluctuates between His beauty and majesty. In every world there is a corresponding locus of manifestation. Thus, the culmina-

1 See the author's commentary on *Manāzil al-sāʾirīn: bāb al-firāsa*, p. 100.

على حسب استعدادها سمي قلبا. وباعتبار تأثره من مبدعه سمي فؤاد، فان الفأد هو الجرح والتأثر لغة. وباعتبار الوجه الذي يلي البدن، وكونه مصدر أنواره وتصدره عن البدن يسمى صدر وغير ذلك.[1]

و كيف ما كان فبالتأييد النوري ينتهي الجميع إلى خلق جديد واحد موحد في مجالي و مظاهر. و مع ذلك نضيف لسابقة ما ذكرت تتعلق بكمال العقل ومنتهاه وكنهه، وهي:

إن أول ما خلق الله العقل، وهو خلق كامل لا احسن منه، ولا أطوع، ولا أرفع، ولا أشرف، ولا أعز، وعليه ترتبت المؤاخذة، والعطاء، والتوحيد، والعبادة، والدعاء، والارتجاء، والابتغاء، والخوف، والحذر، والثواب، والعقاب، كما قال الرب تبارك و تعالى:

ما خلقت خلقا أحسن منك، ولا أطوع لي منك، ولا أرفع منك، ولا أشرف منك، ولا أعز منك، بك أؤخذ، وبك أعطي، وبك أوحد، وبك أعبد، وبك أدعى، وبك أرتجى، وبك أبتغى، وبك أخاف، وبك أحذر، وبك الثواب، وبك العقاب. فله نفس هي العلم في حقيقة العقل، وله روح هي الفهم في حقيقته، وله رأس هو الزهد، وله حياء هي العين، وله الحكمة هي اللسان، وله هم هي الرأفة، وله قلب هي الرحمة، وغير ذلك.

فهذه جميعا من جعل الحق له حين خلقه، فليس ثم نفس غير نفسه، وليس روح غير روحه، وليس قلب غير قلبه، وهكذا، فلا خلق ثان غير خلقه.

فإن ظهر بالعقل عقل عن ربه، إن ظهر بالقلب تقلب بين جماله وجلاله. وله في كل عالم مظهر يناسبه. وهكذا يكون منتهى العقل كما بدا بعد أن يحكم

---

١ - لاحظ شرح كتاب منازل السـائرين/ باب الفراسة/ أكرم الماجد/ ص١٠٠.

tion of the Intellect is like its inception after governing the entirety of the human kingdom, illuminating it with attachment (*ta'alluq*), assuming of traits (*takhalluq*) and realization (*taḥaqquq*).[2] It becomes a new creation and a singular Intellect, whereas it was beforehand an intellect, soul and body. It subsists in its Lord after annihilation and complete immersion in the hidden, treasured light of God. It is alive by His permission and says to a thing, "Be!" and it is, for it is the realization of God's own words at the dawn of its creation, "Go forth and draw near!"

A *hadith qudsī* states, "O mankind, I created you for permanence. I am living and do not die, obey Me in what I have commanded you and desist from what I have forbidden you from, I will make you like Me, alive and undying. I say to a thing, 'Be' and it is. Obey Me in what I have commanded you, I will make you like Me; if you say to a thing, 'Be' it will be."[3]

The Bible says, "In the morning, as he was returning to the city, he became hungry. And seeing a fig tree by the wayside, he went to it and found nothing on it but only leaves. And he said to it, 'May no fruit ever come from you again!' And the fig tree withered at once. When the disciples saw it, they marveled, saying, 'How did the fig tree wither at once?' And Jesus answered them, 'Truly, I say to you, if you have faith and do not doubt, you will not only do what has been done

---

2 The Greatest Master [Ibn al-'Arabī] states in *Kashf al-ma'na 'an sirr asmā al-ḥusnā*, p. 26, "The servant relates to the divine names through attachment (*ta'alluq*), assuming of traits (*takhalluq*) and realization (*taḥaqquq*). Attachment is your absolute neediness towards God with respect to His Essence. Realization is understanding their meanings as they apply to God and as they apply to you. Assumption is to attribute what is appropriate to yourself as you would attribute what is appropriate to Him. It is possible to realize and assume every name besides the name 'Allah'. Theoretically, it can be said that this name has a special attachment if it indicates the Essence.

3 *Mustadrak al-wasā'il*, v. 11, p. 257.

بتمام حكمه مملكة الإنسان، فتستضيء به تعلقا وتخلقا وتحققا[٢]، وتنشا منه خلقا جديدا، ووحدة عقليه بعد أن كان عقلا ونفسا وبدنا، فيكون باقي بربه بعد الفناء وتمام الاستغراق بنور الله المخزون المكنون، يحيي بإذن ربه ويقل للشي كن فيكون لتحققه بقول الله عز وجل في سابق خلقه إقبالا وإدبارا.

وفي الحديث: «يا ابن آدم خلقتك للبقاء وأنا حي لا أموت، اطعني فيما أمرتك به، وانته عما نهيتك عنه، أجعلك مثلي حيا لا تموت، وأنا الذي أقول لشي كن فيكون، اطعني فيما أمرتك به جعلك مثلي إذا قلت لشي كن فيكون».[٣]

و في الإنجيل: وَفِي صَبَاحِ الْيَوْمِ التَّالِي، وَهُوَ رَاجِعٌ إِلَى الْمَدِينَةِ، جَاعَ. وَإِذْ رَأَى شَجَرَةَ تِينٍ عَلَى جَانِبِ الطَّرِيقِ اتَّجَهَ إِلَيْهَا، وَلَكِنَّهُ لَمْ يَجِدْ عَلَيْهَا إِلاَّ الْوَرَقَ، فَقَالَ لَهَا: «لاَ يَكُنْ مِنْكِ ثَمَرٌ بَعْدُ إِلَى الأَبَدِ!» فَيَبِسَتِ التِّينَةُ فِي الْحَالِ. فَلَمَّا رَأَى التَّلاَمِيذُ ذَلِكَ، دُهِشُوا وَقَالُوا: «مَا أَسْرَعَ مَا يَبِسَتِ التِّينَةُ!» فَأَجَابَهُمْ: «الْحَقَّ أَقُولُ لَكُمْ: إِنْ كَانَ لَكُمْ إِيمَانٌ وَلاَ تَشُكُّونَ، فَإِنَّكُمْ تَعْمَلُونَ لاَ مِثْلَ مَا عَمِلْتُ بِالتِّينَةِ وَحَسْبُ، بَلْ إِنْ كُنْتُمْ تَقُولُونَ لِهَذَا الْجَبَلِ: انْقَلِعْ وَانْطَرِحْ فِي الْبَحْرِ،

---

٢ - قال الشيخ الأكبر في كتاب كشف المعنى عن سر أسماء الله الحسنى، / ص٢٦. و للعبد بأسماء الهي تعالى تعلق و تحقق و تخلق:

فتعلق: افتقارك إليه مطلقا من حيث ما هي دالة على الذات،

و التحقق: معرفة معانيها بالنسبة إليه سبحانه، و بالنسبة إليك،

و التخلق أن تنسب إليك على ما يليق بك كما تنسب إليه عما يليق به. فجميع أسمائه سبحانه يمكن تحققها و التخلق بها إلا الاسم الله عند من يجريه مجرى العلمية فيقول: إنه للتعلق خاصة إذا كان مدلوله الذات.

٣ - مستدرك الوسائل/ ١١/ ٢٥٨.

to the fig tree, but even if you say to this mountain, "Be taken up and thrown into the sea," it will happen. And whatever you ask in prayer, you will receive, if you have faith'" (Matthew 21: 18-22).

And he said to his disciples, "Temptations to sin are sure to come, but woe to the one through whom they come! It would be better for him if a millstone were hung around his neck and he were cast into the sea than that he should cause one of these little ones to sin. Pay attention to yourselves! If your brother sins, rebuke him, and if he repents, forgive him, and if he sins against you seven times in the day, and turns to you seven times, saying, 'I repent,' you must forgive him.

The apostles said to the Lord, 'Increase our faith!' And the Lord said, 'If you had faith like a grain of mustard seed, you could say to this mulberry tree, "Be uprooted and planted in the sea," and it would obey you'" (Luke 17:1-6).

It must be so, for it is the realization of the divine command, the manifestation of His complete light and the plane of a new creation. In fact, it is the old, the new, the singular, unified creation, in which the soul and body have fulfilled the divine command of going forth and drawing near, outwardly, through the hidden, treasured light. It is the origin of their new creations after having been encompassed and enveloped in light. None becomes manifest but through Him, by Him and to Him. In fact, both are the manifestations of the singular, unified Intellect, as they were originally annihilated and subsisting in it, and just as the Intellect is annihilated and subsisting in its Lord. A shadow is cast over the secret of its existence, as it is hidden and treasured in the ancient knowledge of God, that neither a sent messenger nor a proximate angel has awareness. There are no words for it except, "All praise be to God!" and the profession of divine unity stated earlier, "Praise be to God who does not have an opposite, nor equal, nor similar, nor equal, nor substitute, nor equivalent, and before whom all things are humble and abased."

فَإِنَّ ذَلِكَ يَحْدُثُ. وَكُلُّ مَا تَطْلُبُونَهُ فِي الصَّلاَةِ بِإِيمَانٍ، تَنَالُونَهُ» [إنجيل متى/ يسوع يلعن شجرة التين].

و في الإنجيل: وَقَالَ لِتَلاَمِيذِهِ: «لاَبُدَّ مِنْ أَنْ تَأْتِيَ الْعَثَرَاتُ. وَلكِنِ الْوَيْلُ لِمَنْ تَأْتِي عَلَى يَدِهِ! كَانَ أَنْفَعَ لَهُ لَوْ عُلِّقَ حَوْلَ عُنُقِه حَجَرُ رَحًى وَطُرِحَ فِي الْبَحْرِ، مِنْ أَنْ يَكُونَ عَثْرَةً لأَحَدِ هؤُلاَءِ الصِّغَارِ. خُذُوا الْحِذْرَ لأَنْفُسِكُمْ: إِنْ أَخْطَأَ أَخُوكَ، فَعَاتِبْهُ. فَإِذَا تَابَ، فَاغْفِرْ لَهُ. وَإِنْ أَخْطَأَ إِلَيْكَ سَبْعَ مَرَّاتٍ فِي الْيَوْمِ، وَعَادَ إِلَيْكَ سَبْعَ مَرَّاتٍ قَائِلاً: أَنَا تَائِبٌ! فَعَلَيْكَ أَنْ تَغْفِرَ لَهُ». وَقَالَ الرُّسُلُ لِلرَّبِّ: «زِدْنَا إِيمَاناً!» وَلكِنَّ الرَّبَّ قَالَ: «لَوْ كَانَ عِنْدَكُمْ إِيمَانٌ مِثْلُ بِزْرَةِ الْخَرْدَلِ، لَكُنْتُمْ تَقُولُونَ لِشَجَرَةِ التُّوتِ هَذِهِ: انْقَلِعِي وَانْغَرِسِي فِي الْبَحْرِ ! فَتُطِيعُكُمْ!» [إنجيل لوقا/ إن أخطأ إليك أخوك].

لابد من ذلك لتحققه بأمر الله وظهوره بتمام نوره ونشأه خلقا جديدا. بل هو الخلق القديم الجديد الواحد الموحد الذي صير النفس والبدن متحققان بأمر الله إقبالا وإدبارا، ظاهران بنوره المخزون المكنون، منشان خلقا جديدا، بعد أن أستوسعهما وأحاطهما نورا، فما ظهرا إلا منه وبه واليه. بل هما ظهور العقل الواحد الموحد، كما خلق أول مرة لفنائهما به وبقائهما فيه، كما هو فاني بربه باقيا فيه. ويظل سر خلقه مخزون مكنون في سابق علم الله لم يطلع عليه نبي مرسل ولا ملك مقرب، وليس له كلام إلا الحمد لله والتوحيد كما تكلم أول مرة: الحمد لله الذي ليس له ضد ولا ند ولا شبيه ولا كفؤ ولا عديل ولا مثل، الذي كل شيء لعظمته خاضع ذليل.

Thus, the first and the last are humbled and abased before His Majesty, in contemplating and realizing it. The first and the last are impoverished as long as the mystery of its existence is attached to the hidden, treasured light of God in His ancient knowledge. All praise be to God, the Lord of the worlds, and peace and blessings be upon the messengers of God, His saints and the guided amongst His servants.

Akram al-Majid, 15th March 2012, London, 4:26 am.
Peace

فأول وآخر خاضع ذليل لعظمته من تعقلها وتحقق بها، وأول وآخر الفقراء من لا يزال سر خلقه متعلق بنور الله المخزون المكنون في سابق علمه.

و الحمد لله رب العالمين، والصلاة والسلام على رسل الله وأوليائه والمهديين من عباده.

أكرم الماجد/ ١٥/ ٣/ ٢٠١٢ / لندن ٤:٢٦ ليلا

والسلام

Bibliography

ʿAbduh, Muḥammad. *Nahj al-balāgha*. Beirut, 1996.

Aḥsāʾī, ibn abī Jumhūr al-. *ʿAwālī al-laʾālī*. Qom, 1404/1983.

Āmidī, ʿAbd al-Wāḥid al-. *Ghurar al-ḥikam wa durar al-kalim*, Qom, 2000.

ʿĀmilī, Zain al-Dīn Ibn-ʿAlī al-. *Munyat al-murīd fī adab al-mufīd waʾl-mustafīd*. Qom, 2000.

ʿAlī b. Abī Ṭālib. *Nahj al-balāgha*, ed. Shaykh ʿAzīzullāh al-ʿUtārdī. Tehran, 1993.

Ali, Mukhtar. *Foundations of Islamic Mysticism*. London, 2018.

———. *The Principles of Correspondences*. Translation of *Qanūn al-tanāsub in Manāzil al-saʾirīn: Bāb al-firāsa*, Akram al-Majid. London, 2018.

Āmulī, Ḥaydar. *Jāmiʿ al-asrār wa-manbaʿ al-anwār*, eds. Henry Corbin and Osman Yahia. Paris 1969.

Bayāḍī, Zayn al-dīn al-ʿĀmili al-Nabaṭī. *Ṣirāt al-mustaqīm*. *N.p.*, 1384.

The Holy Bible: New International Version. Hodder & Stoughton, 1996.

Bukhārī, Muhammad bin Isma'īl bin Ibrahim al-. *Sahih al- Bukhārī*. Beirut, 1378/1958-59.

Bursī, Ḥāfiẓ Rajab al-. *Mashāriq anwār al-yaqīn fī asrār amīr al-mu'minīn*. Beirut, 2001.

Fannārī, Ḥamza. *Misbāḥ al-uns*. Tehran, 1379/1960.

Ghazālī, Abū Ḥāmid al-. *Iḥyā' 'ulūm al-dīn*. Beirut, 1992.

Ḥillī, ibn Faḥd al-. *'Uddat al-dā'ī wa najāḥ al-sā'ī*, ed. F. Ḥassūn Fāris. Qom, 1420/1999.

Hindi, Muttaqī al-. *Kanz al-'ummāl fī sunan al-aqwa wa'l-af'āl*, ed. Bakri Hayyani, Beirut, 1409/1989.

Ibn Abi'l-Ḥadīd. *Sharḥ Nahj al-balāgha li-Ibn Abi'l-Ḥadīd*. Beirut, 1965

Ibn al-'Arabī, Muḥyiddīn. *al-Futūḥāt al-Makkīyya*, 4 vols, Beirut, 1968.

——. *Fuṣūṣ al-ḥikam*, ed. 'Afīfī, A.E., Beirut, 1946.

Ibn Bābawayh, Muḥammad b. 'Alī al-Shaykh al-Ṣadūq. *'Uyūn akhbār al-Riḍa*, ed. M. al-Ḥusaynī al-Lājevardī. Tehran, 1378/1958.

Ibn Ḥanbal, Aḥmad Ibn Muḥammad. *Musnad al-imām Aḥmad ibn Ḥanbal*. Beirut, 1999.

Ibn Ṭāwūs, Abū al-Qāsim 'Alī ibn Mūsā. *Muhaj al-da'wāt wa manhaj al-ibadāt*. Beirut, 1994.

'Irāqī, Zayn al-Dīn. *Takhrīj aḥadīth iḥyā 'ulūm al-dīn*. Beirut, 1425/2005.

Isfahānī, Rāghib. *Mu' jam mufradāt alfāẓ al-Qur'ān*. Beirut, 1997.

Jāmī, 'Abd al-Raḥmān. *Naqd al-Nuṣūṣ fi sharḥ naqsh al-fuṣūṣ*. Tehran, 1977.

——. *Sharḥ fuṣūṣ al-ḥikam*. Beirut, 1425/2004.

Kāshānī, 'Abd al-Razzāq al-. *Laṭā'if al-i'lām fī ishārāt ahl al-ilhām*, ed. M. Hādīzādah. Tehran, 2000.

Kāshānī, Muḥsin Fayḍ al-. *Kalimāt al-maknūna*, ed. al-Ṣādiq Ḥasanzāda. Qom, 2007.

——. *al-Ḥaqā'iq fī maḥāsin al-akhlāq*, Qom, 1423/2002.

——. *al-Mahajjat al-bayḍā' fī tahdhīb al-Ihyā'*. Qom, 1406.

——. *Tuḥfat al-Sannīya. n.p, n.d.*

——. *al-Uṣūl al-asīla*, Tehran, 1390.

——. *al-Wāfī*, 26 vols. N.p., n.d.

——. *Qurrat al-ʿuyūn*. Qom, 1423/2002.

Kulaynī, Muḥammad al-. *Usul al-kāfī*. Tehran, 1418.

Lane, E. W. *An Arabic-English Lexicon*. Repr. Cambridge: Islamic Texts-Society, 1984.

Ma'lūf, Luis. *Qamūs al-Munjid*. Beirut, 1986.

Majah, Ibn. *Sunan Ibn Mājah*. Beirut, 1999.

Mājid, Akram al-. *Manāzil al-sā'irīn: bāb al-firāsa*, Qom, 1429/.

Majlisī,Muḥammad Bāqir al-. *Biḥār al-anwār li-durar akhbār al-a'immat al-aṭhār*, 110 vols. Beirut, 1403 h/1983.

Maluḥī, Mazhar. *Qirā' ṣufiyya li'l-Injīl*. Ann Arbor, 2009.

Manzūr, Yamal al-Dīn Muḥammad Ibn. *Lisān al-ʿarab*. Cairo, 1975.

Mazandarānī, Muḥammad Ṣāliḥ al-. *Sharḥ uṣūl al-kāfī*, ed. ʿAlī ʿAshūr, Beirut, 1421/2000.

Murata, Sachiko. *The Tao of Islam*. Albany, 1992.

Sanʿāni Hāfiẓ al-. *Musannaf of Ibn ʿAbd al-Razzāq*. Beirut, 1390/1970.

Mir Dāmād, Muḥammad Bāqir. *al-Rawāshiḥ al-samāwiya*. Qom, 1984.

Nābulsī, ʿAbd al-Ghanī, *Jawāhir al-fuṣūṣ*. Beirut, 2008.

Namāzī, Ḥasan bin ʿAlī. *Mustadrak safīnat al-biḥār*, 10 vols. Qom, 1418/1977,

Nisābūrī, Niẓām al-Dīn al-Ḥasan ibn Muḥammad. *Gharā'ib al-Qur'ān wa raghā'ib al- furqān*, ed. Zakariyā al-Umayrān. Beirut, 1996.

Nūrī al-Ṭabarsī/Ṭabrīsī, Mīrzā Husayn. *Mustadrak al-wasā'il*. Qom, 1407/1986.

Qayṣarī, Sharaf al-Dīn Dawūd al-. *Sharḥ fuṣūṣ al-ḥikam*, ed. Sayyid Jalāl al-Dīn Āshtiyānī. Qum, 1357 h.

Qummī, 'Abbās, *Mafātīḥ al-jinān*. Tehran, 1381 Sh/2001.

Qūnawī, Ṣadr al-Dīn al-. *Miftāḥ al-ghayb*. Tehran, 1994,

Qushayrī, Abū al-Qāsim. *al-Risāla*, ed. Maḥmūd and Sahrif. Cairo, 1974.

Qushayrī, Muslim bin Hajjaj al-. *Saḥīḥ Muslim*. Beirut, 2001.

Rāzī, Najm al-Dīn al-. *Mirṣad al-'ibād*. Trans. Hamid Algar. The Path of God's Bondsmen from Origin to Return. Delmar, 1980.

Rayshahrī, Muḥammad. *Mīzan al-ḥikma*, Beirut, 1422/2001.

———. *Mawsū'at al-Imām 'Alī ibn abī Ṭālib*, Beirut, 1425.

Sabzavārī, Mulla Hādī. *Sharh al-Manzuma*, ed. Najaf Gholi Habibi. Tehran, 2007.

al-Ṣādiq, Ja'far al-. *Misbāḥ al-sharī'a*. Tehran, 1400/1980.

Sha'rānī, 'Abd al-Wahhab al-. *Lawāqih al-anwār al-qudṣiyya fī bayān al-'uhūd al-Muḥammadiyya*. Beirut, 1936.

Shahrazūrī, Shams al-Dīn Muḥammad ibn Maḥmūd, *Kitāb nuzhat al-arwāḥ wa-rawḍat al-afrāḥ*. Tehran, 1365/1987.

Suyūtī ,Jalaluddin. *al-Durr al-manthūr fī tafsir bi'l-ma'thūr*. Beirut, 1983.

Ṭabrīsī, Abū 'Alī al-Faḍl al-. *Majma' al-bayān fī tafsīr al-Qur'ān*, ed. Sayyid Muḥsin al-Amīn al-Āmilī. Beirut, 1995.

Tehrānī, Agha Bozorg. *al-Dharī'a ilā tasānif al-Shī'a*. Tehran, 1939.

Tirmīdhī, Abu 'Īsa al-. *Sunan al-Tirmīdhī. Cairo*, 1975.

Wāṣiṭī, Muḥammad al-. *'Uyūn al-ḥikam wa'l mawā'iẓ*, 1376 Sh.

Index of Qur'anic Verses

Index of Biblical Verses

(Acts 17:24)

The God who made the world and everything in it is the Lord of heaven and earth and does not live in temples built by human hands, 3

(John 1:12-13)

To all who did receive him, to those who believed in his name, he gave the right to become children of God, children born not of blood, nor the will of the flesh nor the will of man, but born of God, 16

(John 3:3-8)

'None can ascend to the heavens unless he has been born twice.' 'How can someone be born when they are old?' Nicodemus asked. 'Surely they cannot enter a second time into their mother's womb to be born!' Jesus said, 'Flesh gives birth to flesh, but the Spirit gives birth to spirit' You should not be surprised at my saying, you must be born again,' 16

General Index

A

G

H

I

J

K

L

P

Q

R

S

T

Z

www.ingramcontent.com/pod-product-compliance
Lightning Source LLC
Chambersburg PA
CBHW030256100426
42812CB00002B/465